DATE DUE

American
Labor
History
and
Comparative
Labor
Movements

JAMES C. McBREARTY

American Labor History and Comparative Labor Movements

A SELECTED BIBLIOGRAPHY

THE UNIVERSITY OF ARIZONA PRESS
TUCSON, ARIZONA

About the Author . . .

JAMES C. MCBREARTY, as a professor of courses covering comparative labor movements and labor relations law, has a firm grasp of the materials pertinent to a wide-ranging bibliography such as this volume. McBrearty holds graduate degrees in economics from the University of Illinois where his fields of concentration included labor economics and industrial labor relations as well as the history of economic thought and public finance. In 1968, he joined the Department of Economics at the University of Arizona, subsequently becoming director of the Institute of Industrial and Labor Relations. He has served also as director of the annual conference at the University of Arizona on collective bargaining and labor law, sponsored by the National Labor Relations Board, the Federal Mediation and Conciliation Service, and the Arizona Industrial Relations Association.

THE UNIVERSITY OF ARIZONA PRESS

I. S. B. N.-0-8165-0392-3
L. C. No. 78-190624

PREFACE

THIS SELECTED BIBLIOGRAPHY of American labor history and comparative labor movements has been set up and arranged alphabetically by author according to chronological periods and topical subjects for the American labor history section, and by country designation for the comparative labor movements section.

Such a classification system, together with the separation of books and articles and a further breakdown of books into non-fictional and fictional categories, should prove useful to undergraduate and graduate students, professors, librarians, labor unions, management officials, government agencies, adult education classes, and secondary school teachers.

The combining of American labor history and comparative labor movements is an attempt to recognize the latter-day trend toward teaching American labor history in reference to the similarities and contrasts of labor history in other countries. This is done in order to provide broader understanding and appreciation of the global context in which American labor development has been and is now taking place.

No foreign language publications are cited, since many such books and articles are not actually readily available in the United States. An attempt has been made, however, to provide a wide variety of books and articles representative of many viewpoints on the history of both organized and unorganized labor in the United States and abroad.

Moreover, an attempt has been made to put recent problems and practices of labor into proper perspective for the reader by focusing on topics such as unemployment, union membership, collective bargaining, white and blue collar workers in both the private and public sectors, minority groups, internal union affairs, the AFL-CIO, and labor's role in recent foreign policy.

Although every effort has been made to record all entries with the utmost accuracy, some errors have undoubtedly survived, and their identification would be most welcome.

I am much indebted to Marjorie Parker, Ann West, Evelyn Van Dyke, and Leslie Friedman for editing and proofing the manuscript with exemplary attention to detail, as well as for the technical preparation of more than 3,100 cards for publication processing. Further, I express my appreciation to the University of Arizona Press which has regarded the compilation as worthy of book publication and distribution.

J. C. M.

CONTENTS

BOOKS

ARTICLES

PART I

BOOKS

BOOKS—NON-FICTION

I. American Labor History

GENERAL HISTORIES

1

Adamic, Louis. *Dynamite: The Story of Class Violence in America.* Gloucester: Peter Smith, 1934.

2

Allsop, Kenneth. *Hard Travellin': The Hobo and His History.* New York: New American Library, 1967.

3

Anderson, Nels. *Men on the Move.* Chicago: University of Chicago Press, 1940.

4

Auerbach, Jerold S., ed. *American Labor: The Twentieth Century.* Indianapolis: Bobbs-Merrill, 1969.

5

Barbash, Jack. *Labor's Grass Roots.* New York: Harper, 1961.

6

Beebe, Lucius. *The Big Spenders.** Garden City: Doubleday, 1966.

7

Blum, Albert A. *Teacher Unions and Associations: A Comparative Study.* Urbana: University of Illinois Press, 1969.

8

Bremner, Robert H., et al. *Children and Youth in America: A Documentary History, 1600-1865.* Vol. 1. Cambridge: Harvard University Press, 1970.

9

Brody, David, ed. *The American Labor Movement.** New York: Harper & Row, 1971.

10

Brooks, Thomas R. *Picket Lines and Bargaining Tables: Organized Labor Comes of Age, 1935-1955.* New York: Grosset & Dunlap, 1968.

11

————. *Toil and Trouble.** 2nd ed. New York: Dell Publishing Co., 1971.

12
Cahn, William. *A Pictorial History of American Labor.* New York: Crown, 1972.

13
Campbell, Helen S. *Prisoners of Poverty.* Boston: Roberts Brothers, 1887.

14
————. *Women Wage-Earners, Their Trade and Their Lives.* Boston: Roberts Brothers, 1893.

15
Commons, John R. *History of Labor in the United States.* 4 vols. New York: Macmillan, 1926-1935.

16
————, et al., eds. *A Documentary History of American Industrial Society.* 10 vols. New York: Russell & Russell, 1958.

17
Derber, Milton. *The American Idea of Industrial Democracy, 1865-1965.* Urbana: University of Illinois Press, 1970.

18
Dubofsky, Melvin, ed. *American Labor since the New Deal.** Chicago: Quandrangle Books, 1971.

19
Dulles, Foster Rhea. *Labor in America.** 3rd ed. New York: Thomas Y. Crowell, 1966.

20
Faulkner, Harold U., and Starr, Mark. *Labor in America.* New York: Oxford Book Co., 1957.

21
Feied, Frederick. *No Pie in the Sky: The Hobo as an American Cultural Hero.* New York: Citadel Press, 1964.

22
Fish, Carl R. *The Rise of the Common Man, 1830-1850.* New York: Macmillan, 1927.

23
Foner, Philip S. *History of the Labor Movement in the United States.* 4 vols. New York: International Publishers, 1947.

24
Galenson, Walter. *Rival Unionism in the U.S.* New York: American Council on Public Affairs, 1940.

25
Ginzberg, Eli, and Berman, Hyman. *The American Worker in the Twentieth Century: A History through Autobiographies.* New York: Free Press, 1963.

26
Grob, Gerald N. *Workers and Utopia: A Study of Ideological Conflict in the American Labor Movement, 1865-1900.** Evanston: Northwestern University Press, 1961.

27
Harris, Herbert. *American Labor*. New Haven: Yale University Press, 1939.

28
Hays, Samuel P. *The Response to Industrialism, 1885-1914*. Chicago: University of Chicago Press, 1957.

29
Henry, Alice. *Trade Union Woman*. New York: D. Appleton, 1915.

30
Hunter, Robert. *Poverty*. New York: Macmillan, 1904.

31
————. *Violence and the Labor Movement*. New York: Macmillan, 1914.

32
Jerome, Harry. *Mechanization in Industry*. New York: National Bureau of Economic Research, 1934.

33
Johannessen, Edward. *The Hawaiian Labor Movement: A Brief History*. Boston: Bruce Humphries,1956.

34
Josephy, Alvin M. *The Indian Heritage of America*. New York: Alfred A. Knopf, 1970.

35
Kirkland, Edward C. *Dream and Thought in the Business Community, 1860-1900*. Ithaca: Cornell University Press, 1959.

36
Lester, Richard A. *As Unions Mature: An Analysis of the Evolution of American Unionism*. Princeton: Princeton University Press, 1958.

37
Leupp, F.E. *Indian and His Problem*. New York: Scribner, 1910.

38
Levinson, Edward. *Labor on the March*. New York: University Books, 1956.

39
Litwack, Leon. *The American Labor Movement*. Englewood Cliffs: Prentice-Hall, 1962.

40
Marshall, F. Ray. *Labor in the South*. Cambridge: Harvard University Press, 1967.

41
Meltzer, Milton. *Bread and Roses: The Struggle of American Labor, 1865-1914*. New York: Alfred A. Knopf, 1967.

42
Millis, Harry A., and Montgomery, Royal E. *Organized Labor*. New York: McGraw-Hill, 1945.

43
Nadworny, Milton J. *Scientific Management and the Unions, 1900-1932: An Historical Analysis.* Cambridge: Harvard University Press, 1955.

44
Pelling, Henry. *American Labor.** Chicago: University of Chicago Press, 1960.

45
Perlman, Mark. *Labor Union Theories in America: Background and Development.* Evanston: Row, Peterson, 1958.

46
Perlman, Selig, and Taft, Philip. *A History of Trade Unionism in the United States, 1896-1932.* New York: Augustus M. Kelley, 1950.

47
Preston, William, Jr. *Aliens and Dissenters: Federal Suppression of Radicals, 1903-1933.** Cambridge: Harvard University Press, 1963.

48
Rayback, Joseph G. *A History of American Labor.** Rev. ed. New York: Macmillan, 1966.

49
Scott, Anne Firor. *The Southern Lady: From Pedestal to Politics, 1830-1930.* Chicago: University of Chicago Press, 1970.

50
Seligman, Ben B. *The Potentates: Business and Businessmen in American History.* New York: Dial Press, 1971.

51
Sloan, Irving J. *Our Violent Past: An American Chronicle.* New York: Random House, 1970.

52
Streightoff, F.H. *Standard of Living among Industrial People.* Boston: Houghton Mifflin, 1911.

53
Taft, Philip. *Organized Labor in American History.* New York: Harper & Row, 1964.

54
Tully, Jim. *Beggars of Life.* New York: Albert and Charles Boni, 1926.

55
Tyler, Alice F. *Freedom's Ferment: Phases of American Social History from the Revolution to the Outbreak of the Civil War.* Minneapolis: University of Minnesota Press, 1944.

56
Tyler, Gus. *The Political Imperative: The Corporate Character of Unions.* New York: Macmillan, 1968.

57
Ware, Norman J. *The Industrial Worker, 1840-1860.** Boston: Houghton Mifflin, 1924.

58

————. *The Labor Movement in the United States, 1860-1895.** New York: D. Appleton, 1929.

59

Woodward, C. Vann. *Origins of the New South, 1877-1913.* Baton Rouge: Louisiana State University Press, 1951.

60

Yellen, Samuel. *American Labor Struggles.* New York: S.A. Russell, 1956.

PERIODS OF DEVELOPMENT

Workers in Early America (Colonial America)

61

Ballagh, J.C. *White Servitude in Virginia.* Baltimore: Johns Hopkins Press, 1895.

62

Bennett, Lerone. *Before the Mayflower: A History of Black America.* 4th ed. Chicago: Johnson Publishing Co., 1969.

63

Bridenbaugh, Carl. *The Colonial Craftsman.* New York: New York University Press, 1950.

64

————. *Myths and Realities: Societies of the Colonial South.* Baton Rouge: Louisiana State University Press, 1952.

65

Craven, Wesley F. *The Southern Colonies in the Seventeenth Century, 1607-1689.* Baton Rouge: Louisiana State University Press, 1949.

66

Dow, George Francis. *Every Day Life in Massachusetts Bay Colony.* Boston: Society for the Preservation of New England Antiquities, 1935.

67

Dyer, Walter A. *Early American Craftsmen.* New York: Century, 1915.

68

Hansen, Marcus Lee. *The Atlantic Migration 1607-1860.* New York: Harper & Row, 1961.

69

Herrick, Cheesman A. *White Servitude in Pennsylvania: Indentured and Redemption Labor in Colony and Commonwealth.* Philadelphia: McVey, 1926.

70

Holliday, Carl. *Woman's Life in Colonial Days.* Williamstown: Corner House Publishing Co., 1968.

71

Jernegan, Marcus Wilson. *Laboring and Dependent Classes in Colonial America, 1607-1783.* New York: Frederick Ungar, 1931.

72

Jordan, Winthrop. *White over Black: American Attitudes toward the Negro, 1550-1812.* Chapel Hill: University of North Carolina Press, 1968.

73

Josephy, Alvin M. *The Indian Heritage of America.* New York: Alfred A. Knopf, 1970.

74

Klingberg, F.J. *An Appraisal of the Negro in Colonial South Carolina, a Study in Americanization.* Washington, D.C.: Associated Publishers, 1941.

75

Lauber, Almon Wheeler. *Indian Slavery in Colonial Times.* New York: AMS Press, 1969.

76

Locke, M.S. *Anti-Slavery Sentiment in America 1619-1808.* Boston: Ginn & Co., 1901.

77

McKee, Samuel D. *Labor in Colonial New York, 1664-1776.* Port Washington: I.J. Friedman, 1965.

78

Morris, Richard B. *Government and Labor in Early America.** New York: Columbia University Press, 1946.

79

Peckham, Howard, and Bigson, Charles, eds. *Attitudes of the Colonial Powers toward the American Indians.* Salt Lake City: University of Utah Press, 1969.

80

Smith, Abbott E. *Colonists in Bondage: White Servitude and Convict Labor in America, 1607-1776.* Chapel Hill: University of North Carolina Press, 1947.

81

Spruill, J.C. *Women's Life and Work in Southern Colonies.* Chapel Hill: University of North Carolina Press, 1938.

82

Tyler, Alice F. *Freedom's Ferment: Phases of American Social History from the Revolution to the Outbreak of the Civil War.* Minneapolis: University of Minnesota Press, 1944.

83

Wade, Richard C. *Urban Frontier: Pioneer Life in Early Pittsburgh, Cincinnati, Lexington, Louisville and St. Louis, 1790-1830.* Cambridge: Harvard University Press, 1959.

Workingmen in the Era of Jackson

(1820s-1830s)

84
Fish, Carl R. *The Rise of the Common Man, 1830-1850.* New York: Macmillan, 1927.

85
Hugins, Walter E. *Jacksonian Democracy and the Working Class: A Study of the New York Workingmen's Movement, 1829-1837.* Stanford: Stanford University Press, 1960.

86
Miller, Douglas T. *Jacksonian Aristocracy: Class and Democracy in New York, 1830-1860.* New York: Oxford University Press, 1967.

87
Pessen, Edward. *Most Uncommon Jacksonians: The Radical Leaders of the Early Labor Movement.* Albany: State University of New York Press, 1967.

88
Schlesinger, Arthur M., Jr. *The Age of Jackson.* Boston: Little, Brown and Co., 1945.

89
Scoresby, William. *American Factories and Their Female Operatives, 1845.* Reprint. New York: Burt Franklin, 1968.

90
Tyler, Alice F. *Freedom's Ferment: Phases of American Social History from the Revolution to the Outbreak of the Civil War.* Minneapolis: University of Minnesota Press, 1944.

91
Whitman, Alden. *Labor Parties, 1827-1834.* New York: International Publishers, 1943.

Establishing Utopian Communities

(1840s-1850s)

92
Carden, Maren L. *Oneida: Utopian Community to Modern Corporation.* * Baltimore: Johns Hopkins Press, 1969.

93
Cole, Margaret. *Robert Owen of New Lanark, 1771-1858.* New York: Oxford University Press, 1953.

94
Fish, Carl R. *The Rise of the Common Man, 1830-1850.* New York: Macmillan, 1927.

95

Franklin, Julia, trans. *Selections from the Works of Charles Fourier.* London: S. Sonnenschein, 1901.

96

Hinds, William A. *American Communities and Cooperative Colonies.* 2nd rev. ed. Chicago: C.H. Kerr, 1908.

97

Laidler, Harry W. *A History of Socialist Thought.* New York: Thomas Y. Crowell, 1927.

98

Lockwood, George B. *The New Harmony Movement.* New York: D. Appleton, 1905.

99

Mumford, Lewis. *The Story of Utopias.* New York: Boni and Liveright, 1922.

100

Myers, Gustavus. *The History of American Idealism.* New York: Boni and Liveright, 1925.

101

Nordhoff, Charles. *The Communistic Societies of the United States.* New York: Hillary House, 1960.

102

Noyes, John H. *History of American Socialisms.* 1870. Reprint. New York: Hillary House, 1961.

103

Parrington, V.L., Jr. *American Dreams, a Study of American Utopias.* Providence: Brown University Press, 1947.

104

Robertson, Constance Noyes, ed. *Oneida Community: An Autobiography, 1851-1876.* Syracuse: Syracuse University Press, 1970.

105

Swift, Lindsay. *Brook Farm.* New York: Macmillan, 1900.

106

Tyler, Alice F. *Freedom's Ferment: Phases of American Social History from the Revolution to the Outbreak of the Civil War.* Minneapolis: University of Minnesota Press, 1944.

107

Wagner, Donald O. *Social Reformers: Adam Smith to John Dewey.* New York: Macmillan, 1934.

108

Ware, Norman J. *The Industrial Worker, 1840-1860.** Boston: Houghton Mifflin, 1924.

109

Wolfson, Theresa, and and Perkins, Alice J.G. *Frances Wright: Free Enquirer; the Study of a Temperament.* New York: Harper, 1939.

Slavery (Up to 1865)

110
Aptheker, Herbert. *American Negro Slave Revolts*. New York: Columbia University Press, 1944.

111
————. *To Be Free; Studies in American Negro History*. New York: International Publishers, 1948.

112
Ballagh, J.C. *History of Slavery in Virginia*. Baltimore: Johns Hopkins Press, 1902.

113
Bancroft, Frederic. *Slave Trading in the Old South*. Baltimore: J.H. Furst, 1931.

114
Bennett, Lerone. *Before the Mayflower: A History of Black America*. 4th ed. Chicago: Johnson Publishing Co., 1969.

115
Campbell, Penelope. *Maryland in Africa: The Maryland State Colonization Society*. Urbana: University of Illinois Press, 1971.

116
Campbell, Stanley W. *The Slave Catchers: Enforcement of the Fugitive Slave Law, 1850-1860*. Chapel Hill: University of North Carolina Press, 1970.

117
Feldstein, Stanley. *Once a Slave: The Slave's View of Slavery*. New York: William Morrow, 1971.

118
Flanders, R.B. *Plantation Slavery in Georgia*. Chapel Hill: University of North Carolina Press, 1933.

119
Foner, Eric. *Free Soil, Free Labor, Free Men: The Ideology of the Republican Party before the Civil War*. New York: Oxford University Press, 1970.

120
Klein, Herbert S. *Slavery in the Americas: A Comparative Study of Virginia and Cuba*. Chicago: University of Chicago Press, 1967.

121
Land, Aubrey C., ed. *Bases of the Plantation System*. Columbia: University of South Carolina Press, 1969.

122
Lauber, Almon Wheeler. *Indian Slavery in Colonial Times*. New York: AMS Press, 1969.

123
Locke, M.S. *Anti-Slavery Sentiment in America 1619-1808*. Boston: Ginn & Co., 1901.

124
Lynd, Staughton. *Class Conflict, Slavery, and the United States Constitution.* Indianapolis: Bobbs-Merrill, 1967.

125
McDougall, M.G. *Fugitive Slaves.* Boston: Ginn & Co., 1891.

126
Moody, V.A. *Slavery on Louisiana Sugar Plantations.* New Orleans: Louisiana Historical Quarterly, 1924.

127
Nevins, Allan. *Ordeal of the Union.* 2 vols. New York: Scribner, 1947.

128
Olmstead, Frederick Law. *A Journey in the Back Country.* 1860. Reprint. New York: Lenox Hill Publishing Co. (Burt Franklin), 1970.

129
————. *A Journey through Texas.* 1857. Reprint. New York: Lenox Hill Publishing Co. (Burt Franklin), 1970.

130
Owsley, F.L. *Plain Folk of Old South.* Baton Rouge: Louisiana State University Press, 1949.

131
Phillips, Ulrich B. *American Negro Slavery.* New York: D. Appleton, 1918.

132
————. *Life and Labor in the Old South.* Boston: Little, Brown and Co., 1930.

133
Sellers, J.B. *Slavery in Alabama.* University, Ala.: University of Alabama Press, 1950.

134
Siebert, W.H. *The Underground Railroad from Slavery to Freedom.* New York: Macmillan, 1898.

135
Smith, Elbert B. *The Death of Slavery: The United States, 1837-1865.* Chicago History of American Civilization Series. Chicago: University of Chicago Press, 1967.

136
Spears, John R. *The American Slave Trade.* Port Washington: Kennikat Press, 1967.

137
Stampp, Kenneth M. *The Peculiar Institution: Slavery in the Ante-Bellum South.* New York: Alfred A. Knopf, 1968.

138
Starobin, Robert S. *Industrial Slavery in the Old South.* New York: Oxford University Press, 1970.

139
Sydnor, C.S. *Slavery in Mississippi.* New York: Appleton-Century, 1933.

140
Tragle, Henry I. *The Southampton Slave Revolt of 1831: A Compilation of Source Material.* Amherst: University of Massachusetts Press, 1971.

141
Wade, Richard C. *Slavery in the Cities: The South, 1860-1960.* New York: Oxford University Press, 1964.

142
Woodman, Harold D., ed. *Slavery and the Southern Economy.* New York: Harcourt, Brace & World, 1966.

Labor During the Civil War

(1861-1865)

143
Burn, James Dawson. *Three Years Among the Working Classes in the United States during the War.* London: Smith, Elder, 1865.

144
Erickson, Charlotte. *American Industry and the European Immigrant, 1860-1885.* Cambridge: Harvard University Press, 1957.

145
Fite, Emerson David. *Social and Industrial Conditions in the North during the Civil War.* New York: Macmillan, 1910.

146
Lonn, Ella. *Foreigners in Confederacy.* Chapel Hill: University of North Carolina Press, 1940.

147
Ware, Norman J. *The Labor Movement in the United States, 1860-1895.** New York: D. Appleton, 1969.

Formation of National Unions

(1850s-1860s)

148
Grossman, Jonathan. *William Sylvis: Pioneer of American Labor.* New York: Columbia University Press, 1945.

149
Lescohier, Don D. *The Knights of St. Crispen, 1867-1874.* Bulletin 355. Madison: University of Wisconsin, 1910.

150
McNeil, George, ed. *The Labor Movement: The Problem of Today.* Boston: A.W. Bridgman, 1887.

151
Robinson, Jesse S. *The Amalgamated Association of Iron, Steel and Tin Workers.* Baltimore: Johns Hopkins Press, 1920.

152
Roy, Andrew. *A History of the Coal Miners of the United States.* Columbus: J.L. Trauger, 1903.

153
Stockton, Frank T. *The International Molders' Union of North America.* Baltimore: Johns Hopkins Press, 1921.

154
Todes, Charlotte. *William H. Sylvis and the National Labor Union.* New York: International Publishers, 1942.

155
Ulman, Lloyd. *The Rise of the National Trade Union.* Cambridge: Harvard University Press, 1956.

156
Ware, Norman J. *The Labor Movement in the United States, 1860-1895.** New York: D. Appleton, 1929.

157
Wieck, Edward A. *The American Miners' Union.* New York: Russell Sage Foundation, 1940.

An Era of Socio-Economic Transformation
and Violent Protest

(1865-1899)

158
Aurand, Harold W. *From the Molly Maguires to the United Mine Workers: The Social Ecology of an Industrial Union, 1869-1897.* Philadelphia: Temple University Press, 1971.

159
Barnard, Harry. *Eagle Forgotten: The Life of John Peter Altgeld.* Indianapolis: Bobbs-Merrill, 1938.

160
Barrett, Tom. *The Mollies Were Men.* New York: Vantage Press, 1969.

161
Bennett, Lerone. *Black Power, U.S.A.: The Human Side of Reconstruction, 1867-1877.* Chicago: Johnson Publishing Co., 1967.

162
Bimba, Anthony. *The Molly Maguires.* New York: International Publishers, 1932.

163
Bridge, James Howard. *The History of the Carnegie Steel Company.* New York: Aldine Pub. Co., 1903.

164
Broehl, Wayne G. *The Molly Maguires.* Cambridge: Harvard University Press, 1964.

165
Bruce Robert V. *1877: Year of Violence.* Indianapolis: Bobbs-Merrill, 1959.

166
Buchanan, Joseph R. *The Story of a Labor Agitator.* New York: The Outlook Co., 1903.

167
Buder, Stanley. *Pullman: An Experiment in Industrial Order and Community Planning, 1880-1930.* New York: Oxford University Press, 1967.

168
Calmer, Alan. *Labor Agitator: The Story of Albert R. Parsons.* New York: International Publishers, 1937.

169
Christman, Henry M., ed. *The Mind and Spirit of John Peter Altgeld: Selected Writings and Addresses.* Urbana: University of Illinois Press, 1960.

170
Coleman, J. Walter. *The Molly Maguire Riots: Industrial Conflict in the Pennsylvania Coal Region.* Washington, D.C.: Catholic University of America Press, 1936.

171
Dacus, Joseph A. *Annals of the Great Strikes.* 1877. Reprint. New York: Lenox Hill Publishing Co. (Burt Franklin), 1970.

172
David, Henry. *The History of the Haymarket Affair.* * 2nd ed. New York: Russell & Russell, 1958.

173
Erickson, Charlotte. *American Industry and the European Immigrant, 1860-1885.* Cambridge: Harvard University Press, 1957.

174
Evans, W. McKee. *To Die Game: The Story of the Lowry Band, Indian Guerillas of Reconstruction.* Baton Rouge: Louisiana State University, 1971.

175
Garraty, John A. *Labor and Capital in the Guilded Age: 1883.* Boston: Little, Brown and Co., 1969.

176
Ginger, Ray. *The Bending Cross: A Biography of Eugene V. Debs.* New Brunswick: Rutgers University Press, 1949.

177
——————. *Altgeld's America: The Lincoln Ideal v. Changing Realities.* New York: Funk and Wagnalls, 1958.

178
Harvey, G.B.M. *Henry Clay Frick.* New York: Scribner, 1928.

179
Josephson, Matthew. *The Robber Barons: The Great American Capitalists, 1861-1901.* 1934. New York: Harcourt, Brace & World, 1962.

180
Kelsey, Carl. *Negro Farmer.* Chicago: Jennings & Pye, 1903.

181
Kirkland, Edward C. *Industry Comes of Age: Business, Labor and Public Policy, 1860-1897.* New York: Holt, Rinehart and Winston, 1961.

182
Kogan, Bernard, ed. *The Chicago Haymarket Riot: Anarchy on Trial.* * Boston: D.C. Heath, 1959.

183
Lewis, Arthur H. *Lament for the Molly Maguires.* * New York: Harcourt, Brace & World, 1964.

184
Lindsey, Almont. *The Pullman Strike.* * Chicago: University of Chicago Press, 1942.

185
Lloyd, Henry D. *A Strike of Millionaires against Miners or the Story of Spring Valley.* Chicago: Belford-Clarke, 1890.

186
McCabe, James D. (Martin, Edward W., pseud.). *History of the Great Riots.* Philadelphia: National Publishing, 1877.

187
McCarthy, Charles A. *The Great Molly Maguire Hoax.* Wyoming, Pa.: Cro Woods, 1969.

188
McMurry, Donald L. *Coxey's Army: A Study of the Industrial Army Movement of 1894.* Boston: Little, Brown and Co., 1929.

189
––––––. *The Great Burlington Strike of 1888.* Cambridge: Harvard University Press, 1956.

190
Manning, Thomas G. *The Chicago Strike of 1894: Industrial Labor in the Late Nineteenth Century.* New York: Holt, 1960.

191
Meltzer, Milton. *Bread and Roses: The Struggle of American Labor, 1865-1914.* New York: Alfred A. Knopf, 1967.

192
Nordhoff, Charles. *The Cotton States in Spring and Summer of 1875.* 1876. Reprint. New York: Lenox Hill Publishing Co. (Burt Franklin), 1970.

193
Parker, Morris B. *White Oaks: Life in a New Mexico Gold Camp, 1880-1900.* Tucson: University of Arizona Press, 1971.

194
Pinkerton, Allan. *The Molly Maguires and the Detectives.* New York: G.W. Carleton, 1878.

195
————. *Strikers, Communists, Tramps and Detectives: Railroad Strike of 1877.* 1900. Reprint. New York: Arno Press, 1969.

196
Randel, William Pierce. *Centennial: American Life in 1876.* Philadelphia: Chilton, 1969.

197
Rice, Lawrence D. *The Negro in Texas, 1874-1900.* Baton Rouge: Louisiana State University Press, 1971.

198
Rodgers, William Warren. *The One-Gallused Rebellion: Agrarianism in Alabama, 1865-1896.* Baton Rouge: Louisiana State University Press, 1970.

199
Rowan, R.W. *The Pinkertons, a Detective Dynasty.* Boston: Little, Brown and Co., 1931.

200
Salmons, C.H. *The Burlington Strike.* Aurora: Bunnell and Ward, 1889.

201
Saxton, Alexander. *The Indispensable Enemy: Labor and the Anti-Chinese Movement in California.* Berkeley: University of California Press, 1971.

202
Sennett, Richard. *Families against the City: Middle Class Homes of Industrial Chicago, 1872-1890.* Cambridge: Harvard University Press, 1970.

203
Smith, Robert W. *The Coeur d'Alene Mining War of 1892.* Corvallis: Oregon State University Press, 1961.

204
Tindall, George Brown. *South Carolina Negroes, 1877-1900.* Columbia: University of South Carolina Press, 1952.

205
U.S. Congress, House, United States Strike Commission. *Report on the Chicago Strike of June-July 1894.* Washington, D.C.: U.S. Government Printing Office, 1895.

206
Ware, Norman J. *The Labor Movement in the United States, 1860-1895.* New York: D. Appleton, 1929.

207

Warne, Colston E., ed. *The Pullman Boycott of 1894.* * Boston: D.C. Heath, 1955.

208

White, Howard Ashley. *The Freedmen's Bureau in Louisiana.* Baton Rouge: Louisiana State University Press, 1970.

209

Wolff, Leon. *Lockout, the Story of the Homestead Strike of 1892.* New York: Harper & Row, 1965.

210

Wright, Carroll D. *The Battles of Labor.* Philadelphia: Jacobs, 1906.

211

Yellowitz, Irwin. *The Position of the Worker in American Society, 1865-1896.* Englewood Cliffs: Prentice-Hall, 1969.

212

Ziff, Larzer. *The American 1890s: Life and Times of a Lost Generation.* New York: Viking Press, 1966.

Rise and Decline of the Knights of Labor

(1869-1890)

213

Browne, Henry J. *The Catholic Church and the Knights of Labor.* Washington, D.C.: Catholic University of America Press, 1949.

214

Grob, Gerald N. *Workers and Utopia: A Study of Ideological Conflict in the American Labor Movement, 1865-1900.* * Evanston: Northwestern University Press, 1961.

215

Meltzer, Milton. *Bread and Roses: The Struggle of American Labor, 1865-1914.* New York: Alfred A. Knopf, 1967.

216

Powderly, Terrence V. *The Path I Trod.* New York: Columbia University Press, 1940.

217

––––––. *Thirty Years of Labor, 1859-1889.* New York: Augustus M. Kelley, 1967.

The American Federation of Labor

(1885-1955)

218

Danish, Max. *William Green.* New York: Inter-Allied Publications, 1952.

219
Gompers, Samuel. *Seventy Years of Life and Labor.* New York: E.P. Dutton, 1925.

220
Gould, Jean. *Sidney Hillman: Great American.* Boston: Houghton Mifflin, 1952.

221
Grob, Gerald N. *Workers and Utopia: A Study of Idological Conflict in the American Labor Movement, 1865-1900.* Evanston: Northwestern University Press, 1961.

222
Lester, Richard A. *As Unions Mature: An Analysis of the Evolution of American Unionism.* Princeton: Princeton University Press, 1958.

223
Lorwin, Lewis L. (Levine, Louis, pseud.). *The American Federation of Labor: History, Policies and Prospects.* Washington, D.C.: Brookings Institution, 1933.

224
Mandel, Bernard. *Samuel Gompers: A Biography.* Yellow Springs: Antioch Press, 1963.

225
Meltzer, Milton. *Bread and Roses: The Struggle of American Labor, 1865-1914.* New York: Alfred A. Knopf, 1967.

226
Morris, James O. *Conflict within the A.F. of L.: A Study of Craft versus Industrial Unionism, 1901-1938.* Ithaca: Cornell University Press, 1958.

227
Stearn, Gerald Emanuel, ed. *Gompers.* Englewood Cliffs: Prentice-Hall, 1971.

228
Taft, Philip. *The A.F. of L. in the Time of Gompers.* New York: Harper & Row, 1957.

229
————. *The A.F. of L. from the Death of Gompers to the Merger.* New York: Harper & Row, 1959.

230
Walling, William. *American Labor and American Democracy.* New York: Harper, 1926.

The Progressive and Not So Progressive Era

(1900-1914)

231
Adams, Graham. *Age of Industrial Violence, 1910-1915.* New York: Columbia University Press, 1966.

232
Bonnett, Clarence E. *Employers' Associations in the United States*. New York: Macmillan, 1922.

233
Chrislock, Carl H. *The Progressive Era in Minnesota, 1899-1918*. St. Paul: Minnesota Historical Society, 1971.

234
Clopper, E.N. *Child Labor in City Streets*. New York: Macmillan, 1912.

235
Cornell, Robert J. *The Anthracite Coal Strike of 1902*. Washington, D.C.: Catholic University of America Press, 1957.

236
Dubofsky, Melvyn. *When Workers Organize: New York City in the Progressive Era*. Amherst: University of Massachusetts Press, 1968.

237
Gluck, Elsie. *John Mitchell, Miner: Labor's Bargain with the Gilded Age*. New York: John Day, 1929.

238
Grant, Luke. *The National Erectors' Association and the International Association of Bridge and Structural Ironworkers: The United States Commission on Industrial Relations*. Chicago: Barnard and Miller, 1915.

239
Green, Marguerite. *The National Civic Federation and the American Labor Movement, 1900-1925*. Washington, D.C.: Catholic University of America Press, 1956.

240
Gulick, Charles A. *Labor Policy of the United States Steel Corporation*. New York: Columbia University Press, 1924.

241
Holl, Jack M. *Juvenile Reform in the Progressive Era: William R. George and the Junior Republic Movement*. Ithaca: Cornell University Press, 1971.

242
Langdon, Emma F. *The Cripple Creek Strike: A History of Industrial Wars in Colorado, 1903-4-5*. Denver: Great Western Publishing Co., 1904-1905.

243
Person, Carl E. *The Lizard's Trail: A Story from the Illinois Central and Harriman Lines Strike of 1911 to 1915 Inclusive*. Chicago: Lake Publishing Co., 1918.

244
Stein, Leon. *The Triangle Fire*. Philadalphia: Lippincott, 1962.

245
Taylor, Albion Guilford. *Labor Policies of the National Association of Manufacturers*. Urbana: University of Illinois, 1928.

246
Yellowitz, Irwin. *Labor and the Progressive Movement in New York State, 1876-1916*. Ithaca: Cornell University Press, 1965.

Industrial Workers of the World

(1905-1920)

247
Brissenden, Paul F. *The IWW: A Study of American Syndicalism.* 1920. Reprint. New York: Russell & Russell, 1957.

248
Chaplin, Ralph. *Wobbly: The Rough-and-Tumble Story of an American Radical.* Chicago: University of Chicago Press, 1948.

249
Clark, Norman H. *Mill Town: A Social History of Everett, Washington.* Seattle: University of Washington Press, 1970.

250
Conlin, Joseph R. *Big Bill Haywood and the Radical Union Movement.* Syracuse: Syracuse University Press, 1969.

251
————————. *Bread and Roses Too: Studies of the Wobblies.* Westport: Greenwood Press, 1969.

252
Dubofsky, Melvin. *We Shall Be All: A History of the Industrial Workers of the World.* Chicago: Quadrangle Books, 1969.

253
Foner, Philip S. *The Case of Joe Hill.* New York: International Publishers, 1966.

254
Frost, Richard H. *The Mooney Case.* Stanford: Stanford University Press, 1968.

255
Gambs, John. *The Decline of the IWW.* New York: Columbia University Press, 1932.

256
Gentry, Curt. *Frame-Up: The Tom Mooney-Warren Billings Case.* New York: Norton, 1967.

257
Haywood, William D. *Bill Haywood's Book.* New York: International Publishers, 1929.

258
Jensen, Joan M. *The Price of Vigilance.* Chicago: Rand, McNally, 1968.

259
Kornbluh, Joyce L., ed. *Rebel Voices: An IWW Anthology.* * Ann Arbor: University of Michigan Press, 1964.

260
Preston, William, Jr. *Aliens and Dissenters: Federal Suppression of Radicals, 1903-1933.* * Cambridge: Harvard University Press, 1963.

261
Renshaw, Patrick. *The Wobblies: The Story of Syndicalism in the United States.* London: Eyre and Spottiswoode, 1967.

262
Smith, Gibbs M. *Joe Hill.* Salt Lake City: University of Utah Press, 1969.

263
Stegner, Wallace. *Joe Hill: A Biographical Novel.* Garden City: Doubleday, 1969.

264
Tyler, Robert L. *Rebels of the Woods: The IWW in the Pacific Northwest.* Eugene: University of Oregon Books, 1967.

265
Werstein, Irving. *Pie in the Sky: An American Struggle, the Wobblies and Their Times.* New York: Delacorte Press, 1969.

Labor in the First World War

(1914-1920)

266
Baker, R.S. *The New Industrial Unrest.* New York: Doubleday, Page, 1920.

267
Bing, Alexander. *War-Time Strikes and Their Adjustment.* New York: E.P. Dutton, 1921.

268
Brody, David. *Labor in Crisis: The Steel Strike of 1919.** Philadelphia: Lippincott, 1965.

269
Foster, William Z. *The Great Steel Strike and Its Lessons.* New York: B.W. Huebsch, 1920.

270
Friedheim, Robert L. *The Seattle General Strike.* Seattle: University of Washington Press, 1964.

271
Interchurch World Movement of North America, Commission of Inquiry. *Report on the Steel Strike of 1919.* New York: Putnam, 1923.

272
Jensen, Joan M. *The Price of Vigilance.* Chicago: Rand, McNally, 1968.

273
Kennedy, L.V. *Negro Peasant Turns Cityward.* New York: Columbia University Press, 1930.

274
Kluger, James R. *The Clifton-Morenci Strike: Labor Difficulty in Arizona, 1915-1916.* Tucson: University of Arizona Press, 1970.

275
Murray, Robert K. *Red Scare: A Study in National Hysteria, 1919-1920.* Minneapolis: University of Minnesota Press, 1955.

276
O'Connor, Harvey. *Revolution in Seattle: A Memoir.* New York: Monthly Review Press, 1964.

277
Peterson, H.C., and Fite, Gilbert C. *Opponents of War, 1917-1918.** Madison: University of Wisconsin Press, 1957.

278
Preston, William, Jr. *Aliens and Dissenters: Federal Suppression of Radicals, 1903-1933.** Cambridge: Harvard University Press, 1963.

279
Reid, Ira DeA. *Negro Immigrant.* New York: Columbia University Press, 1939.

280
Scott, Emmett J. *Negro Immigration during the War.* New York: Oxford University Press, 1920.

281
Tuttle, William M. *Race Riot: Chicago in the Red Summer of 1919.* New York: Atheneum, 1970.

282
Urofsky, Melvin I. *Big Steel and the Wilson Administration: A Study in Business and Government Relations.* Columbus: Ohio State University Press, 1969.

283
Warne, Colston E., ed. *The Steel Strike of 1919.** Boston: D.C. Heath, 1963.

284
Warne, Frank J. *The Workers at War.* New York: Century, 1920.

285
Watkins, Gordon S. *Labor Problems and Labor Administration in the United States during the World War.* 2 vols. Urbana: University of Illinois Press, 1920.

Welfare Capitalism and the Open Shop Campaign

(1921-1929)

286
Bernstein, Irving. *The Lean Years: A History of the American Worker, 1920-1933.** Boston: Houghton Mifflin, 1960.

287
Dunn, Robert W. *The Americanization of Labor: The Employers' Offensive against the Trade Unions.* New York: International Publishers, 1927.

288

Gallico, Paul. *The Revealing Eye: Personalities of the 1920s.* New York: Atheneum, 1967.

289

Green Marguerite. *The National Civic Federation and the American Labor Movement, 1900-1925.* Washington, D.C.: Catholic University of America Press, 1956.

290

Gulick, Charles A. *Labor Policy of the United States Steel Corporation.* New York: Columbia University Press, 1924.

291

Howard, Sidney Coe. *The Labor Spy.* New York: Republic Publishing Co., 1924.

292

Taylor, Albion Guilford. *Labor Policies of the National Association of Manufacturers.* Urbana: University of Illinois, 1928.

293

Wood, Louis Aubrey. *Union-Management Cooperation on the Railroads.* New Haven: Yale University Press, 1931.

294

Zieger, Robert H. *Republicans and Labor, 1919-1929.* Lexington: University of Kentucky Press, 1969.

The Great Depression

(1929-1940)

295

Aaron, Daniel, and Bendimer, Robert, eds. *The Strenuous Decade.** Garden City: Doubleday, 1970.

296

Ellis, Edward R. *A Nation in Torment: The Great American Depression, 1929-1939.* New York: Coward-McCann, 1970.

297

Goldston, Robert. *The Great Depression: The United States in the Thirties.** Indianapolis: Bobbs-Merrill, 1968.

298

Huthmacher, J. Joseph. *Senator Robert F. Wagner and the Rise of Urban Liberalism.* New York: Atheneum, 1968.

299

McWilliams, Carey. *Factories in the Field: The Story of Migratory Farm Labor in California.* Boston: Little, Brown and Co., 1939.

300

————. *Ill Fares the Land: Migrants and Migratory Labor in the United States.* Boston: Little, Brown and Co., 1942.

301
Simon, Rita James. *As We Saw the Thirties: Essays on Social and Political Movements of a Decade.* Urbana: University of Illinois Press, 1967.

302
Taylor, Paul S., and Lange, Dorothea. *An American Exodus: A Record of Human Erosion in the Thirties.* New Haven: Yale University Press, 1969.

303
Terkel, Studs. *Hard Times: An Oral History of the Great Depression.* * New York: Pantheon Books, 1970.

304
Thompson, W.S. *Research Memorandum on Internal Migration in the Depression.* New York: Social Science Research Council, 1939.

305
Walker, Charles Rumford. *American City: A Rank-and-File History.* New York: Farrar and Rinehart, 1937.

306
Webb, J.N., and Brown, Malcolm. *Migrant Families.* Washington, D.C.: U.S. Government Printing Office, 1939.

307
Wolters, Raymond. *Negroes and the Great Depression.* Westport: Greenwood Press, 1970.

The New Deal and the Rise of Industrial Unionism

(1933-1940)

308
Auerbach, Jerold S. *Labor and Liberty: The La Follette Committee and the New Deal.* Indianapolis: Bobbs-Merrill, 1966.

309
Bernstein, Irving. *The New Deal Collective Bargaining Policy.* Berkeley: University of California Press, 1950.

310
————. *The Turbulent Years: A History of the American Worker, 1933-1941.* Boston: Houghton Mifflin, 1970.

311
Brooks, Thomas R. *Picket Lines and Bargaining Tables: Organized Labor Comes of Age, 1935-1955.* New York: Grosset & Dunlap, 1968.

312
Cantor, Louis. *A Prologue to the Protest Movement: The Missouri Sharecropper Roadside Demonstrations of 1939.* Durham: Duke University Press, 1969.

313
Cayton, Horace R., and Mitchell, George S. *Black Workers and the New Unions.* Chapel Hill: University of North Carolina Press, 1939.

314
Cronon, Edmund D. *Labor and the New Deal.* Chicago: Rand McNally, 1963.

315
DeCaux, Len. *Labor Radical: From the Wobblies to CIO.* Boston: Beacon Press, 1970.

316
Derber, Milton, and Young, Edwin. *Labor and the New Deal.* Madison: University of Wisconsin Press, 1957.

317
Fine, Sidney A. *The Automobile under the Blue Eagle.* Ann Arbor: University of Michigan Press, 1963.

318
————. *Sitdown: The General Motors Strike of 1936-1937.* Ann Arbor: University of Michigan Press, 1969.

319
Galenson, Walter. *Rival Unionism in the U.S.* New York: American Council on Public Affairs, 1940.

320
————. *The CIO Challenge to the A.F. of L.: A History of the American Labor Movement, 1935-1941.* Cambridge: Harvard University Press, 1960.

321
Harris, Herbert. *Labor's Civil War.* New York: Alfred A. Knopf, 1940.

322
Hoffman, Claude E. *Sit-Down in Anderson: UAW Local 663 Anderson, Indiana.* Detroit: Wayne State University Press, 1968.

323
Huberman, Leo. *The Labor Spy Racket.* New York: Modern Age Books, 1937.

324
Kraus, Henry. *The Many and the Few.* Los Angeles: Plantin Press, 1947.

325
Leab, Daniel J. *A Union of Individuals: The Formation of the American Newspaper Guild, 1933-1936.* New York: Columbia University Press, 1970.

326
Lester, Richard A. *As Unions Mature: An Analysis of the Evolution of American Unionism.* Princeton: Princeton University Press, 1958.

327
Levinson, Edward. *Labor on the March.* New York: University Books, 1956.

328
McFarland, C.K. *Roosevelt, Lewis and the New Deal, 1933-1940.* Fort Worth: Texas Christian University Press, 1970.

329
Millis, Harry A., and Brown, E.C. *From the Wagner Act to Taft-Hartley: A Study of National Labor Policy and Labor Relations.* Chicago: University of Chicago Press, 1950.

330
Morris, James O. *Conflict within the A.F. of L.: A Study of Craft versus Industrial Unionism, 1901-1938.* Ithaca: Cornell University Press, 1958.

331
Perlman, Selig. *Labor in New Deal Decade.* New York: Educational Department, International Ladies' Garment Workers' Union, 1945.

332
Preis, Art. *Labor's Giant Step: Thirty Years of the CIO.* New York: Pioneer Publishers, 1964.

333
Quin, Mike. *The Big Strike.* Olema, Calif.: Olema Publishing Co., 1949.

334
Saposs, David J. *Communism in American Unions.* New York: McGraw-Hill, 1959.

335
Stolberg, Benjamin. *The Story of the CIO.* New York: Viking Press, 1938.

Labor in the Second World War and Early Postwar Period

(1941-1949)

336
Adams, L.P. *Wartime Manpower Mobilization, a Study of World War II Experience in the Buffalo-Niagara Area.* Ithaca: Cornell University Press, 1951.

337
Brooks, Thomas R. *Picket Lines and Bargaining Tables: Organized Labor Comes of Age, 1935-1955.* New York: Grosset & Dunlap, 1968.

338
Brown, E.L. *Why Race Riots?* New York: Public Affairs Committee, 1944.

339
Carr, L.J., and Stermer, J.E. *Willow Run: Industrialization and Cultural Inadequacy.* New York: Harper, 1952.

340
Goodman, Jack, ed. *While You Were Gone: A Report on Wartime Life in the U.S.* New York: Simon & Schuster, 1946.

341
Grodzins, Morton. *Americans Betrayed: Politics and the Japanese Evacuation.* Chicago: University of Chicago Press, 1949.

342

Kampelman, Max M. *The Communist Party vs. the CIO: A Study in Power Politics.* New York: Praeger, 1957.

343

McClure, Arthur F. *The Truman Administration and the Problems of Postwar Labor, 1945-1948.* Rutherford: Fairleigh Dickinson University Press, 1969.

344

Millis, Harry A., and Brown, E.C. *From the Wagner Act to Taft-Hartley: A Study of National Labor Policy and Labor Relations.* Chicago: University of Chicago Press, 1950.

345

Myer, Dillon S. *Uprooted Americans.* Tucson: University of Arizona Press, 1971.

346

Ogburn, W.F. *American Society in Wartime.* Chicago: University of Chicago Press, 1943.

347

Rose, A.M. *Negro in Postwar America.* New York: Anti-Defamation League of B'nai B'rith, 1950.

348

Ross, Malcolm. *All Manner of Man.* New York: Reynal & Hitchcock, 1948.

349

Seidman, Joel. *American Labor from Defense to Reconversion.* Chicago: University of Chicago Press, 1953.

350

Warne, Colston E., ed. *Labor in Postwar America.* Brooklyn: Remsen Press, 1949.

351

————, et al., eds. *War Labor Policies.* New York: Philosophical Library, 1943.

352

Witney, Fred. *Wartime Experiences of the National Labor Relations Board, 1941-1945.** Urbana: University of Illinois Press, 1949.

Recent and Current Problems and Practices of Labor

(1950s-1970s)

General

353

Beirne, Joseph A. *Challenge to Labor: New Roles for American Trade Unions.* Englewood Cliffs: Prentice-Hall, 1969.

354
Bok, Derek C., and Dunlop, John T. *Labor and the American Community.* *
New York: Simon & Schuster, 1970.

355
Bowen, William G. *Labor and the National Economy.* * Rev. ed. New
York: Norton, 1972.

356
Cochran, Bert, ed. *American Labor in Midpassage.* New York: Monthly
Review Press, 1959.

357
Davidson, Ray. *Peril on the Job: A Study of Hazards in the Chemical
Industries.* Washington, D.C.: Public Affairs Press, 1970.

358
Griswold, H. Jack. *An Eye for an Eye.* * New York: Holt, Rinehart and
Winston, 1970.

359
Haber, William, ed. *Labor in a Changing America.* New York: Basic Books,
1966.

360
Hardman, J.B.S., ed. *American Labor Dynamics in the Light of Post-War
Developments: An Inquiry by Thirty-Two Labor Men, Teachers, Editors,
and Technicians.* New York: Russell & Russell, 1968.

361
Jacks, Stanley M., ed. *Issues in Labor Policy.* Cambridge: M.I.T. Press, 1971.

362
Lindblom, Charles E. *Unions and Capitalism.* Hamden, Conn.: Archon
Books, 1970.

363
Murton, Tom, and Hyams, Joe. *Accomplices to the Crime.* New York: Grove
Press, 1970.

364
Peterson, Florence. *American Labor Unions: What They Are and How They
Work.* 2nd rev. ed. New York: Harper & Row, 1963.

365
Scoville, James G. *The Job Content of the U.S. Economy, 1940-1970.* New
York: McGraw-Hill, 1969.

366
Stapp, Andy. *Up Against the Brass.* * New York: Simon & Schuster, 1970.

367
Tyler, Gus. *The Labor Revolution: Trade Unions in a New America.* New
York: Viking Press, 1967.

368
Westley, William A., and Westley, Margaret W. *The Emerging
Worker: Equality and Conflict in the Mass Consumption Society.*
Montreal: McGill-Queen's University Press, 1971.

369
Widick, B.J. *Labor Today: The Triumphs and Failures of Unionism in the United States.* Boston: Houghton Mifflin, 1964.

370
Wirtz, William W. *Labor and the Public Interest.* New York: Harper & Row, 1964.

Unemployment

371
Bakke, E. Wight. *The Unemployed Worker: A Study of the Task of Making a Living without a Job.* Hamden, Conn.: Archon Books, 1970.

372
Okun, Arthur M. *The Battle against Unemployment.** Rev. ed. New York: Norton, 1972.

373
Weller, Jack E. *Yesterday's People: Life in Contemporary Appalachia.* Lexington, Ky.: University of Kentucky Press, 1965.

Union Membership

374
Franks, Maurice R. *What's Wrong with Our Labor Unions.* Indianapolis: Bobbs-Merrill, 1963.

375
Jacobs, Paul. *The State of the Unions.* New York: Atheneum, 1963.

376
Lens, Sidney. *The Crisis of American Labor.* New York: Sagamore Press, 1959.

377
Sultan, Paul E. *The Disenchanted Unionist.* New York: Harper & Row, 1963.

Collective Bargaining

378
Baumback, Clifford M. *Structural Wage Issues in Collective Bargaining.* Lexington, Mass.: D.C. Heath, 1971.

379
Brooks, Thomas R. *Picket Lines and Bargaining Tables: Organized Labor Comes of Age, 1935-1955.* New York: Grosset & Dunlap, 1968.

380
Bureau of National Affairs. *Collective Bargaining Today, 1970.* Washington, D.C.: Bureau of National Affairs, 1970.

381
Bureau of National Affairs. *Collective Bargaining Today, 1971.* Washington, D.C.: Bureau of National Affairs, 1971.

382
Chernish, William N. *Coalition Bargaining: A Study of Union Tactics and Public Policy.* Philadelphia: University of Pennsylvania Press, 1969.

383
Gillmer, Richard S. *Death of a Business: The Red Wing Potteries.* Minneapolis: Ross and Haines, 1968.

384
Gouldner, Alvin W. *Wildcat Strikes: A Study in Worker-Management Relationships.* New York: Harper & Row, 1965.

385
Gunter, Hans, ed. *Trans-National Industrial Relations.* New York: St. Martin's Press, 1972.

386
Karsh, Bernard. *Diary of a Strike.* Urbana: University of Illinois Press, 1958.

387
Kuechle, David. *The Story of the Savannah: An Episode in Maritime Labor-Management Relations.* Cambridge: Harvard University Press, 1971.

388
Levinson, Harold M; Rehmus, Charles M.; Goldberg, Joseph P.; and Kahn, Mark L. *Collective Bargaining and Technological Change in American Transportation.* Evanston: Transportation Center, Northwestern University, 1971.

389
Mills, Daniel Q. *Industrial Relations and Manpower in Construction.* Cambridge: M.I.T. Press, 1972.

390
Munts, Raymond. *Bargaining for Health: Labor Unions, Health Insurance, and Medical Care.* Madison: University of Wisconsin Press, 1967.

391
Rowan, Richard L., ed. *Collective Bargaining: Survival in the '70s?* Philadelphia: Industrial Research Unit, University of Pennsylvania, 1972.

392
Seidman, Joel, ed. *Trade Union Government and Collective Bargaining: Some Critical Issues.* New York: Praeger, 1970.

393
Siegel, Abraham, J., ed. *The Impact of Computers on Collective Bargaining.* Cambridge: M.I.T. Press, 1969.

394
Slote, Alfred. *Termination: The Closing at Baker Plant.* Indianapolis: Bobbs-Merrill, 1969.

395

Tandon, B.K. *Collective Bargaining and the Indian Scene.* Mystic: Verry, Laurence, 1971.

396

Thieblot, Armand J., and Cowin, Ronald M. *Welfare and Strikes: The Use of Public Funds to Support Strikers.* Philadelphia: Industrial Research Unit, University of Pennsylvania, 1972.

397

Uphoff, Walter H. *Kohler on Strike: Thirty Years of Conflict.* * Boston: Beacon Press, 1966.

398

Wolfbein, Seymour L., ed. *Emerging Sectors of Collective Bargaining.* * Braintree, Mass.: D.H. Mark, 1970.

Professional, Technical and Office Workers

399

Arian, Edward. *Bach, Beethoven, and Bureaucracy: The Case of the Philadelphia Orchestra.* University, Ala.: University of Alabama Press, 1971.

400

Baitsell, John M. *Airline Industrial Relations: Pilots and Flight Engineers.* Boston: Harvard Business School, 1966.

401

Blum, Albert A.; Estey, Marten; Kuhn, James W.; Wildman, Wesley A.; and Troy, Leo. *White-Collar Workers.* New York: Random House, 1971.

402

Koenig, Allen E., ed. *Broadcasting and Bargaining: Labor Relations in Radio and Television.* Madison: University of Wisconsin Press, 1970.

403

Moskow, Michael H. *Labor Relations in the Performing Arts: An Introductory Survey.* New York: Associated Councils of the Arts, 1969.

404

Parrish, Bernie. *They Call It a Game.* New York: Dial Press, 1971.

405

Walton, Richard. *The Impact of the Professional Engineering Union.* Boston: Graduate School of Business Administration, Harvard University, 1961.

Public and Non-Profit Employees

406

Blum, Albert A.; Estey, Marten; Kuhn James W.; Wildman, Wesley A.; and Troy, Leo. *White-Collar Workers.* New York: Random House, 1971.

407
Bureau of National Affairs. *The Crisis in Public Employee Relations in the Decade of the Seventies.* * Washington, D.C.: Bureau of National Affairs, 1970.

408
Burpo, John H. *The Police Labor Movement: Problems and Perspectives.* Springfield, Ill.: Charles C. Thomas, 1971.

409
Cole, Stephen, *United Federation of Teachers: A Case Study of the UFT.* New York: Praeger, 1969.

410
Elam, Stanley, and Moskow, Michael H., eds. *Employment Relations in Higher Education.* Bloomington, Ind.: Phi Delta Kappa, 1969.

411
Moskow, Michael H. *Teachers and Unions: The Applicability of Collective Bargaining to Public Education.* Philadelphia: University of Pennsylvania Press, 1966.

412
Roberts, Harold S. *Labor-Management Relations in the Public Service.* Honolulu: University of Hawaii Press, 1970.

413
Smith, Dennis. *Report from Engine Co. 82.* New York: McCall, 1971.

414
Stanley, David T., and Cooper, Carole L. *Managing Local Government under Union Pressure.* Washington, D.C.: Brookings Institution, 1972.

415
Stinnett, T.M. *Turmoil in Teaching: A History of the Organizational Struggle for America's Teachers.* New York: Macmillan, 1968.

416
Walsh, Robert E., ed. *Sorry . . . No Government Today: Unions vs. City Hall.* Boston: Beacon Press, 1969.

417
Wellington, Harry H., and Winter, Ralph K. *The Unions and the Cities.* Washington, D.C.: Brookings Institution, 1971.

418
Zagoria, Sam, ed. *Public Workers and Public Unions.* * Englewood Cliffs: Prentice-Hall, 1972.

419
Zitron, Celia Lewis. *The New York City Teachers Union, 1916-1964.* New York: Humanities Press, 1968.

Black Workers

420
Armstrong, Gregory, ed. *Life at the Bottom.* New York: Bantam Books, 1971.

421

Blumrosen Alfred W. *Black Employment and the Law.* New Brunswick: Rutgers University Press, 1971.

422

Bracey, John H.; Meier, August; and Rudwick, Elliot, eds. *Black Workers and Organized Labor.* Belmont, Calif.: Wadsworth Publishing Co., 1971.

423

Cantor, Milton, ed. *Black Labor in America.* Westport: Negro Universities Press, 1969.

424

Daniel, Pete. *The Shadow of Slavery: Peonage in the South, 1901-1969.* Urbana: University of Illinois Press, 1972.

425

Ferman, Louis A., et al., eds. *Negroes and Jobs: A Book of Readings.* * Ann Arbor: University of Michigan Press, 1968.

426

Jacobson, Julius, ed. *The Negro and the American Labor Movement.* * New York: Doubleday, 1968.

427

Kovarsky, Irving, and Albrecht, William. *Black Employment: The Impact of Religion, Economic Theory, Politics and Law.* Ames: Iowa State University Press, 1970.

428

Marshall, F. Ray. *The Negro and Organized Labor.* New York: John Wiley, 1965.

429

————, and Briggs, Vernon M., Jr. *The Negro and Apprenticeship.* Baltimore: Johns Hopkins Press, 1967.

430

Marshall, Ray. *The Negro Worker.* * New York: Random House, 1967.

431

Meier, August, and Rudwick, Elliot M. *From Plantation to Ghetto.* * Rev. ed. New York: Hill & Wang, 1970.

432

Osofsky, Gilbert. *Harlem: The Making of a Ghetto.* 2nd ed. New York: Harper, 1971.

433

Rose, A.M. *Negro in Postwar America.* New York: Anti-Defamation League of B'nai B'rith, 1950.

434

Ross, Arthur M., and Hill, Herbert, eds. *Employment, Race and Poverty: A Critical Study of the Disadvantaged Status of Negro Workers from 1865-1965.* * New York: Harcourt, Brace & World, 1967.

435
Spero, Sterling D., and Harris, Abram L. *The Black Worker: The Negro and the Labor Movement.* Port Washington: Kennikat Press, 1931.

436
Twentieth Century Fund Task Force on Employment Problems of Black Youth. *The Job Crisis for Black Youth.* New York: Praeger, 1971.

437
Weaver, Robert C. *Negro Labor: A National Problem.* New York: Harcourt, Brace & World, 1946.

438
Weinstein, Allen, and Gatell, Frank Otto. *The Segregation Era, 1863-1954: A Modern Reader.* New York: Oxford University Press, 1970.

Mexican-Americans

439
Allen, Steve. *The Ground is Our Table.* Garden City: Doubleday, 1966.

440
Armstrong, Gregory, ed. *Life at the Bottom.** New York: Bantam Books, 1971.

441
Bishop, C.E., ed. *Farm Labor in the United States.* New York: Columbia University Press, 1967.

442
Craig, Richard B. *The Bracero Program: Interest Groups and Foreign Policy.* Austin: University of Texas Press, 1971.

443
Day, Mark. *Forty Acres: César Chávez and the Farm Workers.* New York: Praeger, 1971.

444
Dunne, John Gregory. *Delano: The Story of the California Grape Strike.* Rev. ed. New York: Farrar, Straus & Giroux, 1971.

445
Galarza, Ernesto. *Merchants of Labor: The Mexican Bracero Story.** Santa Barbara: McNally & Loftin, 1964.

446
————. *Spiders in the House and Workers in the Field.* Notre Dame: University of Notre Dame Press, 1970.

447
Howard, John R., ed. *Awakening Minorities: American Indians, Mexican Americans, Puerto Ricans.* Chicago: Aldine Pub. Co, 1970.

448
London, Joan, and Anderson, Henry. *So Shall Ye Reap: The Story of César Chávez and the Farm Workers' Movement.* New York: Thomas Y. Crowell, 1970.

449
McWilliams, Carey. *Factories in the Field: The Story of Migratory Farm Labor in California.* Boston: Little, Brown and Co., 1939.

450
––––––. *Ill Fares the Land: Migrants and Migratory Labor in the United States.* Boston: Little, Brown and Co., 1942.

451
Matthiessen, Peter. *Sal Si Puedes: César Chávez and the New American Revolution.* * New York: Random House, 1969.

452
Moore, Truman. *The Slaves We Rent.* New York: Random House, 1965.

453
Norquest, Carrol. *Rio Grande Wetbacks: Migrant Mexican Workers.* Albuquerque: University of New Mexico Press, 1972.

454
Samora, Julian, ed. *La Raza: Forgotten Americans.* * Notre Dame: University of Notre Dame Press, 1966.

455
––––––. *Los Mojados: The Wetback Story.* Notre Dame: University of Notre Dame Press, 1971.

456
Servin, Manuel P. *The Mexican-Americans: An Awakening Minority.* Beverly Hills: Glencoe Press, 1970.

457
Shotwell, Louisa R. *The Harvesters: The Story of the Migrant People.* Garden City: Doubleday, 1961.

458
Steiner, Stan. *La Raza: The Mexican Americans.* * New York: Harper & Row, 1970.

459
Webb, J.N. *Migratory-Casual Worker.* Washington, D.C.: U.S. Government Printing Office, 1937.

460
Wright, Dale. *They Harvest Despair: The Migrant Farm Worker.* Boston: Beacon Press, 1965.

461
Young, Jan. *Migrant Workers and César Chávez.* New York: Julian Messner, 1972.

White Blue-Collar Workers

462
Blauner, Robert. *Alienation and Freedom: The Factory Worker and His Industry.* Chicago: University of Chicago Press, 1964.

463
Lasson, Kenneth. *The Workers: Portraits of Nine American Job Holders.*
New York: Grossman, 1971.

464
Levitan, Sar A. *Blue Collar Workers: A Symposium on Middle America.* New
York: McGraw-Hill, 1971.

Women

465
Bird, Caroline. *Born Female: The High Cost of Keeping Women Down.* New
York: David McKay, 1968.

466
Cain, Glen C. *Married Women in the Labor Force: An Economic Analysis.*
Chicago: University of Chicago Press, 1966.

467
Kreps, Juanita. *Sex in the Marketplace: American Women at Work.* Baltimore: Johns Hopkins Press, 1971.

468
U.S. Women's Bureau. *American Women at the Crossroads: Directions for
the Future.* Report of the 50th Anniversary of the Women's Bureau,
Department of Labor. Washington, D.C.: U.S. Government Printing
Office.

Internal Union Affairs

469
Cook, Alice H. *Union Democracy: Practice and Ideal.* Ithaca: Cornell
University, 1963.

470
Garnel, Donald. *The Rise of Teamster Power in the West.* Berkeley: University of California Press, 1971.

471
Graham, Harry Edward. *The Paper Rebellion: Development and Upheaval in
Pulp and Paper Unionism.* Iowa City: University of Iowa, 1970.

472
Hume, Brit. *Death and the Mines: Rebellion and Murder in the UMW.* New
York: Grossman, 1971.

473
Hutchinson, John. *The Imperfect Union: A History of Corruption in
American Trade Unions.* New York: E.P. Dutton, 1970.

474
James, Ralph, and James, Estelle. *Hoffa and the Teamsters: A Study of
Union Power.* * Princeton: D. Van Nostrand, 1965.

475
Johnson, Malcolm M. *Crime on the Labor Front.* New York: McGraw-Hill,
1950.

476
Kennedy, Robert F. *The Enemy Within.** New York: Harper & Row, 1960.

477
McClellan, John L. *Crime without Punishment.* New York: Duell, Sloan & Pearce, 1962.

478
Mills, C. Wright. *The New Men of Power: America's Labor Leaders.* New York: Harcourt, Brace, 1948.

479
Mollenhoff, Clark D. *Tentacles of Power: The Story of Jimmy Hoffa.* Cleveland: World Pub. Co., 1965.

480
Seidman, Joel, ed. *Trade Union Government and Collective Bargaining: Some Critical Issues.* New York: Praeger, 1970.

481
————; London, Jack; Karsh, Bernard; and Tagliacozzo, Daisy L. *The Worker Views His Union.* Chicago: University of Chicago Press, 1958.

482
Tyler, Gus. *The Political Imperative: The Corporate Character of Unions.* New York: Macmillan, 1968.

AFL and CIO

483
Goldberg, Arthur. *AFL-CIO Labor United.* New York: McGraw-Hill, 1956.

Foreign Policy

484
Craig, Richard B. *The Bracero Program: Interest Groups and Foreign Policy.* Austin: Univerisity of Texas Press, 1971.

485
Foner, Philip S. *American Labor and the Indochina War: The Growth of Union Opposition.* New York: International Publishers, 1971.

486
Hero, Alfred O. *The UAW and World Affairs.* Boston: World Peace Foundation, 1965.

487
————. *The Reuther-Meany Foreign Policy Dispute.* Dobbs Ferry: Oceana Publications, 1970.

488
Morris, George. *The CIA and American Labor: The Subversion of the AFL-CIO's Foreign Policy.* New York: International Publishers, 1967.

489
Radosh, Ronald. *American Labor and United States Foreign Policy.* New York: Random House, 1969.

SPECIALIZED TOPICS

Biographical and Autobiographical Material

490

Alinsky, Saul. *John L. Lewis: An Unauthorized Biography.* New York: Putnam, 1949.

491

Barnard, Harry. *Eagle Forgotten: The Life of John Peter Altgeld.* Indianapolis: Bobbs-Merrill, 1938.

492

Beebe, Lucius. *The Big Spenders.* * Garden City: Doubleday, 1966.

493

Beshoar, Barron B. *Out of the Depths: The Story of John R. Lawson a Labor Leader.* Denver: World Press, 1942.

494

Bisno, Abraham. *Abraham Bisno: Union Pioneer in the Women's Garment Industry.* Madison: University of Wisconsin Press, 1967.

495

Bonosky, Phillip. *Brother Bill McKie: Building the Union at Ford.* New York: International Publishers, 1953.

496

Boucher, Arline, and Tehan, John. *Prince of Democracy: James Cardinal Gibbons.* Garden City: Doubleday, 1962.

497

Bridge, James Howard. *The History of the Carnegie Steel Company.* New York: Aldine Pub. Co., 1903.

498

Buchanan, Joseph R. *The Story of a Labor Agitator.* New York: The Outlook Co., 1903.

499

Buder, Stanley. *Pullman: An Experiment in Industrial Order and Community Planning, 1880-1930.* New York: Oxford University Press, 1967.

500

Calmer, Alan. *Labor Agitator: The Story of Albert R. Parsons.* New York: International Publishers, 1937.

501

Caudill, Harry. *Night Comes to the Cumberlands: A Biography of a Depressed Area.* Boston: Little, Brown and Co, 1963.

502

Christman, Henry M., ed. *The Mind and Spirit of John Peter Altgeld: Selected Writings and Addresses.* Urbana: University of Illinois Press, 1960.

503

Cole, Margaret. *Robert Owen of New Lanark, 1771-1858.* New York: Oxford University Press, 1953.

504

Conlin, Joseph R. *Big Bill Haywood and the Radical Union Movement.* Syracuse: Syracuse University Press, 1969.

505

Cormier, Frank, and Eaton, William J. *Reuther.* Englewood Cliffs: Prentice-Hall, 1970.

506

Danish, Max D. *William Green.* New York: Inter-Allied Publications, 1952.

507

––––––. *The World of David Dubinsky.* Cleveland: World Pub. Co., 1957.

508

Darrow, Clarence. *The Story of My Life: An Autobiography.* New York: Scribner, 1932.

509

Day, Mark. *Forty Acres: César Chávez and the Farm Workers.* New York: Praeger, 1971.

510

DeCaux, Len. *Labor Radical: From the Wobblies to CIO.* Boston: Beacon Press, 1970.

511

Dunne, John Gregory. *Delano: The Story of the California Grape Strike.* Rev. ed. New York: Farrar, Straus & Giroux, 1971.

512

Evans, W. McKee. *To Die Game: The Story of the Lowry Band, Indian Guerillas of Reconstruction.* Baton Rouge: Louisiana State University, 1971.

513

Fast, Howard M. *The Passion of Sacco and Vanzetti: A New England Legend.* New York: Blue Heron Press, 1953.

514

Feldstein, Stanley. *Once a Slave: The Slave's View of Slavery.* New York: William Morrow, 1971.

515

Foner, Philip S. *Jack London, American Rebel.* New York: Citadel Press, 1947.

516

––––––. *The Case of Joe Hill.* New York: International Publishers, 1966.

517

Fox, Mary Harrita. *Peter E. Dietz, Labor Priest.* Notre Dame: University of Notre Dame Press, 1953.

518
Frost, Richard H. *The Mooney Case*. Stanford: Stanford University Press, 1968.

519
Gallico, Paul. *The Revealing Eye: Personalities of the 1920s*. New York: Atheneum, 1967.

520
Gentry, Curt. *Frame-Up: The Tom Mooney-Warren Billings Case*. New York: Norton, 1967.

521
Gilfillan, Lauren. *I Went to Pit College*. New York: Viking Press, 1934.

522
Ginger, Ray. *The Bending Cross: A Biography of Eugene V. Debs*. New Brunswick: Rutgers University Press, 1949.

523
————————. *Altgeld's America: The Lincoln Ideal v. Changing Realities*. New York: Funk and Wagnalls, 1958.

524
Ginzberg, Eli, and Berman, Hyman. *The American Worker in the Twentieth Century: A History through Autobiographies*. New York: The Free Press, 1963.

525
Gluck, Elsie. *John Mitchell, Miner: Labor's Bargain with the Gilded Age*. New York: John Day, 1929.

526
Goldmark, Josephine. *Impatient Crusader: Florence Kelley's Life Story* Urbana: University of Illinois Press, 1953.

527
Gompers, Samuel. *Seventy Years of Life and Labor*. New York: E.P. Dutton, 1925.

528
Gould, Jean. *Sidney Hillman: Great American*. Boston: Houghton Mifflin, 1952.

529
Grossman, Jonathan. *William Sylvis: Pioneer of American Labor*. New York: Columbia University Press, 1945.

530
Hanna, Hilton E., and Belsky, Joseph. *Picket and the Pen: The Pat Gorman Story*. Yonkers: American Institute of Social Science, 1960.

531
Harvey, G.B.M. *Henry Clay Frick*. New York: Scribner, 1928.

532
Haywood, William D. *Bill Haywood's Book*. New York: International Publishers, 1929.

533
Hero, Alfred O. *The Reuther-Meany Foreign Policy Dispute.* Dobbs Ferry: Oceana Publications, 1970.

534
Hoffa, James R. *The Trials of Jimmy Hoffa: An Autobiography.* Chicago: Henry Regnery, 1970.

535
Holl, Jack M. *Juvenile Reform in the Progressive Era: William R. George and the Junior Republic Movement.* Ithaca: Cornell University Press, 1971.

536
Hopkins, George E. *The Airline Pilots: A Study in Elite Unionization.* Cambridge: Harvard University Press, 1971.

537
Howe, Irving, and Widick, B.J. *The UAW and Walter Reuther.* New York: Random House, 1949.

538
Huthmacher, J. Joseph. *Senator Robert F. Wagner and the Rise of Urban Liberalism.* New York: Atheneum, 1968.

539
James, Ralph, and James Estelle. *Hoffa and the Teamsters: A Study of Union Power.* * Princeton: D. Van Nostrand, 1965.

540
Jones, Mary. *Autobiography of Mother Jones.* Chicago: C.H. Kerr, 1925.

541
Josephson, Matthew. *Sidney Hillman, Statesman of American Labor.* Garden City: Doubleday, 1952.

542
————. *The Robber Barons: The Great American Capitalists, 1861-1901.* 1934. New York: Harcourt, Brace & World, 1962.

543
Joughin, G.L., and Morgan, E.M. *Legacy of Sacco and Vanzetti.* New York: Harcourt, Brace, 1948.

544
Kraus, Henry. *The Many and the Few.* Los Angeles: Plantin Press, 1947.

545
Kurland, Gerald. *Seth Low: The Reformer in an Urban and Industrial Age.* New York: Twayne Publishers, 1971.

546
Leiter, Robert D. *The Musicians and Petrillo.* New York: Bookman Associates, 1953.

547
London, Joan, and Anderson, Henry. *So Shall Ye Reap: The Story of César Chávez and the Farm Workers' Movement.* New York: Thomas Y. Crowell, 1970.

548
McDonald, David J. *Union Man*. New York: E.P. Dutton, 1969.

549
McFarland, C.K. *Roosevelt, Lewis and the New Deal, 1933-1940*. Fort Worth: Texas Christian University Press, 1970.

550
McMurry, Donald L. *Coxey's Army: A Study of the Industrial Army Movement of 1894*. Boston: Little, Brown and Co., 1929.

551
Madison, Charles A. *American Labor Leaders: Personalities and Forces in the Labor Movement*. New York: Frederick Ungar, 1962.

552
Mandel, Bernard. *Samuel Gompers: A Biography*. Yellow Springs: Antioch Press, 1963.

553
Matthiessen, Peter. *Sal Si Puedes: César Chávez and the New American Revolution.* * New York: Random House, 1969.

554
Mollenhoff, Clark D. *Tentacles of Power: The Story of Jimmy Hoffa*. Cleveland: World Pub. Co., 1965.

555
Mortimer, Wyndham. *Organize! My Life as a Union Man*. Boston: Beacon Press, 1971.

556
Payton, Boyd E. *Scapegoat: Prejudice, Politics, Prison*. Philadelphia: Whitmore Pub. Co., 1970.

557
Powderly, Terrence. *The Path I Trod*. New York: Columbia University Press, 1940.

558
————. *Thirty Years of Labor, 1859-1889*. New York: Augustus M. Kelley, 1967.

559
Raymond, Allen. *Waterfront Priest*. New York: Holt, 1955.

560
Roney, Frank. *Frank Roney: Irish Rebel and California Labor Leader*. Berkeley: University of California Press, 1931.

561
Royko, Mike. *Boss: Richard J. Daley of Chicago*. New York: E.P. Dutton, 1971.

562
Seidman, Harold. *Labor Czars: A History of Labor Racketeering*. New York: Liveright, 1958.

563
Seligman, Ben B. *The Potentates: Business and Businessmen in American History.* New York: Dial Press, 1971.

564
Shefferman, Nathan. *The Man in the Middle.* Garden City, Doubleday, 1961.

565
Smith, Gibbs M. *Joe Hill.* Salt Lake City: University of Utah Press, 1969.

566
Stearn, Gerald Emanuel, ed. *Gompers.* Englewood Cliffs: Prentice-Hall, 1971.

567
Steffens, Lincoln. *The Autobiography of Lincoln Steffens.* 2 vols. New York: Harcourt, Brace, 1937.

568
Stegner, Wallace. *Joe Hill: A Biographical Novel.* Garden City: Doubleday, 1969.

569
Sward, Keith. *The Legend of Henry Ford.* * New York: Rinehart, 1948.

570
Taft, Philip. *The A.F. of L. in the Time of Gompers.* New York: Harper & Row, 1957.

571
Tarr, Joel A. *A Study of Boss Politics: William Lorimer of Chicago.* Urbana: University of Illinois Press, 1971.

572
Todes, Charlotte. *William H. Sylvis and the National Labor Union.* New York: International Publishers, 1942.

573
Tussey, Jean Y., ed. *Eugene V. Debs Speaks.* New York: Pathfinder Press, 1970.

574
Wall, Joseph F. *Andrew Carnegie.* New York: Oxford University Press, 1970.

575
Ward, Estolv E. *Harry Bridges on Trial.* * New York: Modern Age Books, 1940.

576
Washington, Booker T. *Up From Slavery.* Garden City: A.L. Bert Co., 1901.

577
Wechsler, James A. *Labor Baron: A Portrait of John L. Lewis.* New York: William Morrow, 1944.

578
Weintraub, Hyman G. *Andrew Furuseth: Emancipator of the Seamen.* Berkeley: University of California Press, 1959.

579
Whittemore, L.H. *The Man Who Ran the Subways: The Story of Mike Quill.*
New York: Holt, Rinehart and Winston, 1968.

580
Williams, T. Harry. *Huey Long.* * New York: Alfred A. Knopf, 1969.

581
Wolfson, Theresa, and Perkins, Alice J.G. *Frances Wright: Free Enquirer; the Study of a Temperament.* New York: Harper, 1939.

Immigrant and Minority Groups in the Labor Force

582
Allen, Steve. *The Ground is Our Table.* Garden City: Doubleday, 1966.

583
Allsop, Kenneth. *Hard Travellin': The Hobo and His History.* New
York: New American Library, 1967.

584
Ander, O. Fritiof, ed. *In the Trek of the Immigrants.* Rock Island,
Ill.: Augustana College Library, 1964.

585
Anderson, Nels. *Men on the Move.* Chicago: University of Chicago Press,
1940.

586
Aptheker, Herbert. *To Be Free: Studies in American Negro History.* New
York: International Publishers, 1948.

587
Bennett, Lerone. *Black Power, U.S.A.: The Human Side of Reconstruction,
1867-1877.* Chicago: Johnson Pub. Co., 1967.

588
Berthoff, Rowland. *British Immigrants in Industrial America, 1790-1950.*
Cambridge: Harvard University Press, 1953.

589
Bishop, C.E., ed. *Farm Labor in the United States.* New York: Columbia
University Press, 1967.

590
Blumrosen, Alfred W. *Black Employment and the Law.* New Brunswick: Rutgers University Press, 1971.

591
Bracey, John H.; Meier, August; and Budwick, Elliot, eds. *Black Workers and
Organized Labor.* Belmont, Calif.: Wadsworth Pub. Co., 1971.

592
Brown, E.L. *Why Race Riots?* New York: Public Affairs Committee, 1944.

593
Burdick, Eugene. *The Ninth Wave.* Boston: Houghton Mifflin, 1956.

594
Cain, Glen C. *Married Women in the Labor Force: An Economic Analysis.* Chicago: University of Chicago Press, 1966.
595
Campbell, Helen S. *Prisoners of Poverty.* Boston: Roberts Brothers, 1887.
596
————. *Women Wage-Earners, Their Trade and Their Lives.* Boston: Roberts Brothers, 1893.
597
Cantor, Milton, ed. *Black Labor in America.* Westport: Negro Universities Press, 1969.
598
Cayton, Horace R., and Mitchell, George S. *Black Workers and the New Unions.* Chapel Hill: University of North Carolina Press, 1939.
599
Collidge, Mary Roberts. *Chinese Immigration.* New York: Holt, 1909.
600
Craig, Richard B. *The Bracero Program: Interest Groups and Foreign Policy.* Austin: University of Texas Press, 1971.
601
Day, Mark. *Forty Acres: César Chávez and the Farm Workers.* New York: Praeger, 1971.
602
Dunaway, Wayland F. *The Scotch-Irish of Colonial Pennsylvania.* Chapel Hill: University of North Carolina Press, 1944.
603
Dunne, John Gregory. *Delano: The Story of the California Grape Strike.* Rev. ed. New York: Farrar, Straus & Giroux, 1971.
604
Epstein, Melech. *Jewish Labor in U.S.A.* Vols. 1 and 2. New York: KTAV Pub. House, 1969.
605
Erickson, Charlotte. *American Industry and the European Immigrant, 1860-1885.* Cambridge: Harvard University Press, 1957.
606
Feied, Frederick. *No Pie in the Sky: The Hobo as an American Cultural Hero.* New York: Citadel Press, 1964.
607
Ferman, Louis A., et al., eds. *Negroes and Jobs: A Book of Readings.** Ann Arbor: University of Michigan Press, 1968.
608
Fermi, Laura. *Illustrious Immigrants: The Intellectual Migration from Europe, 1930-1941.* 2nd ed. Chicago: University of Chicago Press, 1972.
609
Fortune, Timothy Thomas. *Black and White: Land, Labor and Politics in the South.* New York: Arno Press, 1968.

610
Friedland, William H., and Nelkin, Dorothy. *Migrant-Agricultural Workers in America's Northeast.* New York: Holt, Rinehart and Winston, 1972.

611
Galarza, Ernesto. *Merchants of Labor: The Mexican Bracero Story.** Santa Barbara: McNally & Loftin, 1964.

612
––––––. *Spiders in the House and Workers in the Field.* Notre Dame: University of Notre Dame Press, 1970.

613
Greene, Victor R. *The Slavic Community on Strike: Immigrant Labor in Pennsylvania Anthracite.* Notre Dame: University of Notre Dame Press, 1968.

614
Griswold, H. Jack. *An Eye for an Eye.** New York: Holt, Rinehart and Winston, 1970.

615
Grodzins, Morton. *Americans Betrayed: Politics and the Japanese Evacuation.* Chicago: University of Chicago Press, 1949.

616
Handlin, Oscar, ed. *This Was America.* Cambridge: Harvard University Press, 1949.

617
––––––. *The Uprooted: The Epic Story of the Great Migrations.** Boston: Little, Brown and Co., 1951.

618
––––––. *Race and Nationality in American Life.* Boston: Little, Brown and Co., 1957.

619
––––––. *Boston's Immigrants, 1790-1880.* Cambridge: Harvard University Press, 1959.

620
Hansen, Marcus Lee. *The Atlantic Migration 1607-1860.* New York: Harper & Row, 1961.

621
Henry, Alice. *Trade Union Woman.* New York: D. Appleton, 1915.

622
Higham, John. *Strangers in the Land: Patterns of American Nativism, 1860-1925.* New York: Atheneum, 1970.

623
Hourwich, Isaac. *Immigration and Labor: The Economic Aspects of European Immigration to the United States.* New York: B.W. Huebsch, 1922.

624
Howard, John R., ed. *Awakening Minorities: American Indians, Mexican Americans, Puerto Ricans.* Chicago: Aldine Pub. Co., 1970.

625

Hunter, Robert. *Poverty.* New York: Macmillan, 1904.

626

Jacobson, Julius, ed. *The Negro and the American Labor Movement.* * New York: Doubleday, 1968.

627

Jordan, Winthrop. *White over Black: American Attitudes toward the Negro, 1550-1812.* Chapel Hill: University of North Carolina Press, 1968.

628

Joughin, G.L., and Morgan, E.M. *Legacy of Sacco and Vanzetti.* New York: Harcourt, Brace, 1948.

629

Kelsey, Carl. *Negro Farmer.* Chicago: Jennings & Pye, 1903.

630

Kennedy, L.V. *Negro Peasant Turns Cityward.* New York: Columbia University Press, 1930.

631

Korman, Gerd. *Industrialization, Immigrants and Americanizers: The View from Milwaukee, 1866-1921.* Madison: State Historical Society of Wisconsin, 1967.

632

Leupp, F.E. *Indian and His Problem.* New York: Scribner, 1910.

633

Lewis, Oscar. *Sea Routes to the Gold Fields: The Migration to California by Water, 1849-1852.* * New York: Alfred A. Knopf, 1949.

634

————. *La Vida: A Puerto Rican Family in the Culture of Poverty—San Juan and New York.* * New York: Random House, 1966.

635

Ljungmark, Lars. *For Sale—Minnesota: Organized Promotion of Scandinavian Immigration, 1866-1873.* Chicago: Swedish Pioneer Historical Society, 1971.

636

London, Joan, and Anderson, Henry. *So Shall Ye Reap: The Story of César Chávez and the Farm Workers' Movement.* New York: Thomas Y. Crowell, 1970.

637

McWilliams, Carey. *Factories in the Field: The Story of Migratory Farm Labor in California.* Boston: Little, Brown and Co., 1939.

638

————. *Ill Fares the Land: Migrants and Migratory Labor in the United States.* Boston: Little, Brown and Co., 1942.

639

Manning, Caroline. *The Immigrant Woman and Her Job.* New York: Arno Press, 1970.

640
Marshall, F. Ray. *The Negro and Organized Labor.* New York: John Wiley, 1965.

641
—————, and Briggs, Vernon M., Jr. *The Negro and Apprenticeship.* Baltimore: Johns Hopkins Press, 1967.

642
Marshall, Ray. *The Negro Worker.* * New York: Random House, 1967.

643
Matthiessen, Peter. *Sal Si Puedes: César Chávez and the New American Revolution.* * New York: Random House, 1969.

644
Meier, August, and Rudwick, Elliot M. *From Plantation to Ghetto.* * Rev. ed. New York: Hill & Wang, 1970.

645
Miller, Stuart Creighton. *The Unwelcome Immigrant: The American Image of the Chinese, 1785-1822.* Berkeley: University of California Press, 1969.

646
Millis, H.A. *Japanese Problem in United States.* New York: Macmillan, 1915.

647
Mills, C. Wright. *The Puerto Rican Journey: New York's Newest Migrants.* New York: Harper, 1950.

648
Moore, Truman. *The Slaves We Rent.* New York: Random House, 1965.

649
Murton, Tom, and Hyams, Joe. *Accomplices to the Crime.* New York: Grove Press, 1970.

650
Nelli, Humbert S. *The Italians in Chicago, 1880-1930: A Study in Ethnic Mobility.* New York: Oxford University Press, 1970.

651
Norquest, Carrol. *Rio Grande Wetbacks: Migrant Mexican Workers.* Albuquerque: University of New Mexico Press, 1972.

652
Odencrantz, Louise C. *Italian Women in Industry: A Study of Conditions in New York City.* New York: Russell Sage Foundation, 1919.

653
Peckham, Howard, and Bigson, Charles, eds. *Attitudes of the Colonial Powers toward the American Indians.* Salt Lake City: University of Utah Press, 1969.

654
Reid, Ira DeA. *Negro Immigrant.* New York: Columbia University Press, 1939.

655

————. *The Negro Immigrant: His Background, Characteristics and Social Adjustment, 1889-1937.* New York: AMS Press, 1968.

656

Rice, Lawrence D. *The Negro in Texas, 1874-1900.* Baton Rouge: Louisiana State University Press, 1971.

657

Riis, Jacob A. *How the Other Half Lives: Studies among the Tenements of New York.* New York: Scribner, 1890.

658

Roberts, Edward F. *Ireland in America.* New York: Putnam, 1931.

659

Rose, A.M. *Negro in Postwar America.* New York: Anti-Defamation League of B'nai B'rith, 1950.

660

Ross, Arthur M., and Hill, Herbert, eds. *Employment, Race and Poverty: A Critical Study of the Disadvantaged Status of Negro Workers from 1865-1965.* * New York: Harcourt, Brace & World, 1967.

661

Samora, Julian, ed. *La Raza: Forgotten Americans.* * Notre Dame: University of Notre Dame Press, 1966.

662

————. *Los Mojados: The Wetback Story.* Notre Dame: University of Notre Dame Press, 1971.

663

Saxton, Alexander. *The Indispensable Enemy: Labor and the Anti-Chinese Movement in California.* Berkeley: University of California Press, 1971.

664

Scoresby, William. *American Factories and Their Female Operatives.* 1845. Reprint. New York: Burt Franklin, 1968.

665

Scott, Emmett J. *Negro Immigration during the War.* New York: Oxford University Press, 1920.

666

Servin, Manuel P. *The Mexican-Americans: An Awakening Minority.* Beverly Hills: Glencoe Press, 1970.

667

Seward, George F. *Chinese Immigration and Its Social and Economic Aspects.* New York: Arno Press, 1970.

668

Shotwell, Louisa R. *The Harvesters: The Story of the Migrant People.* Garden City: Doubleday, 1961.

669

Spero, Sterling D., and Harris, Abram L. *The Black Worker: The Negro and the Labor Movement.* Port Washington: Kennikat Press, 1931.

670
Steiner, Stan. *La Raza: The Mexican Americans.** New York: Harper & Row, 1970.

671
Tarr, Joel A. *A Study of Boss Politics: William Lorimer of Chicago.* Urbana: University of Illinois Press, 1971.

672
Taylor, Paul S. *Mexican Labor in the United States.* 2 vols. Berkeley: University of California Press, 1928-1934.

673
Tindall, George Brown. *South Carolina Negroes, 1877-1900.* Columbia: University of South Carolina Press, 1952.

674
Todd, Arthur C. *The Cornish Miner in America.* Glendale, Calif.: Arthur H. Clark, 1967.

675
Tragle, Henry I. *The Southampton Slave Revolt of 1831: A Compilation of Source Material.* Amherst: University of Massachusetts Press, 1971.

676
Tully, Jim. *Beggars of Life.* New York: Albert and Charles Boni, 1926.

677
Twentieth Century Fund Task Force on Employment Problems of Black Youth. *The Job Crisis for Black Youth.* New York: Praeger, 1971.

678
Warne, Frank J. *The Slav Invasion and the Mine Workers: A Study in Immigration.* Philadelphia: Lippincott, 1904.

679
————. *The Immigrant Invasion.* New York: Dodd, Mead, 1913.

680
Washington, Booker T. *Up From Slavery.* Garden City: A.L. Bert Co., 1901.

681
Weaver, Robert C. *Negro Labor: A National Problem.* New York: Harcourt, Brace & World, 1946.

682
Webb, J.N. *Migratory-Casual Worker.* Washington, D.C.: U.S. Government Printing Office, 1937.

683
————, and Brown, Malcolm. *Migrant Families.* Washington, D.C.: U.S. Government Printing Office, 1939.

684
Weinstein, Allen, and Gatell, Frank Otto. *The Segregation Era, 1863-1954: A Modern Reader.* New York: Oxford University Press, 1970.

685
Weller, Jack E. *Yesterday's People: Life in Contemporary Appalachia.* Lexington, Ky.: University of Kentucky Press, 1965.

686

Westley, William A., and Westley, Margaret W. *The Emerging Worker: Equality and Conflict in the Mass Consumption Society.* Montreal: McGill-Queen's University Press, 1971.

687

Wittke, Carl. *The Irish in America.* Baton Rouge: Louisiana State University Press, 1956.

688

————. *We Who Built America: The Saga of the Immigrant.* Rev. ed. Cleveland: Case Western Reserve University, 1967.

689

Wolters, Raymond. *Negroes and the Great Depression.* Westport: Greenwood Press, 1970.

690

Wright, Dale. *They Harvest Despair: The Migrant Farm Worker.* Boston: Beacon Press, 1965.

691

Yearley, Clifton K., Jr. *Britons in American Labor: A History of the Influence of the United Kingdom Immigrants on American Labor, 1820-1914.* Baltimore: Johns Hopkins Press, 1957.

Cities and States

692

Allen, Ruth A. *East Texas Lumber Workers: An Economic and Social Picture, 1870-1950.* Austin: University of Texas Press, 1961.

693

Arian, Edward. *Bach, Beethoven, and Bureaucracy: The Case of the Philadelphia Orchestra.* University, Ala.: University of Alabama Press, 1971.

694

Ballagh, J.C. *White Servitude in Virginia.* Baltimore: Johns Hopkins Press, 1895.

695

————. *History of Slavery in Virginia.* Baltimore: Johns Hopkins Press, 1902.

696

Bean, Walton. *Boss Ruef's San Francisco: The Story of the Union Labor Party, Big Business, and the Graft Prosecution.* Berkeley: University of California Press, 1952.

697

Bedford, Henry F. *Socialism and the Workers in Massachusetts, 1886-1912.* Amherst: University of Massachusetts Press, 1966.

698
Campbell, Penelope. *Maryland in Africa: The Maryland State Colonization Society*. Urbana: University of Illinois Press, 1971.

699
Cantor, Louis. *A Prologue to the Protest Movement: The Missouri Sharecropper Roadside Demonstrations of 1939*. Durham: Duke University Press, 1969.

700
Chrislock, Carl H. *The Progressive Era in Minnesota, 1899-1918*. St. Paul: Minnesota Historical Society, 1971.

701
Clark, Norman H. *Mill Town: A Social History of Everett, Washington*. Seattle: University of Washington Press, 1970.

702
Cross, I.B. *Labor Movement in California*. Berkeley: University of California Press, 1935.

703
Dow, George Francis. *Every Day Life in Massachusetts Bay Colony*. Boston: The Society for the Preservation of New England Antiquities, 1935.

704
Dubofsky, Melvyn. *When Workers Organize: New York City in the Progressive Era*. Amherst: University of Massachusetts Press, 1968.

705
Dunaway, Wayland F. *The Scotch-Irish of Colonial Pennsylvania*. Chapel Hill: University of North Carolina Press, 1944.

706
Dunne, John Gregory. *Delano: The Story of the California Grape Strike.* * Rev. ed. New York: Farrar, Straus & Giroux, 1971.

707
Flanders, R.B. *Plantation Slavery in Georgia*. Chapel Hill: University of North Carolina Press, 1933.

708
Friedheim, Robert L. *The Seattle General Strike*. Seattle: University of Washington Press, 1964.

709
Greene, Victor R. *The Slavic Community on Strike: Immigrant Labor in Pennsylvania Anthracite*. Notre Dame: University of Notre Dame Press, 1968.

710
Handlin, Oscar. *Boston's Immigrants, 1790-1880*. Cambridge: Harvard University Press, 1959.

711

Harris, Evelyn L., and Krebs, Frank J. *From Humble Beginnings: West Virginia State Federation of Labor, 1903-1957.* Charleston: West Virginia Labor History Publishing Fund, 1960.

712

Harvey, Katherine A. *The Best-Dressed Miners: Life and Labor in the Maryland Coal Region, 1835-1910.* Ithaca: Cornell University Press, 1969.

713

Herrick, Cheesman A. *White Servitude in Pennsylvania: Indentured and Redemption Labor in Colony and Commonwealth.* Philadelphia: McVey, 1926.

714

Herring, Harriet L. *Welfare Work in Mill Villages: The Story of Extra-Mill Activities in North Carolina.* Chapel Hill: University of North Carolina Press, 1929.

715

Hugins, Walter E. *Jacksonian Democracy and the Working Class: A Study of the New York Workingmen's Movement, 1829-1837.* Stanford: Stanford University Press, 1960.

716

Johannessen, Edward. *The Hawaiian Labor Movement: A Brief History.* Boston: Bruce Humphries, 1956.

717

Kahn, Melvin A. *The Politics of American Labor: The Indiana Microcosm.* Carbondale: Southern Illinois University Labor Institute, 1970.

718

Klingberg, F.J. *An Appraisal of the Negro in Colonial South Carolina, a Study in Americanization.* Washington, D.C.: Associated Publishers, 1941.

719

Kluger, James R. *The Clifton-Morenci Strike: Labor Difficulty in Arizona, 1915-1916.* Tucson: University of Arizona Press, 1970.

720

Knight, Harold V. *Working in Colorado: A Brief History of the Colorado Labor Movement.** Boulder: Center for Labor Education and Research, University of Colorado, 1971.

721

Korman, Gerd. *Industrialization, Immigrants and Americanizers: The View from Milwaukee, 1866-1921.* Madison: State Historical Society of Wisconsin, 1967.

722

Lane, Winthrop D. *Civil War in West Virginia.* New York: B.W. Huebsch, 1921.

723

Langdon, Emma F. *The Cripple Creek Strike: A History of Industrial Wars in Colorado 1903-4-5.* Denver: Great Western Pub. Co., 1904-1905.

724

Larrowe, Charles P. *Shape-Up and Hiring Hall: A Comparison of Hiring Methods and Labor Relations on the New York and Seattle Waterfronts.* Berkeley: University of California Press, 1955.

725

Lewis, Oscar. *La Vida: A Puerto Rican Family in the Culture of Poverty — San Juan and New York.* * New York: Random House, 1966.

726

Ljungmark, Lars. *For Sale—Minnesota: Organized Promotion of Scandinavian Immigration, 1866-1873.* Chicago: Swedish Pioneer Historical Society, 1971.

727

Lloyd, Henry D. *A Strike of Millionaires against Miners or the Story of Spring Valley.* Chicago: Belford-Clarke, 1890.

728

McKee, Samuel D. *Labor in Colonial New York, 1664-1776.* Port Washington: I.J. Friedman, 1965.

729

Manning, Thomas G. *The Chicago Strike of 1894: Industrial Labor in the Late Nineteenth Century.* New York: Holt and Rinehart, 1960.

730

Miller, Douglas T. *Jacksonian Aristocracy: Class and Democracy in New York, 1830-1860.* New York: Oxford University Press, 1967.

731

Montgonery, Royal E. *Industrial Relations in the Chicago Building Trades.* Chicago: University of Chicago Press, 1927.

732

Moody, V.A. *Slavery on Louisiana Sugar Plantations.* New Orleans: Louisiana Historical Quarterly, 1924.

733

Mushkat, Jerome. *Tammany: The Evolution of a Political Machine, 1789-1865.* Syracuse: Syracuse University Press, 1971.

734

Nelli, Humbert S. *The Italians in Chicago, 1880-1930: A Study in Ethnic Mobility.* New York: Oxford University Press, 1970.

735

Newell, Barbara W. *Chicago and the Labor Movement: Metropolitan Unionism in the 1930s.* Urbana: University of Illinois Press, 1961.

736

O'Connor, Harvey. *Revolution in Seattle: A Memoir.* New York: Monthly Review Press, 1964.

737

Olmstead, Frederick Law. *A Journey through Texas.* 1857. Reprint. New York: Lenox Hill Pub. Co. (Burt Franklin), 1970.

738
Parker, Morris B. *White Oaks: Life in a New Mexico Gold Camp, 1880-1900.* Tucson: University of Arizona Press, 1971.

739
Perry, Louis B., and Perry, Richard S. *A History of the Los Angeles Labor Movement, 1911-1941.* Berkeley: University of California Press, 1963.

740
Phelan, James, and Pozen, Robert. *The Company State: Du Pont in Delaware.* New York: Grossman, 1972.

741
Rice, Lawrence D. *The Negro in Texas, 1874-1900.* Baton Rouge: Louisiana State University Press, 1971.

742
Richardson, James F. *The New York Police: Colonial Times to 1901.* New York: Oxford University Press, 1970.

743
Riis, Jacob A. *How the Other Half Lives: Studies among the Tenements of New York.* New York: Scribner, 1890.

744
Rodgers, William Warren. *The One-Gallused Rebellion: Agrarianism in Alabama, 1865-1896.* Baton Rouge: Louisiana State University Press, 1970.

745
Rogin, Michael P., and Shover, John L. *Political Change in California: Critical Elections and Social Movements, 1890-1966.* Westport: Greenwood Press, 1970.

746
Roney, Frank. *Frank Roney: Irish Rebel and California Labor Leader.* Berkeley: University of California Press, 1931.

747
Ross, Murray. *Stars and Strikes: Unionization of Hollywood.* New York: Columbia University Press, 1941.

748
Saxton, Alexander. *The Indispensable Enemy: Labor and the Anti-Chinese Movement in California.* Berkeley: University of California Press, 1971.

749
Sellers, J.B. *Slavery in Alabama.* University, Ala.: University of Alabama Press, 1950.

750
Sennett, Richard. *Families against the City: Middle Class Homes of Industrial Chicago, 1872-1890.* Cambridge: Harvard University Press, 1970.

751
Smith, Robert W. *The Coeur d'Alene Mining War of 1892.* Corvallis: Oregon State University Press, 1961.

752
Stimson, Grace H. *The Rise of the Labor Movement in Los Angeles, 1870-1914*. Berkeley: University of California Press, 1955.

753
Sydnor, C.S. *Slavery in Mississippi*. New York: Appleton-Century, 1933.

754
Taft, Philip. *Labor Politics American Style: The California State Federation of Labor*. Cambridge: Harvard University Press, 1968.

755
Tarr, Joel A. *A Study of Boss Politics: William Lorimer of Chicago*. Urbana: University of Illinois Press, 1971.

756
Tindall, George Brown. *South Carolina Negroes, 1877-1900*. Columbia: University of South Carolina Press, 1952.

757
Tragle, Henry I. *The Southampton Slave Revolt of 1831: A Compilation of Source Material*. Amherst: University of Massachusetts Press, 1971.

758
Troy, Leo. *Organized Labor in New Jersey*. Princeton: D. Van Nostrand, 1965.

759
Tuttle, William M. *Race Riot: Chicago in the Red Summer of 1919*. New York: Atheneum, 1970.

760
U.S. Congress, House, United States Strike Commission. *Report on the Chicago Strike of June-July 1894*. Washington, D.C.: U.S. Government Printing Office, 1895.

761
Wade, Richard C. *Urban Frontier: Pioneer Life in Early Pittsburgh, Cincinnati, Lexington, Louisville and St. Louis, 1790-1830*. Cambridge: Harvard University Press, 1959.

762
————. *Slavery in the Cities: The South, 1860-1960*. New York: Oxford University Press, 1964.

763
White, Howard Ashley. *The Freedmen's Bureau in Louisiana*. Baton Rouge: Louisiana State University Press, 1970.

764
Widick, B.J. *Detroit: City of Race and Class Violence*. Chicago: Quadrangle Books, 1972.

765
Zitron, Celia Lewis. *The New York City Teachers Union, 1916-1964*. New York: Humanities Press, 1968.

Individual Unions, Companies and Occupations

766
Alinsky, Saul. *John L. Lewis: An Unauthorized Biography.* New York: Putnam, 1949.

767
Allen, Ruth A. *East Texas Lumber Workers: An Economic and Social Picture, 1870-1950.* Austin: University of Texas Press, 1961.

768
Allen, Steve. *The Ground is Our Table.* Garden City: Doubleday, 1966.

769
Arian, Edward. *Bach, Beethoven, and Bureaucracy: The Case of the Philadelphia Orchestra.* University, Ala.: University of Alabama Press, 1971.

770
Aurand, Harold W. *From the Molly Maguires to the United Mine Workers: The Social Ecology of an Industrial Union, 1869-1897.* Philadelphia: Temple University Press, 1971.

771
Baitsell, John M. *Airline Industrial Relations: Pilots and Flight Engineers.* Boston: Harvard Business School, 1966.

772
Baratz, Morton S. *The Union and the Coal Industry.* New Haven: Yale University Press, 1955.

773
Barbash, Jack. *Unions and Telephones: The Story of the Communications Workers of America.* New York: Harper, 1952.

774
Barnard, Harry. *Eagle Forgotten: The Life of John Peter Altgeld.* Indianapolis: Bobbs-Merrill, 1938.

775
Barnes, Charles B. *The Longshoremen.* New York: Russell Sage Foundation, 1915.

776
Barry, Desmond A. *Too Hot to Handle.* * Garden City: Doubleday, 1962.

777
Beshoar, Barron B. *Out of the Depths: The Story of John R. Lawson, Labor Leader.* Denver: World Press, 1942.

778
Bishop, C.E., ed. *Farm Labor in the United States.* New York: Columbia University Press, 1967.

779
Bisno, Abraham. *Abraham Bisno: Union Pioneer in the Women's Garment Industry.* Madison: University of Wisconsin Press, 1967.

780
Blum, Albert A. *Teacher Unions and Associations: A Comparative Study.* Urbana: University of Illinois Press, 1969.

781
Bonosky, Phillip. *Brother Bill McKie: Building the Union at Ford.* New York: International Publishers, 1953.

782
Bridge, James Howard. *The History of the Carnegie Steel Company.* New York: Aldine Pub. Co., 1903.

783
Brody, David. *Steelworkers in America: The Nonunion Era.* Cambridge: Harvard University Press, 1960.

784
————. *The Butcher Workmen: A Study in Unionization.* Cambridge: Harvard University Press, 1964.

785
————. *Labor in Crisis: The Steel Strike of 1919.* * Philadelphia: Lippincott, 1965.

786
Brown, Leo C., S.J. *Union Policies in the Leather Industry.* Cambridge: Harvard University Press, 1947.

787
Buder, Stanley. *Pullman: An Experiment in Industrial Order and Community Planning, 1880-1930.* New York: Oxford University Press, 1967.

788
Budish, Jacob M., and Soule, George. *The New Unionism in the Clothing Industry.* New York: Harcourt, Brace and Howe, 1920.

789
Burpo, John H. *The Police Labor Movement: Problems and Perspectives.* Springfield, Ill.: Charles C. Thomas, 1971.

790
Carpenter, Jesse. *Competition and Collective Bargaining in the Needle Trades, 1910-1967.* Ithaca: New York State School of Industrial and Labor Relations, 1971.

791
Chinoy, Ely. *Automobile Workers and the American Dream.* Garden City: Doubleday, 1955.

792
Christie, Robert A. *Empire in Wood: A History of the Carpenters Union.* Ithaca: Cornell University Press, 1956.

793
Clark, William H. *Ships and Sailors: The Story of Our Merchant Marine.* Boston: Page, 1938.

794
Cole, Stephen. *United Federation of Teachers: A Case Study of the UFT.* New York: Praeger, 1969.

795
Coleman, McAlister. *Men and Coal.* New York: Farrar and Rinehart, 1943.

796
Cormier, Frank, and Eaton, William J. *Reuther.* Englewood Cliffs: Prentice-Hall, 1970.

797
Cornell, Robert J. *The Anthracite Coal Strike of 1902.* Washington, D.C.: Catholic University of America Press, 1957.

798
Craig, Richard B. *The Bracero Program: Interest Groups and Foreign Policy.* Austin: University of Texas Press, 1971.

799
Danish, Max D. *The World of David Dubinsky.* Cleveland: World Pub. Co., 1957.

800
Davidson, Ray. *Peril on the Job: A Study of Hazards in the Chemical Industries.* Washington, D.C.: Public Affairs Press, 1970.

801
Day, Mark. *Forty Acres: César Chávez and the Farm Workers.* New York: Praeger, 1971.

802
Doherty, William C. *Mailman, U.S.A.* New York: David McKay, 1960.

803
Dunne, John Gregory. *Delano: The Story of the California Grape Strike.** Rev. ed. New York: Farrar, Straus & Giroux, 1971.

804
Elam, Stanley, and Moskow, Michael H., eds. *Employment Relations in Higher Education.* Bloomington, Indiana: Phi Delta Kappa, 1969.

805
Feinsinger, Nathan P. *Collective Bargaining in the Trucking Industry.* Philadelphia: University of Pennsylvania Press, 1949.

806
Fine, Sidney. *The Automobile under the Blue Eagle.* Ann Arbor: University of Michigan Press, 1963.

807
————. *Sitdown: The General Motors Strike of 1936-1937.* Ann Arbor: University of Michigan Press, 1969.

808
Fitch, John Andrew. *The Steel Worker.* New York: Charities Publication Committee, 1910.

809
Foster, William Z. *The Great Steel Strike and Its Lessons.* New York: B.W. Huebsch, 1920.

810
Friedland, William H., and Nelkin, Dorothy. *Migrant-Agricultural Workers in America's Northeast.* New York: Holt, Rinehart and Winston, 1972.

811
Galarza, Ernesto. *Merchants of Labor: The Mexican Bracero Story.** Santa Barbara: McNally & Loftin, 1964.

812
————. *Spiders in the House and Workers in the Field.** Notre Dame: University of Notre Dame Press, 1970.

813
Garnel, Donald. *The Rise of Teamster Power in the West.* Berkeley: University of California Press, 1971.

814
Gilfillan, Lauren. *I Went to Pit College.* New York: Viking Press, 1934.

815
Gillmer, Richard S. *Death of a Business: The Red Wing Potteries.* Minneapolis: Ross and Haines, 1968.

816
Goldberg, Joseph P. *The Maritime Story: A Study in Labor-Management Relations.* Cambridge: Harvard University Press, 1958.

817
Gooden, Orville Thrasher. *The Missouri and North Arkansas Railroad Strike.* New York: Columbia University Press, 1926.

818
Graham, Harry Edward. *The Paper Rebellion: Development and Upheaval in Pulp and Paper Unionism.* Iowa City: University of Iowa, 1970.

819
Grant, Luke. *The National Erectors' Association and the International Association of Bridge and Structural Ironworkers: The United States Commission on Industrial Relations.* Chicago: Barnard and Miller, 1915.

820
Green, Archie. *Only a Miner: Studies in Recorded Coal-Mining Songs.* Urbana: University of Illinois Press, 1971.

821
Greene, Victor R. *The Slavic Community on Strike: Immigrant Labor in Pennsylvania Anthracite.* Notre Dame: University of Notre Dame Press, 1968.

822
Gulick, Charles A. *Labor Policy of the United States Steel Corporation.* New York: Columbia University Press, 1924.

823
Haber, William, and Levinson, Harold M. *Labor Relations and Productivity in the Building Trades.* Ann Arbor: Bureau of Industrial Relations, University of Michigan, 1956.

824
Hanna, Hilton E., and Belsky, Joseph. *Picket and the Pen: The Pat Gorman Story.* Yonkers: American Institute of Social Science, 1960.

825
Harvey, Katherine A. *The Best-Dressed Miners: Life and Labor in the Maryland Coal Region, 1835-1910.* Ithaca: Cornell University Press, 1969.

826
Hoffa, James R. *The Trials of Jimmy Hoffa: An Autobiography.* Chicago: Henry Regnery, 1970.

827
Hoffman, Claude E. *Sit-Down in Anderson: UAW Local 663 Anderson, Indiana.* Detroit: Wayne State University Press, 1968.

828
Hohman, Elmo P. *History of American Merchant Seamen.* Hamden, Conn.: The Shoe String Press, 1956.

829
Hopkins, George E. *The Airline Pilots: A Study in Elite Unionization.* Cambridge: Harvard University Press, 1971.

830
Horowitz, Morris A. *The New York Hotel Industry: A Labor Relations Study.* Cambridge: Harvard University Press, 1960.

831
Howe, Irving, and Widick, B.J. *The UAW and Walter Reuther.* New York: Random House, 1949.

832
Hume, Brit. *Death and the Mines: Rebellion and Murder in the UMW.* New York: Grossman, 1971.

833
Interchurch World Movement of North America, Commission of Inquiry. *Report on the Steel Strike of 1919.* New York: Putnam, 1923.

834
James, Ralph, and James, Estelle. *Hoffa and the Teamsters: A Study of Union Power.* * Princeton: D. Van Nostrand, 1965.

835
Jensen, Vernon H. *Lumber and Labor.* New York: Farrar and Rinehart, 1945.

836
––––––. *Heritage of Conflict: Labor Relations in the Nonferrous Metals Industry up to 1930.* Ithaca: New York State School of Industrial and Labor Relations, Cornell University, 1950.

837

————. *Nonferrous Metals Industry Unionism, 1932-1954.* Ithaca: New York State School of Industrial and Labor Relations, Cornell University, 1954.

838

Josephson, Matthew. *Sidney Hillman, Statesman of American Labor.* Garden City: Doubleday, 1952.

839

————. *Union House, Union Bar: The History of the Hotel and Restaurant Employees and Bartenders International Union.* New York: Random House, 1956.

840

Karsh, Bernard. *Diary of a Strike.* Urbana: University of Illinois Press, 1958.

841

Kaufman, Jacob Joseph. *Collective Bargaining in the Railroad Industry.* New York: King's Crown Press, 1954.

842

Kirkland, Edward C. *Dream and Thought in the Business Community, 1860-1900.* Ithaca: Cornell University Press, 1959.

843

Kirstein, George C. *Stores and Unions: A Study of the Growth of Unionism in Dry Goods and Department Stores.* New York: Fairchild, 1950.

844

Kluger, James R. *The Clifton-Morenci Strike: Labor Difficulty in Arizona, 1915-1916.* Tucson: University of Arizona Press, 1970.

845

Koenig, Allen E. *Broadcasting and Bargaining: Labor Relations in Radio and Television.* Madison: University of Wisconsin Press, 1970.

846

Kraus, Henry. *The Many and the Few.* Los Angeles: Plantin Press, 1947.

847

Kuechle, David. *The Story of the Savannah: An Episode in Maritime Labor-Management Relations.* Cambridge: Harvard University Press, 1971.

848

LaDame, Mary. *The Filene Store: A Study of Employees' Relation to Management in a Retail Store.* New York; Russell Sage Foundation, 1930.

849

Larrowe, Charles P. *Shape-Up and Hiring Hall: A Comparison of Hiring Methods and Labor Relations on the New York and Seattle Waterfronts.* Berkeley: University of California Press, 1955.

850

Leab, Daniel J. *A Union of Individuals: The Formation of the American Newspaper Guild, 1933-1936.* New York: Columbia University Press, 1970.

851

Leiter, Robert D. *The Musicians and Petrillo.* New York: Bookman Associates, 1953.

852

Levinson, Harold M.; Rehmus, Charles M.; Goldberg, Joseph P.; and Kahn, Mark L. *Collective Bargaining and Technological Change in American Transportation.* Evanston: Transportation Center at Northwestern University, 1971.

853

Lloyd, Henry D. *A Strike of Millionaires against Miners or the Story of Spring Valley.* Chicago: Belford-Clarke, 1890.

854

London, Joan, and Anderson, Henry. *So Shall Ye Reap: The Story of César Chávez and the Farm Workers' Movement.* New York: Thomas Y. Crowell, 1970.

855

Lorwin, Louis (Louis Levine pseud.). *The Women's Garment Workers: A History of the International Ladies' Garment Workers' Union.* New York: B.W. Huebsch, 1924.

856

McDonald, David J. *Union Man.* New York: E.P. Dutton, 1969.

857

MacDonald, Robert M. *Collective Bargaining in the Automobile Industry.* New Haven: Yale University Press, 1963.

858

McWilliams, Carey. *Factories in the Field: The Story of Migratory Farm Labor in California.* Boston: Little, Brown and Co., 1939.

859

––––––. *Ill Fares the Land: Migrants and Migratory Labor in the United States.* Boston: Little, Brown and Co., 1942.

860

Matthiessen, Peter. *Sal Si Puedes: César Chávez and the New American Revolution.* * New York: Random House, 1969.

861

Mills, Daniel Q. *Industrial Relations and Manpower in Construction.* Cambridge: The M.I.T. Press, 1972.

862

Mollenhoff, Clark D. *Tentacles of Power: The Story of Jimmy Hoffa.* Cleveland: World Pub. Co., 1965.

863

Montgomery, Royal E. *Industrial Relations in the Chicago Building Trades.* Chicago: University of Chicago Press, 1927.

864

Moody, V.A. *Slavery on Louisiana Sugar Plantations.* New Orleans: Louisiana Historical Quarterly, 1924.

865
Moskow, Michael H. *Teachers and Unions: The Applicability of Collective Bargaining to Public Education.* Philadelphia: University of Pennsylvania Press, 1966.

866
————. *Labor Relations in the Performing Arts: An Introductory Survey.* New York: Associated Councils of the Arts, 1969.

867
Munson, Fred C. *Labor Relations in the Lithographic Industry.* Cambridge: Harvard University Press, 1963.

868
Orear, Leslie F., and Diamond, Stephan H. *Out of the Jungle.* * Chicago: Hyde Park Press, 1968.

869
Parrish, Bernie. *They Call It a Game.* New York: Dial Press, 1971.

870
Payton, Boyd E. *Scapegoat: Prejudice, Politics, Prison.* Philadelphia: Whitmore Pub. Co., 1970.

871
Person, Carl E. *The Lizard's Trail: A Story from the Illinois Central and Harriman Lines Strike of 1911 to 1915 Inclusive.* Chicago: Lake Publishing Co., 1918.

872
Pflug, Warner W. *UAW in Pictures.* Detroit: Wayne State University Press, 1971.

873
Quin, Mike. *The Big Strike.* Olema, Calif.: Olema Pub. Co., 1949.

874
Richardson, James F. *The New York Police: Colonial Times to 1901.* New York: Oxford University Press, 1970.

875
Richardson, Reed C. *The Locomotive Engineer, 1863-1963: A Century of Railway Labor Relations and Work Rules.* Ann Arbor: Bureau of Industrial Relations, University of Michigan, 1963.

876
Roberts, Peter. *Anthracite Coal Industry.* New York: Macmillan, 1901.

877
Rodgers, William Warren. *The One-Gallused Rebellion: Agrarianism in Alabama, 1865-1896.* Baton Rouge: Louisiana State University Press, 1970.

878
Ross, Murray. *Stars and Strikes: Unionization of Hollywood.* New York: Columbia University Press, 1941.

879

Russell, Maud. *Men along the Shore: The ILA and Its History.* New York: Brussel and Brussel, 1966.

880

Segal, Martin. *The Rise of the United Association: National Unionism in the Pipe Trades, 1884-1924.* Cambridge: Harvard University Press, 1970.

881

Smith, Dennis. *Report from Engine Co. 82.* New York: McCall, 1971.

882

Smith, Robert W. *The Coeur d'Alene Mining War of 1892.* Corvallis: Oregon State University Press, 1961.

883

Stapp, Andy. *Up Against the Brass.* * New York: Simon & Schuster, 1970.

884

Stein, Leon. *The Triangle Fire.* Philadelphia: Lippincott, 1962.

885

Stinnett, T.M. *Turmoil in Teaching: A History of the Organizational Struggle for America's Teachers.* New York: Macmillan, 1968.

886

Suffern, Arthur E. *Conciliation and Arbitration in the Coal Industry.* Boston and New York: Houghton Mifflin, 1915.

887

Sward, Keith. *The Legend of Henry Ford.* * New York; Rinehart, 1948.

888

Todd, Arthur C. *The Cornish Miner in America.* Glendale, Calif.: Arthur H. Clark, 1967.

889

Uphoff, Walter H. *Kohler on Strike: Thirty Years of Conflict.* * Boston: Beacon Press, 1966.

890

Urofsky, Melvin I. *Big Steel and the Wilson Administration: A Study in Business and Government Relations.* Columbus: Ohio State University Press, 1969.

891

Walker, Charles R. *American City: A Rank and File History.* New York: Farrar and Rinehart, 1937.

892

————. *Steeltown, an Industrial Case History of the Conflict between Progress and Security.* New York: Harper, 1950.

893

Wall, Joseph F. *Andrew Carnegie.* New York: Oxford University Press, 1970.

894

Walsh, Robert E., ed. *Sorry . . . No Government Today: Unions vs. City Hall.* Boston: Beacon Press, 1969.

895
Ward, Estolv E. *Harry Bridges on Trial.** New York: Modern Age Books, 1940.

896
Warne, Colston E., ed. *The Steel Strike of 1919.** Boston: D.C. Heath, 1963.

897
Warne, Frank J. *The Slav Invasion and the Mine Workers: A Study in Immigration.* Philadelphia: Lippincott, 1904.

898
Wechsler, James A. *Labor Baron: A Portrait of John L. Lewis.* New York: William Morrow, 1944.

899
Weintraub, Hyman G. *Andrew Furuseth: Emancipator of the Seamen.* Berkeley: University of California Press, 1959.

900
Weisbord, Albert. *Passaic: The Story of a Struggle against Starvation Wages and the Right to Organize.* Chicago: Daily Worker Pub. Co., 1926.

901
Wellington, Harry H., and Winter, Ralph K. *The Unions and the Cities.* Washington, D.C.: Brookings Institution, 1971.

902
Whittemore, L.H. *The Man Who Ran the Subways: The Story of Mike Quill.* New York: Holt, Rinehart and Winston, 1968.

903
Widick, B.J. *Detroit: City of Race and Class Violence.* Chicago: Quadrangle Books, 1972.

904
Wright, Dale. *They Harvest Despair: The Migrant Farm Worker.* Boston: Beacon Press, 1965.

905
Wyman, Walker D. *The Lumberjack Frontier: The Life of a Logger in the Early Days on the Chippeway.* Lincoln: University of Nebraska Press, 1969.

906
Young, Jan. *Migrant Workers and César Chávez.* New York: Julian Messner, Inc., 1972.

907
Zagoria, Sam, ed. *Public Workers and Public Unions.** Englewood Cliffs: Prentice-Hall, 1972.

908
Zitron, Celia Lewis. *The New York City Teachers Union, 1916-1964.* New York: Humanities Press, 1968.

Labor and the Law

909
Abodeely, John E. *The NLRB and the Appropriate Bargaining Unit.** Philadelphia: Industrial Research Unit, University of Pennsylvania, 1971.

910
Angle, Paul M. *Bloody Williamson: A Chapter in American Lawlessness.* New York: Alfred A. Knopf, 1952.

911
Barry, Desmond A. *Too Hot to Handle.** Garden City: Doubleday, 1962.

912
Bean, Walton. *Boss Ruef's San Francisco: The Story of the Union Labor Party, Big Business, and the Graft Prosecution.* Berkeley: University of California Press, 1952.

913
Berman, Edward. *Labor and the Sherman Act.* New York: Harper, 1930.

914
Blackman, John L. *Presidential Seizure in Labor Disputes.* Cambridge: Harvard University Press, 1967.

915
Blumrosen, Alfred W. *Black Employment and the Law.* New Brunswick: Rutgers University Press, 1971.

916
Cohen, Sanford. *Labor Law.* Indianapolis: Charles E. Merrill, 1964.

917
Cortner, Richard C. *The Jones and Laughlin Case.** New York: Alfred A. Knopf, 1970.

918
Davidson, E.H. *Child Labor Legislation in Southern Textile States.* Chapel Hill: University of North Carolina Press, 1939.

919
Dereshinsky, Ralph M. *The NLRB and Secondary Boycotts.** Philadelphia: Industrial Research Unit, University of Pennsylvania, 1972.

920
Eggert, Gerald G. *Railroad Labor Disputes: The Beginnings of Federal Strike Policy.* Ann Arbor: University of Michigan Press, 1967.

921
Falcone, Nicholas. *Labor Law.* New York: John Wiley, 1962.

922
Frankfurter, Felix, and Greene, Nathan. *The Labor Injunction.* New York: Macmillan, 1930.

923
Frost, Richard H. *The Mooney Case.* Stanford: Stanford University Press, 1968.

924
Gentry, Curt. *Frame-Up: The Tom Mooney-Warren Billings Case.* New York: Norton, 1967.

925
Hoffa, James R. *The Trials of Jimmy Hoffa: An Autobiography.* Chicago: Henry Regnery, 1970.

926
Hutchinson, John. *The Imperfect Union: A History of Corruption in American Trade Unions.* * New York: E.P. Dutton, 1970.

927
Johnson, Malcolm M. *Crime on the Labor Front.* New York: McGraw-Hill, 1950.

928
Kennedy, Robert F. *The Enemy Within.* * New York: Harper & Row, 1960.

929
Kirkland, Edward C. *Industry Comes of Age: Business, Labor and Public Policy, 1860-1897.* New York: Holt, Rinehart and Winston, 1961.

930
Kovarsky, Irving, and Albrecht, William. *Black Employment: The Impact of Religion, Economic Theory, Politics and Law.* Ames: Iowa State University Press, 1970.

931
Laidler, H.W. *Boycotts and Labor Struggle.* New York: Columbia University Press, 1914.

932
Lieberman, Elias. *Unions before the Bar.* * Rev. ed. New York: Oxford Book Co., 1960.

933
Lynd, Staughton. *Class Conflict, Slavery, and the United States Constitution.* Indianapolis: Bobbs-Merrill, 1967.

934
McClellan, John L. *Crime without Punishment.* New York: Duell, Sloan & Pearce, 1962.

935
Millis, Harry A., and Brown, E.C. *From the Wagner Act to Taft-Hartley: A Study of National Labor Policy and Labor Relations.* Chicago: University of Chicago Press, 1950.

936
Mills, C. Wright. *The New Men of Power: America's Labor Leaders.* New York: Harcourt, Brace, 1948.

937
Mollenhoff, Clark D. *Tentacles of Power: The Story of Jimmy Hoffa.* Cleveland: World Pub. Co., 1965.

938
Morris, Richard B. *Government and Labor in Early America.** New York: Columbia University Press, 1946.

939
Payton, Boyd E. *Scapegoat: Prejudice, Politics, Prison.* Philadelphia: Whitmore Pub. Co., 1970.

940
Rowan, R.W. *The Pinkertons, a Detective Dynasty.* Boston: Little, Brown and Co., 1931.

941
Seidman, Harold. *Labor Czars: A History of Labor Racketeering.* New York: Liveright, 1958.

942
Shefferman, Nathan. *The Man in the Middle.* Garden City: Doubleday, 1961.

943
Ward, Estolv E. *Harry Bridges on Trial.** New York: Modern Age Books, 1940.

944
Webb, Garn H., and Bianco, Thomas C. *Labor Law and Antitrust: Analysis and Explanation.* New York: Holt, Rinehart and Winston, 1970.

945
Wellington, Harry H. *Labor and the Legal Process.* New Haven: Yale University Press, 1968.

946
Witney, Fred. *Wartime Experiences of the National Labor Relations Board, 1941-1945.** Urbana: University of Illinois Press, 1949.

947
Wolman, Leo. *Boycott in American Trade Unions.* Baltimore: Johns Hopkins Press, 1916.

948
Yellen, Samuel. *American Labor Struggles.* New York: S.A. Russell, 1956.

949
Ziskind, David. *One Thousand Strikes of Government Employees.* New York: Columbia University Press, 1940.

Labor and Politics

950
Bean, Walton. *Boss Ruef's San Francisco: The Story of the Union Labor Party, Big Business, and the Graft Prosecution.* Berkeley: University of California Press, 1952.

951
Bedford, Henry F. *Socialism and the Workers in Massachusetts, 1886-1912.* Amherst: University of Massachusetts Press, 1966.

952
Bornet, Vaughn Davis. *Labor Politics in a Democratic Republic: Moderation, Division and Disruption in the Presidential Election of 1928.* Washington, D.C.: Spartan Books, 1964.

953
Foner, Eric. *Free Soil, Free Labor, Free Men: The Ideology of the Republican Party before the Civil War.* New York: Oxford University Press, 1970.

954
Foner, Philip S. *American Labor and the Indochina War: The Growth of Union Opposition.* New York: International Publishers, 1971.

955
Fortune, Timothy Thomas. *Black and White: Land, Labor and Politics in the South.* New York: Arno Press, 1968.

956
Greenstone, J. David. *Labor in American Politics.* New York: Alfred A. Knopf, 1969.

957
Hero, Alfred O. *The UAW and World Affairs.* Boston: World Peace Foundation, 1965.

958
————————. *The Reuther-Meany Foreign Policy Dispute.* Dobbs Ferry: Oceana Publications, 1970.

959
Hofstadter, Richard. *The American Political Tradition and the Men Who Made It.* New York: Alfred A. Knopf, 1948.

960
Hugins, Walter E. *Jacksonian Democracy and the Working Class: A Study of the New York Workingmen's Movement, 1829-1837.* Stanford: Stanford University Press, 1960.

961
Kahn, Melvin A. *The Politics of American Labor: The Indiana Microcosm.* Carbondale: Southern Illinois University Labor Institute, 1970.

962
Kampelman, Max M. *The Communist Party vs. the CIO: A Study in Power Politics.* New York: Praeger, 1957.

963
Karson, Marc. *American Labor Unions and Politics, 1900-1918.* Carbondale: Southern Illinois University Press, 1958.

964
Laslett, John. *Labor and the Left: A Study of Socialist and Radical Influences in the American Labor Movement, 1881-1924.* New York: Basic Books, 1970.

965
McClure, Arthur F. *The Truman Administration and the Problems of Postwar Labor, 1945-1948.* Rutherford: Fairleigh Dickinson University Press, 1969.

966
Montgomery, David. *Beyond Equality: Labor and the Radical Republicans, 1862-1872.* New York: Alfred A. Knopf, 1967.

967
Morris, George. *The CIA and American Labor: The Subversion of the AFL-CIO's Foreign Policy.* New York: International Publishers, 1967.

968
Mushkat, Jerome. *Tammany: The Evolution of a Political Machine, 1789-1865.* Syracuse: Syracuse University Press, 1971.

969
Pessen, Edward. *Most Uncommon Jacksonians: The Radical Leaders of the Early Labor Movement.* Albany: State University of New York Press, 1967.

970
Radosh, Ronald. *American Labor and United States Foreign Policy.* New York: Random House, 1969.

971
Rehmus, Charles M., and McLaughlin, Doris B., eds. *Labor and American Politics: A Book of Readings.* Ann Arbor: University of Michigan Press, 1967.

972
Rogin, Michael P., and Shover, John L. *Political Change in California: Critical Elections and Social Movements, 1890-1966.* Westport: Greenwood Press, 1970.

973
Royko, Mike. *Boss: Richard J. Daley of Chicago.** New York: E.P. Dutton, 1971.

974
Saposs, David J. *Communism in American Unions.* New York: McGraw-Hill, 1959.

975
Sexton, Patricia Cayo, and Sexton, Brendan. *Blue Collars and Hard Hats: The Working Class and the Future of American Politics.* New York: Random House, 1971.

976
Taft, Philip. *Labor Politics American Style: The California State Federation of Labor.* Cambridge: Harvard University Press, 1968.

977
Tarr, Joel A. *A Study of Boss Politics: William Lorimer of Chicago.* Urbana: University of Illinois Press, 1971.

978
Trattner, Walter I. *Crusade for the Children—A History of the National Child Labor Committee and Child Labor Reform in America.* Chicago: Quadrangle Books, 1970.

979
Vale, Vivian. *Labour in American Politics.* New York: Barnes & Noble, 1971.

980
Whitman, Alden. *Labor Parties, 1827-1834.* New York: International Publishers, 1943.

981
Yellowitz, Irwin. *Labor and the Progressive Movement in New York State, 1876-1916.* Ithaca: Cornell University Press, 1965.

982
Zieger, Robert H. *Republicans and Labor, 1919-1929.* Lexington, Ky.: University of Kentucky Press, 1969.

II. Comparative Labor Movements

GENERAL SURVEYS

983
Alba, Victor. *Politics and the Labor Movement in Latin America.* Stanford: Stanford University Press, 1968.

984
Alcock, Anthony. *History of the International Labor Organization.* New York: Octagon Books, 1971.

985
Alexander, Robert J. *Organized Labor in Latin America.* New York: The Free Press, 1965.

986
Ayusawa, Iwao F. *International Labor Legislation.* New York: Columbia University Press, 1920.

987
Barbash, Jack. *Trade Unions and National Economic Policy.* Baltimore: Johns Hopkins Press, 1972.

988
Barkin, Solomon, et al. *International Labor.* New York: Harper & Row, 1967.

989
Beling, Willard A. ed. *The Role of Labor in African Nation-Building.* New York: Praeger, 1968.

990
Blum, Albert A. *Teacher Unions and Associations: A Comparative Study.* Urbana: University of Illinois Press, 1969.

991

Boissonnade, P. *Life and Work in Medieval Europe.* * New York; Harper & Row, 1964.

992

Brentano, Lujo. *On the Origin and Development of Gilds and the Origin of Trade-Unions.* 1870. New York: Burt Franklin, 1970.

993

Clune, George. *The Medieval Gild System.* Dublin: Browne and Nolan, 1943.

994

Davies, Joan. *African Trade Unions.* * Great Britain: Penguin Books, 1966.

995

Feder, Ernest. *The Rape of the Peasantry: Latin America's Landholding System.* * Garden City: Doubleday, 1971.

996

Galenson, Walter. *Labor in Developing Economies.* Berkeley: University of California Press, 1962.

997

−−−−−−, ed. *Comparative Labor Movements.* New York: Prentice-Hall, 1952.

998

Ginzberg, Eli. *Manpower for Development: Perspectives on Five Continents.* New York: Praeger, 1971.

999

Gunter, Hans, ed. *Transnational Industrial Relations.* New York: St. Martin's Press, 1972.

1000

Houde, Bryn J. *The Scandinavian Countries.* Ithaca: Cornell University Press, 1948.

1001

Jones, G.P. *Workers Abroad.* London: Thomas Nelson and Sons, 1939.

1002

Kamin, Alfred. *Western European Labor and the American Corporation.* Washington, D.C.: Bureau of National Affairs, 1970.

1003

Kassalow, Everett M., ed. *National Labor Movements in the Postwar World.* Evanston: Northwestern University Press, 1963.

1004

Kuczynski, Jurgen. *The Rise of the Working Class.* * New York: McGraw-Hill, 1967.

1005

Landy, E.A. *The Effectiveness of International Supervision: Thirty Years of ILO Experience.* Dobbs Ferry: Oceana Publications, 1966.

1006

Lorwin, Val R. *Labor and Working Conditions in Modern Europe.* * New York: Macmillan, 1967.

1007
Lynd, George E. *The Politics of African Trade Unionism.* New York: Praeger, 1968.

1008
Meyers, Frederic. *European Coal Mining Unions: Structure and Function.* Los Angeles: Institute of Industrial Relations, University of California, 1961.

1009
Mitchell, Harvey, and Stearns, Peter N. *The European Labor Movement, the Working Classes, and the Origins of Social Democracy, 1890-1914.* Itasca, Illinois: F.E. Peacock, 1971.

1010
Mossé, Claude. *The Ancient World at Work.* London: Chatto & Windus, 1969.

1011
New York State Public Employment Relations Board. *Proceedings of the International Symposium on Public Employment Labor Relations, May 3-5, 1971.* New York: New York State Public Employment Relations Board, 1971.

1012
Niland, John R. *The Asian Engineering Brain Drain.* Lexington, Mass.: D.C. Heath, 1970.

1013
Oram, R.B. *The Dockers' Tragedy.* London: Hutchinson & Co., 1970.

1014
Ponomaryov, B.N., ed. *World Revolutionary Movement of the Working Class.* 3rd ed. Moscow: Progress Publishers, 1967.

1015
Ramos, Joseph R. *Labor and Development in Latin America.* New York: Columbia University Press, 1970.

1016
Rimlinger, Gaston V. *Welfare Policy and Industrialization in Europe, America and Russia.* New York: John Wiley & Sons, 1971.

1017
Roberts, B.C. *Labour in the Tropical Territories of the Commonwealth.* Durham: Duke University Press, 1965.

1018
Roberts, Harold S., and Brissenden, Paul F., eds. *The Challenge of Industrial Relations in the Pacific-Asian Countries.* Honolulu: East-West Center Press, 1965.

1019
Romualdi, Serafino. *Presidents and Peons: Recollections of a Labor Ambassador in Latin America.* New York: Funk & Wagnalls, 1967.

1020
Rose, Arnold M. *Migrants in Europe: Problems of Acceptance and Adjustment.* Minneapolis: University of Minnesota Press, 1969.

1021
Schwartz, Albin. *Trade Unions and National Economic Policy in Western Unions.* New York: Viking Press, 1972.

1022
Snow, Sinclair. *The Pan-American Federation of Labor.* Durham: Duke University Press, 1964.

1023
Stewart, Margaret. *Britain and the ILO: The Story of Fifty Years.* London: Her Majesty's Stationery Office, 1969.

1024
Sturmthal, Adolf. *Workers Councils.* Cambridge: Harvard University Press, 1964.

1025
––––––, ed. *White-Collar Trade Unions: Contemporary Developments in Industrialized Societies.* * Urbana: University of Illinois Press, 1966.

1026
Van de Vall, Mark. *Labor Organizations: A Macro- and Micro-Sociological Analysis on a Comparative Basis.* London: Cambridge University Press, 1970.

SPECIFIC COUNTRIES

Argentina

1027
Alexander, Robert. *Labor Relations in Argentina, Brazil and Chile.* New York: McGraw-Hill, 1962.

1028
Baily, Samuel L. *Labor, Nationalism, and Politics in Argentina.* New Brunswick: Rutgers University Press, 1967.

Australia

1029
Caiden, Gerald E. *Public Employment Compulsory Arbitration in Australia.* Ann Arbor: Institute of Industrial and Labor Relations, University of Michigan, 1971.

1030
Childe, Vere Gordon. *How Labour Governs: A Study of Workers' Representation in Australia.* New York: Cambridge University Press, 1964.

1031
Cooksey, Robert, ed. *The Great Depression in Australia.* No. 17. Canberra: Australian Society for the Study of Labour History, 1969.

1032
Docker, Edward W. *The Blackbirders: The Recruiting of South Seas Labour for Queensland, 1863-1907.* Sydney: Angus & Robertson, 1970.

1033
Harris, Joe. *The Bitter Fight: A Pictorial History of the Australian Labor Movement.* Queensland: University of Queensland Press, 1970.

1034
Louis, L.J. *Trade Unions and the Depression: A Study of Victoria, 1930-1932.* Canberra: Australian National University Press, 1968.

1035
Matthews, P.W.D., and Ford, G.W., eds. *Australian Trade Unions: Their Development, Structure and Horizons.* Melbourne: Sun Books, 1968.

1036
Sutcliffe, J.T. *A History of Trade Unionism in Australia.* Melbourne: Macmillan, 1921.

1037
Turner, Ian. *Industrial Labour and Politics: The Labour Movement in Eastern Australia, 1900-1921.* New York: Cambridge University Press, 1965.

1038
Walker, Kenneth F. *Australian Industrial Relations Systems.* Cambridge: Harvard University Press, 1970.

Belgium

1039
Blanpain, Roger. *Public Employee Unionism in Belgium.* Ann Arbor: Institute of Industrial and Labor Relations, University of Michigan, 1971.

1040
Seyfarth, H.E.; Shaw, Lee C.; Fairweather, Owen; and Geraldson, Raymond I. *Labor Relations and the Law in Belgium and the United States.* International Labor Studies, vol. 2. Ann Arbor: University of Michigan, 1969.

Brazil

1041
Alexander, Robert. *Labor Relations in Argentina, Brazil and Chile.* New York: McGraw-Hill, 1962.

Canada

1042
Adell, B.L. *The Legal Status of Collective Bargaining Agreements in England, the United States, and Canada.* Research series No. 10. Kingston: Industrial Relations Centre, Queen's University, 1970.

1043

Arthurs, H.W. *Collective Bargaining by Public Employee Unions in Canada: Five Models.* Ann Arbor: Institute of Industrial and Labor Relations, University of Michigan, 1971.

1044

Bairstow, Frances, ed. *The Dynamics of Change – Labour Relations on the Montreal Waterfront.* Montreal: Industrial Relations Centre, McGill University, 1970.

1045

Bradwin, Edmund W. *The Bunkhouse Man: A Study of Work and Pay in the Camps of Canada, 1903-1914.* New York: Columbia University Press, 1928.

1046

Crispo, John. *International Unionism: A Study in Canadian-American Relations.* Toronto: McGraw-Hill, 1967.

1047

Horowitz, Gad. *Canadian Labour in Politics.* Toronto: University of Toronto Press, 1968.

1048

Macdowell, G.F. *The Brandon Packers Strike: A Tragedy of Errors.* Toronto: McClelland and Stewart, 1971.

1049

Phillips, Paul A. *No Power Greater: A Century of Labour in British Columbia.* Vancouver: British Columbia Federation of Labour, 1967.

1050

Robin, Martin. *Radical Politics and Canadian Labour, 1880-1930.* Kingston, Ontario: Industrial Relations Centre, Queen's University, 1968.

Ceylon

1051

Kearney, Robert N. *Trade Unions and Politics in Ceylon.* Berkeley: University of California Press, 1971.

Chile

1052

Alexander, Robert. *Labor Relations in Argentina, Brazil and Chile.* New York: McGraw-Hill, 1962.

1053

Morris, James O. *Élites, Intellectuals, and Consensus: A Study of the Social Questions and the Industrial Relations System in Chile.* Ithaca: New York State School of Industrial and Labor Relations, Cornell University, 1966.

China

1054
Chesneaux, Jean. *The Chinese Labor Movement, 1919-1927.* Stanford: Stanford University Press, 1968.

1055
Hoffman, Charles. *Work Incentive Practices and Policies in the People's Republic of China, 1953-1965.* Albany: State University of New York Press, 1967.

1056
Mousnier, Roland. Translated by Brian Pearce. *Peasant Uprisings in Seventeenth Century France, Russia and China.** New York: Harper & Row, 1970.

1057
Myers, Ramon H. *The Chinese Peasant Economy: Agricultural Development in Hopei and Shantung, 1890-1949.* Cambridge: Harvard University Press, 1970.

Colombia

1058
Urrutia, Miguel. *The Development of the Colombian Labor Movement.* New Haven: Yale University Press, 1969.

Cuba

1059
Cuban Economic Research Project. *A Study on Cuba.* Coral Gables: University of Miami Press, 1965.

1060
Klein, Herbert S. *Slavery in the Americas: A Comparative Study of Virginia and Cuba.* Chicago: University of Chicago Press, 1967.

1061
Mesa-Lago, Carmelo. *The Labor Sector and Socialist Distribution in Cuba.* New York: Praeger, 1968.

1062
Zeitlin, Maurice. *Revolutionary Politics and the Cuban Working Class.** Princeton: Princeton University Press, 1967.

Dahomey

1063
Polanyi, Karl. *Dahomey and the Slave Trade: An Analysis of an Archaic Economy.* Seattle: University of Washington Press, 1966.

Denmark

1064
Raffaele, Joseph A. *Labor Leadership in Italy and Denmark.* Madison: University of Wisconsin Press, 1962.

Finland

1065
Knoellinger, Carl E. *Labor in Finland.* Cambridge: Harvard University Press, 1960.

France

1066
Crozier, Michel. *The World of the Office Worker.* Translated by David Landau. Chicago: University of Chicago Press, 1971.

1067
Hamilton, Richard F. *Affluence and the French Worker in the Fourth Republic.* Princeton: Princeton University Press, 1967.

1068
Lorwin, Val R. *The French Labor Movement.* Cambridge: Harvard University Press, 1954.

1069
Mendras, Henri. *The Vanishing Peasant: Innovation and Change in French Agriculture.* Cambridge: M.I.T. Press, 1971.

1070
Meyers, Frederic. *The State and Government Employee Unions in France.* Ann Arbor: Institute of Industrial and Labor Relations, University of Michigan, 1971.

1071
Mousnier, Roland. Translated by Brian Pearce. *Peasant Uprisings in Seventeenth Century France, Russia and China.** New York: Harper & Row, 1970.

1072
Ridley, F.F. *Revolutionary Syndicalism in France.* Cambridge: University of Cambridge Press, 1970.

1073
Saposs, David J. *The Labor Movement in Post-World War I France.* New York: Columbia University Press, 1931.

1074
Williams, Gwyn A. *Artisans and Sans-Culottes: Popular Movements in France and Britain during the French Revolution.* New York: Norton, 1969.

Germany

1075
Armeson, Robert B. *Total Warfare and Compulsory Labor: Germany during World War I.* The Hague: Martinus Nijhoff, 1965.

1076
de Schweinitz, Dorothea. *Labor-Management Consultation in the Factory: The Experience of Sweden, England, and the Federal Republic of Germany.* Honolulu: Industrial Relations Center, University of Hawaii, 1966.

1077
Dietrich, George P. *The Trade Union Role in the Reconstruction of Germany.* Berlin: Office of Military Government, Manpower Division, 1949.

1078
Feldman, Gerald D. *Army, Industry and Labor in Germany, 1914-1918.* Princeton: Princeton University Press, 1966.

1079
Grebing, Helga. *The History of the German Labour Movement.* London: Oswald Wolff, 1969.

1080
Homze, Edward L. *Foreign Labor in Nazi Germany.* Princeton: Princeton University Press, 1967.

1081
Kampffmeyer, Paul. *Changes in the Theory and Tactics of German Social Democracy.* Chicago: Charles H. Kerr, 1908.

1082
Lösche, Peter. *The German Labor Movement and Economic Development.* Urbana: University of Illinois Press, 1972.

1083
MacDonald, D.F. *Employers' Associations in Western Germany.* Berlin: Office of Military Government, Manpower Division, 1949.

1084
McPherson, William H. *Public Employee Relations in West Germany.* Ann Arbor: Institute of Industrial and Labor Relations, University of Michigan, 1971.

1085
Musgrave, P.W. *Technical Change, the Labour Force and Education: A Study of the British and German Iron and Steel Industries, 1860-1964.* Long Island City: Pergamon Press, 1967.

1086
Neuman, Robert P. *Industrialization and Sexual Behavior: Some Aspects of Working Class Life in Imperial Germany.* Lexington, Mass.: D.C. Heath, 1972.

1087

Noyes, P.H. *Organization and Revolution: Working-Class Associations in the German Revolutions of 1848-1849.* Princeton: Princeton University Press, 1966.

1088

Redlich, Fritz. *The German Military Enterpriser and His Work Force: A Study in European Economic and Social History.* Wiesbaden: Franz Steiner Verlag, 1964.

1089

Reich, Nathan. *Labour Relations in Republican Germany.* New York: Oxford University Press, 1938.

1090

Reichard, Richard W. *Crippled from Birth: German Social Democracy, 1844-1870.* Ames: Iowa State University Press, 1969.

1091

Roth, Guenther. *The Social Democrats in Imperial Germany: A Study in Working Class Isolation and National Integration.* Totowa, N.J.: Bedminster Press, 1963.

1092

Seyfarth, H.E.; Shaw, Lee C.; Fairweather, Owen; and Geraldson, Raymond I. *Labor Relations and the Law in West Germany and the United States.* International Labor Studies, vol. 3. Ann Arbor: University of Michigan, 1969.

1093

Sheehan, James J. *The Career of Lujo Brentano: A Study of Liberalism and Social Reform in Imperial Germany.* Chicago: University of Chicago Press, 1966.

1094

Wunderlich, Frieda. *German Labor Courts.* Chapel Hill: University of North Carolina Press, 1947.

1095

————. *Farm Labor in Germany, 1810-1945.* Princeton: Princeton University Press, 1961.

Great Britain

1096

Adell, B.L. *The Legal Status of Collective Bargaining Agreements in England, the United States, and Canada.* Research series No. 10. Kingston: Industrial Relations Centre, Queen's University, 1970.

1097

Arnot, R. Page. *The General Strike, May 1926: Its Origin and History.* London: Labour Research Department, 1926.

1098

————. *A History of the Scottish Miners.* London: Allen & Unwin, 1955.

1099
Baernreither, J.M. *English Associations of Working Men.* London: Swan Sonnenschein, 1889.

1100
Bell, Florence Eveleen (Olliffe) Lady. *At the Works: A Study of a Manufacturing Town (Middlesbrough).* 1907. New York: Augustus M. Kelley, 1969.

1101
Bell, J.D.M. *Industrial Unionism: A Critical Analysis.* Glasgow: University of Glasgow, 1949.

1102
Bennett, Eric. *The Worshipful Company of Wheelwrights of the City of London, 1670-1970.* Newton Abbot, England: David & Charles, 1970.

1103
Briggs, Asa, and Saville, John, eds. *Essays in Labor History.* Rev. ed. London: Macmillan, 1967.

1104
Chancellor, Valerie E. *Master and Artisan in Victorian England: The Diary of William Andrews and the Autobiography of Joseph Gutteridge.* New York: Augustus M. Kelley, 1969.

1105
Chang, Duck Soo. *British Methods of Industrial Peace.* New York: Columbia University Press, 1936.

1106
Clegg, H.A. *The System of Industrial Relations in Great Britain.* Oxford: Basil Blackwell, 1970.

1107
————; Fox, Allan; and Thompson, A.F. *A History of British Trade Unions, 1889-1910.* Oxford: Clarendon Press, 1964.

1108
Coates, Ken, and Topham, Anthony. *Industrial Democracy in Great Britain.* London: MacGibbon and Kee, 1968.

1109
Cole, G.D.H. *Chartist Portraits.* London: Macmillan, 1941.

1110
————. *Fabian Socialism.* London: Allen & Unwin, 1943.

1111
————. *British Working Class Politics, 1832-1914.* London: Routledge and Kegan Paul, 1950.

1112
————. *Labour in the Commonwealth: A Book for the Younger Generation.* 1918. Freeport, N.Y.: Books for Libraries Press, 1971.

1113
Committee on Trades' Societies. *Trades' Societies and Strikes.* London: John W. Parker & Son, 1860.

1114
Cowling, Maurice. *The Impact of Labour, 1920-1924: The Beginning of Modern British Politics*. New York: Cambridge University Press, 1971.

1115
Craik, William. *Sydney Hill and the National Union of Public Employees*. London: Allen & Unwin, 1968.

1116
Department of Employment and the Central Office of Information. *Industrial Relations: A Guide to the Industrial Relations Act, 1971*. London: Her Majesty's Stationery Office, 1971.

1117
de Schweinitz, Dorothea. *Labor-Management Consultation in the Factory: The Experience of Sweden, England, and the Federal Republic of Germany*. Honolulu: Industrial Relations Center, University of Hawaii, 1966.

1118
Engels, Friedrich. *The Conditions of the Working Class in England*. 1845. Translated and edited by W.D. Henderson and W.H. Chaloner. Stanford: Stanford University Press, 1968.

1119
Finlayson, Geoffrey. *Decade of Reform: England in the Eighteen Thirties*. New York: Norton, 1970.

1120
Gammage, R.G. *History of the Chartist Movement, 1837-1854*. 2nd ed. London: Truslove & Hanson, 1894.

1121
Goodman, J.F.B., and Whittingham, T.G. *Shop Stewards in British Industry*. New York: McGraw-Hill, 1971.

1122
Groves, Reg. *Sharpen the Sickle! The History of the Farm Workers' Union*. London: The Porcupine Press, 1949.

1123
Hammond, J.L., and Hammond, Barbara. *The Age of the Chartists, 1832-1854*. London: Longmans, Green, 1930.

1124
Hepple, B.A., and O'Higgins, Paul. *Public Employee Trade Unionism in the United Kingdom: The Legal Framework*. Ann Arbor: Institute of Industrial and Labor Relations, University of Michigan, 1971.

1125
Hibbert, Francis A. *The Influence and Development of English Gilds*. Cambridge: Cambridge University Press, 1891.

1126
Hindess, Barry. *The Decline of Working-Class Politics*. London: MacGibbon and Kee, 1971.

1127
Hobsbaum, E.J. *Labouring Men: Studies in the History of Labour.* * New York: Basic Books, 1964.

1128
Hutchins, B.L., and Harrison, A. *A History of Factory Legislation.* 3rd ed. London: P.S. King & Son, 1926.

1129
Jencks, Clinton E. *Men Underground: Working Conditions of British Coal Miners since Nationalization.* San Diego: San Diego State College Press, 1969.

1130
Kingsford, P.W. *Victorian Railwaymen: The Emergence and Growth of Railway Labour, 1830-1870.* London: Cass, 1970.

1131
Knoop, Douglas, and Jones, G.P. *The Medieval Mason: An Economic History of English Stone Building in the Later Middle Ages and Early Modern Times.* Manchester: Manchester University Press, 1967.

1132
Kramer, Stella. *The English Craft Gilds and the Government.* New York: Columbia University Press, 1905.

1133
Leventhal, F.M. *Respectable Radical: George Howell and Victorian Working Class Politics.* Cambridge: Harvard University Press, 1971.

1134
Levinson, Harold M. *Collective Bargaining by British Local Authority Employees.* Ann Arbor: Institute of Industrial and Labor Relations, University of Michigan, 1971.

1135
Lovell, John. *Stevedores and Dockers: A Study of Trade Unionism in the Port of London, 1870-1914.* New York: Augustus M. Kelley, 1969.

1136
————, and Roberts, B.C. *A Short History of the TUC.* London: Macmillan, 1968.

1137
Loveridge, Raymond. *Collective Bargaining by National Employees in the United Kingdom.* Ann Arbor: Institute of Industrial and Labor Relations, University of Michigan, 1971.

1138
McKenzie, Robert, and Silver, Allan. *Angels in Marble: Working Class Conservatives in Urban England.* Chicago: University of Chicago Press, 1968.

1139
Martin, Roderick. *Communism and the British Trade Unions, 1924-1933: A Study of the National Minority Movement.* New York: Oxford University Press, 1970.

1140

Mason, Anthony. *The General Strike in the North East*. Hull, England: University of Hull, 1970.

1141

Musgrave, P.W. *Technical Change, the Labour Force and Education: A Study of the British and German Iron and Steel Industries, 1860-1964*. Long Island City: Pergamon Press, 1967.

1142

Neff, Wanda F. *Victorian Working Women: An Historical and Literary Study of Women in British Industries and Professions, 1832-1850*. 2nd ed. London: Frank Cass & Co., 1966.

1143

Oram, R.B. *The Dockers' Tragedy*. London: Hutchinson & Co., 1970.

1144

Parnaby, O.W. *Britain and the Labor Trade in the Southwest Pacific*. Durham: Duke University Press, 1964.

1145

Paynter, Will. *British Trade Unions and the Problem of Change*. London: Allen & Unwin, 1970.

1146

Pelling, Henry. *A History of British Trade Unionism*. London: Macmillan, 1966.

1147

Pinchbeck, Ivy. *Women Workers and the Industrial Revolution, 1750-1850*. 2nd ed. London: Frank Cass & Co., 1969.

1148

Plummer, Alfred. *Bronterre: A Political Biography of Bronterre O'Brien, 1804-1864*. London: Allen & Unwin, 1971.

1149

Seabrook, Jeremy. *City Close-Up*. Indianapolis: Bobbs-Merrill, 1972.

1150

Seyfarth, H.E.; Shaw, Lee C.; Fairweather, Owen; and Geraldson, Raymond I. *Labor Relations and the Law in the United Kingdom and the United States*. International Labor Studies, vol 1. Ann Arbor: University of Michigan, 1968.

1151

Slosson, Preston W. *The Decline of the Chartist Movement*. New York: Columbia University Press, 1916.

1152

Stewart, Margaret. *Frank Cousins: A Study*. London: Hutchinson and Co., 1968.

1153

————. *Britain and the ILO: The Story of Fifty Years*. London: Her Majesty's Stationery Office, 1969.

1154
Thompson, Laurence. *The Enthusiasts: A Biography of John and Katharine Bruce Glasier.* London: Victor Gollancz, 1971.

1155
Tunstall, Jeremy. *The Fishermen.* London: MacGibbon and Kee, 1962.

1156
Turner, H.A. *Labour Relations in the British Motor Car Industry.* London: Allen & Unwin, 1967.

1157
Webb, Sydney, and Webb, Beatrice. *Industrial Democracy.* London: Longmans, Green, 1920.

1158
————. *The History of Trade Unionism, 1666-1920.* London: Longmans, Green 1920.

1159
Wedderburn, K.W., and Davies, P.L. *Employment Grievances and Disputes Procedures in Britain.* Berkeley: University of California Press, 1969.

1160
West, Julius. *A History of the Chartist Movement.* London: Constable & Co., 1926.

1161
Williams, Alfred. *Life in a Railway Factory.* London: Duckworth & Co., 1915.

1162
Wilson, Alexander. *The Chartist Movement in Scotland.* Manchester: University of Manchester Press, 1970.

1163
Wright, Peter L. *The Coloured Worker in British Industry.* London: Oxford University Press, 1968.

Greece

1164
Jecchinis, Christos. *Trade Unionism in Greece: A Study in Political Paternalism.* Chicago: Labor Education Division, Roosevelt University, 1967.

Hungary

1165
Timár János. *Planning the Labor Force in Hungary.* White Plains: International Arts and Sciences Press, 1966.

India

1166
Aggarwal, Arjun P. *Indian and American Labor Legislation and Practices: A Comparative Study.* New York; Asia Publishing House, 1967.

1167
Agnihortri, Vidhyadhar. *Industrial Relations in India.* New Delhi: Atma Ram, 1970.

1168
Crouch, Harold. *Trade Unions and Politics in India.* Bombay: Manaktalas, 1966.

1169
Johri, Chandra K. *Unionism in a Developing Economy: A Study of the Interaction between Trade Unionism and Government Policy in India, 1950-1965.* New York: Asia Publishing House, 1967.

1170
Morris, Morris David. *The Emergence of an Industrial Labor Force in India: A Study of the Bombay Cotton Mills, 1854-1947.* Berkeley: University of California Press, 1965.

1171
Munson, Fred C. *Indian Trade Unions: Structure and Function.* Ann Arbor: Institute for International Commerce and Bureau of Industrial Relations, University of Michigan, 1970.

1172
Pant, Suresh C. *Indian Labour Problems.* 2nd ed. Allahabad: Chaitanya Publishing House, 1970.

1173
Sharma, G. *The Labour Movement in India: Its Past and Present.* New York: International Publications Service, 1971.

1174
Subramanian, K.N. *Labour-Management Relations in India.* New York: Asia Publishing House, 1967.

Ireland

1175
Clarkson, Jesse D. *Labour and Nationalism in Ireland.* New York: AMS Press, 1970.

1176
Connell, Kenneth Hugh. *Irish Peasant Society: Four Historical Essays.* New York: Oxford University Press, 1968.

1177
Daly, George F. *Industrial Relations: Comparative Aspects with Particular Reference to Ireland.* Cork: The Mercier Press, 1958.

1178
Larkin, Emmet. *James Larkin: Irish Labour Leader, 1876-1947.* Cambridge: M.I.T. Press, 1965.

Israel

1179
Lefkowitz, Jerome. *Public Employee Unionism in Israel.* Ann Arbor: Institute of Industrial and Labor Relations, University of Michigan, 1971.

Italy

1180
Gualtieri, Humbert L. *The Labor Movement in Italy.* New York: S.F. Vanni, 1946.

1181
Newfeld, Maurice F. *Italy: School for Awakening Countries.* Ithaca: Cornell University Press, 1961.

1182
Raffaele, Joseph A. *Labor Leadership in Italy and Denmark.* Madison: University of Wisconsin Press, 1962.

1183
Seyfarth, H.E.; Shaw, Lee C.; Fairweather, Owen; and Geraldson, Raymond I. *Labor Relations and the Law in Italy and the United States.* International Labor Studies, vol. 4. Ann Arbor: University of Michigan, 1970.

Japan

1184
Ayusawa, Iwao F. *A History of Labor in Modern Japan.* Honolulu: East-West Center Press, 1966.

1185
Ballon, Robert J. *The Japanese Employee.* Tokyo: Sophia University; Rutland, Vt.: C.E. Tuttle, 1969.

1186
Cole, Robert E. *Japanese Blue Collar: The Changing Tradition.* Berkeley: University of California Press, 1971.

1187
Cook, Alice H. *An Introduction to Japanese Trade Unionism.* * Ithaca: New York State School of Industrial and Labor Relations, Cornell University, 1966.

1188
————; Levine, Solomon B.; and Mitsufuji, Tadashi. *Public Employee Labor Relations in Japan: Three Aspects.* Ann Arbor: Institute of Industrial and Labor Relations, University of Michigan, 1971.

1189
Taira, Koji. *Economic Development and the Labor Market in Japan.* New York: Columbia University Press, 1970.

1190
Whitehill, Arthur M. *The Other Worker: A Comparative Study of Industrial Relations in the United States and Japan.* Honolulu: East-West Center Press, 1968.

1191
Wilkenson, Thomas O. *The Urbanization of Japanese Labor, 1868-1965.* Amherst: University of Massachusetts Press, 1965.

Kenya

1192
Singh, Makham. *History of Kenya's Trade Union Movement to 1952.* Nairobi, Kenya: East African Publishing House, 1969.

Libya

1193
Norman, John. *Labor and Politics in Libya and Arab Africa.* New York: Bookman Associates, 1965.

Malaya

1194
Jain, Ravindra K. *South Indians on the Plantation Frontier in Malaya.* New Haven: Yale University Press, 1970.

1195
Stenson, M.R. *Industrial Conflict in Malaya: Prelude to the Communist Revolt of 1948.* London: Oxford University Press, 1970.

Mexico

1196
Ashby, Joe C. *Organized Labor and the Mexican Revolution under Lazáro Cárdenas.* Chapel Hill: University of North Carolina Press, 1967.

1197
Brading, D.A. *Miners and Merchants in Bourbon Mexico, 1763-1810.* New York: Cambridge University Press, 1971.

1198
Levenstein, Harvey A. *Labor Organizations in the United States and Mexico: A History of Their Relations.* Westport: Greenwood Press, 1971.

Netherlands

1199
Windmuller, John P. *Labor Relations in the Netherlands.* Ithaca: Cornell University Press, 1969.

Nigeria

1200
Ananaba, Wogu. *The Trade Union Movement in Nigeria.* New York: Africana Publishing Corp., 1969.

Norway

1201
Dorfman, Herbert. *Labor Relations in Norway.* Oslo: Norwegian Joint Committee on International Social Policy, 1966.

Peru

1202
Chaplin, David. *The Peruvian Industrial Labor Force.* Princeton: Princeton University Press, 1967.

1203
Payne, James L. *Labor and Politics in Peru: The System of Political Bargaining.* New Haven: Yale University Press, 1965.

Poland

1204
Johnpoll, Bernard K. *The Politics of Futility: The General Jewish Workers Bund of Poland, 1917-1943.* Ithaca: Cornell University Press, 1967.

Portuguese West Africa

1205
Cadbury, William A. *Labour in Portuguese West Africa.* 1910. New York: Negro Universities Press, 1969.

Puerto Rico

1206
Friedlander, Stanley L. *Labor Migration and Economic Growth: A Case Study of Puerto Rico.* Cambridge: The M.I.T. Press, 1965.

Russia

1207
Anonymous. *The Dark Side of the Moon.* New York: Scribner, 1947.

1208
Blum, Jerome. *Lord and Peasant in Russia from the Ninth to the Nineteenth Century.* * Princeton: Princeton University Press, 1961.

1209
Brodersen, Arvid. *The Soviet Worker: Labor and Government in Soviet Society.* * New York: Random House, 1966.

1210
Brown, Emily C. *Soviet Trade Unions and Labor Relations.* Cambridge: Harvard University Press, 1966.

1211
Conquest, Robert, ed. *Industrial Workers in the USSR.* New York: Praeger, 1967.

1212
Dallin, David J., and Nicolaevsky, Boris I. *Forced Labor in Soviet Russia.* New Haven: Yale University Press, 1947.

1213
Deutscher, Isaac. *Soviet Trade Unions: Their Place in Soviet Labour Policy.* London: Royal Institute of International Affairs, 1950.

1214
Dewar, Margaret. *Labour Policy in the USSR, 1917-1928.* London: Royal Institute of International Affairs, 1956.

1215
Dodge, Norton T. *Women in the Soviet Economy: Their Role in Economic, Scientific, & Technical Development.* Baltimore: Johns Hopkins Press, 1966.

1216
Freeman, Joseph. *The Soviet Worker.* New York: Liveright, 1932.

1217
Gorbatov, Aleksander V. *Years off My Life: The Memoirs of General of the Soviet Army, A.V. Gorbatov.* Translated by Gordon Clough and Anthony Cash. New York: Norton, 1965.

1218
Gordon, Manya. *Workers Before and After Lenin.* New York: E.P. Dutton, 1941.

1219
Herling, Albert K. *The Soviet Slave Empire.* New York: Wilfred Funk, 1951.

1220
Kaplan, Frederick I. *Bolshevik Ideology and the Ethics of Soviet Labor, 1917-1920.* New York: Philosophical Library, 1968.

1221
Kirsch, Leonard J. *Soviet Wages.* Cambridge: The M.I.T. Press, 1972.

1222
Lengyel, József. *From Beginning to End.* Translated by Ilona Duczynska. London: Owen, 1966.

1223
McAuley, Mary. *Labor Disputes in Soviet Russia, 1957-1965.* New York: Oxford University Press, 1969.

1224
Male, D.J. *Russian Peasant Organization before Collectivisation.* New York: Cambridge University Press, 1971.

1225
Mendelsohn, Ezra. *Class Struggle in the Pale: The Formative Years of the Jewish Workers' Movement in Tsarist Russia.* Cambridge, England: Cambridge University Press, 1970.

1226
Mousnier, Roland. *Peasant Uprisings in Seventeenth Century France, Russia and China.* * Translated by Brian Pearce. New York: Harper & Row, 1970.

1227
Orr, Charles A. *Stalin's Slave Camps: An Indictment of Modern Slavery.* Boston: Beacon Press, 1952.

1228
Osipov, G.V., ed. *Industry and Labour in the USSR.* * London: Tavistock Publications, 1971.

1229
Pipes, Richard. *Social Democracy and the St. Petersburg Labor Movement, 1885-1897.* Cambridge: Harvard University Press, 1963.

1230
Rimlinger, Gaston V. *Welfare Policy and Industrialization in Europe, America and Russia.* New York: John Wiley & Sons, 1971.

1231
Schwarz, Solomon. *Labor in the Soviet Union.* New York: Praeger, 1951.

1232
Serebrennikov, G.N. *The Position of Women in the USSR.* 1937. Freeport, N.Y.: Books for Libraries Press, 1970.

1233
Swianiewicz, S. *Forced Labour and Economic Development: An Enquiry into the Experience of Soviet Industrialization.* New York: Oxford University Press, 1965.

1234
Treadgold, Donald W. *The Great Siberian Migration, 1861-1913.* Princeton: Princeton University Press, 1957.

1235
Tupper, Harmon. *To the Great Ocean: Siberia and the Trans-Siberian Railway.* Boston: Little, Brown and Co., 1965.

1236
Turin, S.P. *From Peter the Great to Lenin: A History of the Russian Labour Movement.* London: Frank Cass and Co., 1935.

Singapore

1237
Chalmers, W. Ellison. *Crucial Issues in Industrial Relations in Singapore.* Singapore: Donald Moore Press, 1967.

Sweden

1238
de Schweinitz, Dorothea. *Labor-Management Consultation in the Factory: The Experience of Sweden, England, and the Federal Republic of Germany.* Honolulu: Industrial Relations Center, University of Hawaii, 1966.

1239
Jagerskiold, Stig. *Collective Bargaining Rights of State Officials in Sweden.* Ann Arbor: Institute of Industrial and Labor Relations, University of Michigan, 1971.

1240
Norgren, Paul. *The Swedish Collective Bargaining System.* Cambridge: Harvard University Press, 1941.

1241
Robbins, James J. *The Government of Labor Relations in Sweden.* Chapel Hill: University of North Carolina, 1942.

1242
Schmidt, Folke. *The Law of Labour Relations in Sweden.* Stockholm: Almquist and Wiksell, 1962.

Tanganyika

1243
Friedland, William H. *VUTA KAMBA: The Development of Trade Unions in Tanganyika.* Stanford: Hoover Institution Press, Stanford University, 1969.

Tunisia

1244
Beling, Willard A. *Modernization and African Labor: A Tunisian Case Study.* New York: Praeger, 1965.

Turkey

1245
Hirsch, Eva. *Poverty and Plenty on the Turkish Farm.* New York: Middle East Institute (distributed by Columbia University Press), 1970.

Uganda

1246
Scott, Roger. *The Development of Trade Unions in Uganda.* Nairobi, Kenya: East African Publishing House, 1966.

Venezuela

1247
Lombardi, John V. *The Decline and Abolition of Negro Slavery in Venezuela, 1820-1854.* Westport: Greenwood Press, 1971.

Yugoslavia

1248
Adizes, Ichak. *Industrial Democracy: Yugoslav Style.* New York: The Free Press, 1971.

BOOKS—NOVELS

1249

Adamic, Louis. *Grandsons* (about a Yugoslav family with three sons: an IWW member, a gangster, a war veteran). New York: Harper, 1935.

1250

Adams, Samuel Hopkins. *Sunrise to Sunset* (involves work, love, mystery in cotton mill setting, Troy, N.Y., in 1930s). New York: Random House, 1950.

1251

Albery, Faxon F.D. *Michael Ryan, Capitalist* (depicts steelworkers union in Midwest; early 1900s). Columbus: Rowfant, 1913.

1252

Algren, Nelson. *Somebody in Boots* (story of jobless youths and their disillusionment with the social system of the 1930s). New York: Vanguard, 1935.

1253

————. *Never Come Morning* (shows the Polish on Chicago's Northwest Side—reminiscent of James T. Farrell's "Irish"). New York: Harper, 1942.

1254

Alman, David. *World Full of Strangers* (documentary treatment of fatigue, defeat, and corruption among immigrants in New York City). New York: Doubleday, 1949.

1255

Anderson, Sherwood. *Poor White* (about an inventor among industrialists; 1880-1900). New York: B.W. Huebsch, 1920.

1256

Anderson, Thomas. *Here Comes Pete Now* (deals with educated young man with a hankering to work with his hands on the docks; setting: longshoremen's hiring hall). New York: Random House, 1961.

1257

Arnow, Harriette L. *The Dollmaker* (life of Cumberland Mountain people who migrate to Detroit for work during World War II). New York: Macmillan, 1954.

1258

Asch, Shalom. *East River* (concerns Jews and Catholics as workers and factory owners in modern New York). New York: Putnam, 1946.

1259

Atherton, Sarah H. *Mark's Own* (follows rise of the union in coal-mining Pennsylvania; 1850-1930). Indianapolis: Bobbs-Merrill, 1941.

1260

Attaway, William. *Let Me Breathe Thunder* (strong story of two migratory workers and small Mexican boy they pick up on the road). New York: Doubleday, 1939.

1261

————. *Blood on the Forge* (pictures Negro steelworkers' bitter struggles; World War I). New York: Doubleday, Doran, 1941.

1262

Barrio, Raymond. *The Plum Plum Pickers** (sets forth a descriptive and humane story of migrant Mexican-American workers). New York: Harper & Row, 1971.

1263

Beard, Daniel C. *Moonblight and Six Feet of Romance* (set in Pennsylvania, 1890s; coal miners' protest). New York: Charles Webster, 1892.

1264

Bell, Thomas. *Out of This Furnace* (about a three-generation struggle of steelworkers; development of CIO; 1880-1938; Pennsylvania). Boston: Little, Brown and Co., 1941.

1265

————. *There Comes a Time* (involves bank employees and CIO organizing; New York; 1940s). Boston: Little, Brown and Co., 1946.

1266

Bellamy, Edward. *Looking Backward: 2000-1887** (projects a perfect Socialist state of the year 2000). Boston: Houghton Mifflin, 1966.

1267

Bellow, Saul. *The Adventures of Augie March** (best-seller pictures young man trying to fit into life; wide setting; 1930s). New York: Viking Press, 1953.

1268

Bezzerides, A.I. *Thieves' Market* (shows the hard life of an independent fruit and vegetable trucker). New York: Scribner, 1949.

1269

Bisno, Beatrice. *Tomorrow's Bread* (about rise of a labor leader among Jewish garment workers; Chicago; late 1800s-1920s). New York: Liveright, 1938.

1270

Bissell, Richard. *A Stretch on the River* (narrates life of towboat workers on the Mississippi; early 1940s). Boston: Little, Brown and Co., 1950.

1271

————. *7 1/2 Cents* (treats comically a pajama factory strike in Iowa River town). Boston: Little, Brown and Co., 1953.

1272

Bland, Alden. *Behold a Cry* (shows an urban Negro worker who has migrated to Chicago from the South; set during World War I and the early 1920s). New York: Scribner, 1947.

1273

Bontemps, Arna. *Black Thunder* (portrays an attempted slave insurrection in early 19th century). New York: Macmillan, 1936.

1274

Boyd, Thomas. *In Time of Peace* (shows one man's struggle with unemployment, boom times, and labor violence; 1919-1929). New York: Minton, 1935.

1275

Boyer, Richard O. *The Dark Ship* (about World War II maritime workers; union and leaders). Boston: Little, Brown and Co., 1947.

1276

Brody, Catharine. *Nobody Starves* (portrays a man and his wife, their work, and their tragedy growing out of the Depression). New York: Longmans, 1932.

1277

Bromfield, Louis. *The Green Bay Tree* (first of series dealing with factory town founders and descendants). New York: Grosset & Dunlap, 1927.

1278

Brown, Rollo W. *Firemakers* (portrays worker's hopeless effort to escape coal mines; southern Ohio; early 1900s). New York: Coward-McCann, 1931.

1279

Bullard, Arthur (Albert Edwards, pseud.). *Comrade Yetta* (about New York sweatshop workers and trade union movement; early 1900s). New York: Macmillan, 1913.

1280

Caldwell, Erskine. *Kneel to the Rising Sun* (depicts the Southern Negro as a member of the working class, crushed by the economic system). New York: Viking Press, 1935.

1281

Caldwell, Janet Taylor. *The Strong City* (pictures young German immigrant's climb to power in Pennsylvania steel mills: late 19th century). New York: Scribner, 1942.

1282

Campbell, Frances. *Men of the Enchantress* (story of Mexico, centering in an American-owned silver mine worked by Mexican laborers). Indianapolis: Bobbs-Merrill, 1947.

1283

Cantwell, Robert. *Land of Plenty* (gives realistic, brutal portrait of lumber mill workers, owners). New York: Farrar and Rinehart, 1934.

1284

Carter, John F., Jr. *The Destroyers* (about coal mine strike and its defeat; Illinois; early 1900s). Washington, D.C.: Neale, 1907.

1285

Chevalier, Haakon M. *For Us the Living* (uses murder mystery as vehicle for story of farm laborers and longshoremen in organizing struggle; California; 1929-41). New York: Alfred A. Knopf, 1948.

1286

Chidester, Ann. *The Long Year* (turmoil is caused in a small Minnesota town by a ruthless woman who is part owner of its factory). New York: Scribner, 1946.

1287

Child, Nellise. *If I Come Home* (contrasts the wealthy and the pauperized, Fascist and democratic, intolerant and sympathetic people to be found in Los Angeles). New York: Doubleday, 1943.

1288

Churchill, Winston. *The Dwelling Place of Light* (describes U.S. industrialism; plight of women workers; the IWW). New York: Macmillan, 1917.

1289

Clayton, John B. *Six Angels at My Back* (intimate view of have-nots in Florida–their essential decency, their uneducated groping for a home and a good life, and their attitudes toward tourists and flashy resorts). New York: Macmillan, 1952.

1290

Cohen, Hyman, and Cohen, Lester. *Aaron Traum* (portrays life of N.Y. garment workers–Jew and Slav, and union). New York: Liveright, 1930.

1291

Coleman, McAlister, and Raushenbush, H.S. *Red Neck* (with "red-neck" miners of Pennsylvania, asserts familiar story of uncompromising opposition of capital to labor). New York: Random House, 1936.

1292

Colman, Louis. *Lumber* (about a Northwest lumber mill worker; his difficulties, downfall). Boston: Little, Brown and Co., 1931.

1293

Conrad, Lawrence H. *Temper* (concerns lives of Midwest auto workers; 1920s). New York: Dodd, Mead, 1924.

1294

Conroy, Jack. *The Disinherited* (narrates life of industrial "bum"; 1920s). New York: Covici-Friede, 1933.

1295

Cooke, Grace M. *The Grapple* (describes Illinois mine workers in early 1900s). Boston: Page, 1905.

1296

Corle, Edwin. *Fig Tree John* (shows adjustment problems of an Apache Indian who leaves his tribe and settles on an isolated spot near Salton Sea). New York: Liveright, 1935.

1297

Cournos, John. *The Mask* (describes Russian Jews who come to America and find themselves economically trapped in the textile mills of Philadelphia). New York: Boni, 1920.

1298

Crane, Stephen. *Maggie: A Girl of the Streets: A Story of New York** (contains stark realism and pathos in a New England town). Gainesville: Scholars' Fascimiles and Reprints, 1966.

1299

Cuthbert, Clifton. *Another Such Victory* (about a textile workers strike; New England; 1934). New York: Hillman-Curl, 1937.

1300

Dahlberg, Edward. *Bottom Dogs* (makes realistic indictment of American institutions and futility of life for the lower classes). New York: Simon & Schuster, 1930.

1301

Dargan, Olive T. (Fielding Burke, pseud.) *Call Home the Heart* (describes life of a Blue Ridge Mountain woman who goes to work in a factory). New York: Longmans, Green, 1932.

1302

————. *A Stone Came Rolling* (a sequel to *Call Home the Heart;* North Carolina in Depression). New York: Longmans, Green, 1935.

1303

————. *Sons of the Stranger* (concerns miners in Denver Rockies; 1900s). New York: Longmans, Green, 1947.

1304

Davenport, Marcia. *The Valley of Decision* (dramatizes the struggle between ownership and labor, showing enlightened labor policy in American heavy industry since 1860s). New York: Scribner, 1943.

1305

Davidson, Lallah S. *South of Joplin* (involves CIO and lead mine workers; Midwest; 1930s). New York: Norton, 1939.

1306

Davis, Rebecca Harding. *Margaret Howth* (a realistic early tale of woolen mill workers; Indiana; 1860s). Boston: Ticknor and Fields, 1862.

1307

Dell, Floyd. *Diana Stair* (deals with mill workers and strike leader; Boston; 1840s). New York: Farrar and Rinehart, 1932.

1308

Denison, Thomas S. *An Iron Crown: A Tale of the Great Republic.* Chicago: T.S. Denison, 1885.

1309

Dibner, Martin. *Showcase* (treats life in a big department store). New York: Doubleday, 1958.

1310

Di Donato, Pietro. *Christ in Concrete* (portrays the piety, customs, and economic helplessness of an Italian family in New York). Indianapolis: Bobbs-Merrill, 1939.

1311

Dos Passos, John. *The Big Money* (kalieidoscopic picture of the "roaring twenties" focusing on the business world, the laboring classes and the leisure class). New York: Harcourt, 1936.

1312

Dostoevskii, Fedor T. *The House of the Dead* (deals with forced labor in Russia during the 1840s). Translated by H. Sutherland Edwards. English edition 1911. New York: E.P. Dutton, 1967.

1313

Dreiser, Theodore. *Sister Carrie** (is the eye-opener tale of 18-year old girl in Chicago of 1900). Cleveland: World Pub. Co., 1927.

1314

Duncan, David. *The Serpent's Egg* (focuses on a labor-dispute panel abritrating a controversy about overtime pay for bus drivers). New York: Macmillan, 1950.

1315

Eddy, Arthur J. *Ganton and Company* (about Chicago teamsters and meat packers; early 1900s). Chicago: McClurg, 1908.

1316

Edmonds, Walter D. *Rome Haul** (captures the bustle and vitality of life along the Erie Canal, once the lifeline between New York, New England, and the West). Boston: Little, Brown and Co., 1929.

1317

Farrell, James T. *Gas House McGinty* (describes the lives of employees and their boss in a large distributing company). New York: Vanguard, 1933.

1318

————. *A World I Never Made* (first in series on life of Danny O'Neill, young Irish-American, growing up in Chicago in early 1920s). New York: Vanguard Press, 1936.

1319

————. *Studs Lonigan: A Trilogy* (follows realistically the life of a middle-class Chicago boy growing up on the streets). New York: Vanguard Press, 1937.

1320

————. *No Star Is Lost* (second in Danny O'Neill series, concentrating on tragic consequences of poverty in Chicago). New York: Vanguard Press, 1938.

1321

————. *Father and Son* (third book in the Danny O'Neill series, focusing on a workingman's fight with his own destiny). New York: Vanguard Press, 1940.

1322
––––––. *My Days of Anger** (fourth in Danny O'Neill series; he attends University of Chicago). New York: Vanguard Press, 1943.

1323
Fast, Howard. *The American* (fictionalizes the life of John Peter Altgeld, Illinois governor, who pardoned the Haymarket anarchists). New York: Duell, Sloan & Pierce, 1946.

1324
––––––. *Power* (about a man who rises to power in a mine workers' union and automobile industry). Garden City: Doubleday, 1962.

1325
Ferber, Edna. *Giant* (points out maladjustments of Texans, their bigotry, hypocrisy, and undignified treatment of Mexican-Americans). New York: Doubleday, 1952.

1326
Ferber, Nat J. *The Sidewalks of New York* (show the life of the ghetto and its effect on a Russian boy who comes to America and grows up on the East Side of New York). New York: Covici-Friede, 1927.

1327
Field, Ben. *Piper Tompkins* (concerns a defense plant worker who becomes a fervent unionist in New England; World War II). New York: Doubleday, 1946.

1328
Fisher, William. *The Waiters* (portrays a man who works in a restaurant as a waiter; restaurant conditions). Cleveland and New York: World Pub. Co., 1936.

1329
Foote, Mary H. *Coeur d'Alene* (concerns a labor war between union and mining syndicate). Boston: Houghton Mifflin, 1894.

1330
Freeman, Mary E. Wilkins. *The Portion of Labor* (depicts the struggle between labor and capital in early New England). New York: Harper, 1901.

1331
Gaither, Frances O. *Follow the Drinking Gourd* (shows economic wastefulness of slavery, and social effects on all concerned; set in pre-Civil War Georgia and Alabama). New York: Macmillan, 1940.

1332
––––––. *The Red Cock Crows* (depicts a slave revolt on a model Mississippi plantation). New York: Macmillan, 1944.

1333
––––––. *Double Muscadine* (tells story of love and slavery on a Mississippi plantation). New York: Macmillan, 1949.

1334
Garland, Hamlin. *Hesper* (concerns miners at turn of century in Colorado). New York: Harper, 1903.

1335

Garside, Edward B. *Cranberry Red.* (describes oppression of poor Irish workers in the Cape Cod Cranberry Region). New York: Little, Brown and Co., 1938.

1336

Gibbons, William F. *Those Black Diamond Men* (concerns the coal miners in Pennsylvania at early part of century). New York; Revell, 1902.

1337

Gilkyson, Thomas W. *Oil* (vividly describes actual scouting and drilling for oil; the ruthless business methods of some oil men). New York: Scribner, 1924.

1338

Givens, Charles G. *The Devil Takes a Hill Town* (portrays the devil and God as Tennessee hillbillies discussing capitalism and class struggle). Indianapolis: Bobbs-Merrill, 1939.

1339

Grant, Robert. *Face to Face* (presents problems of labor and capital and changes brought about by labor unrest). New York: Scribner, 1886.

1340

Greene, Josiah E. *Not in Our Stars* (develops the relationships of individuals and families working on a dairy farm; East; 1940s). New York: Macmillan, 1945.

1341

————. *The Man with One Talent.* New York: McGraw-Hill, 1951.

1342

Grey, Zane. *Desert of Wheat* (follows the IWW in the state of Washington; 1917-20). New York: Grossett & Dunlap, 1918.

1343

Grubb, Davis. *The Barefoot Man* (describes hardships suffered by Appalachian coal miners in their attempts to organize, better working conditions). New York: Simon & Schuster, 1971.

1344

Halper, Albert. *The Foundry* (contains a realistic description of workers in a foundry, all classes). New York: Viking Press, 1934.

1345

————. *The Chute* (character studies of young Jews in a mail-order house; Chicago). New York: Viking Press, 1937.

1346

————. *The Little People* (narrates lives of department store workers). New York: Harper, 1942.

1347

Hapgood, Hutchins. *The Spirit of Labor* (concerns a woodworker and labor leader; Chicago; early 1900s). New York: Duffield, 1907.

1348

Harris, Cyril. *The Trouble at Hungersford* (about miners, ironworkers and sawmill workers; Peekskill, New York; 1850s). Boston: Little, Brown and Co., 1952.

1349

Harris, Frank. *The Bomb* (an imaginative story of a German boy who, after arriving in Chicago, tosses the bomb that starts the Haymarket riots). New York: Mitchell Kennerly, 1909.

1350

Hart, Alan. *In the Lives of Men* (about the IWW and lumberworkers; northwestern frontier town; 1890-1909). New York: Norton, 1937.

1351

Hatcher, Harlan H. *Central Standard Time* (describes industrial conflict of manufacturing workers; Ohio; 1934). New York: Farrar and Rinehart, 1937.

1352

Havighurst, Walter. *Pier 17* (covers a shipping strike from seamen's point of view; west coast; 1930s). New York: Macmillan, 1935.

1353

Hay, John. *The Breadwinners: A Social Study* (realistically depicts railroad workers in a provincial town). New York: Harper, 1884.

1354

Hayes, Alfred. *Shadow of Heaven* (about a labor leader who becomes disenchanted; New York; mid-1940s). New York: Howell, Soskin, 1947.

1355

Hayes, Dorsha. *Who Walk with the Earth* (concerns union education director and intra-union conflicts). New York: Harper, 1945.

1356

Hedges, Marion Hawthorne. *Iron City* (depicts change in a smug New England town in the form of unionsim, strikes, and the war; involves a young college instructor and a labor agitator). New York: Boni and Liveright, 1919.

1357

Hemingway, Ernest. *To Have and Have Not* (satirizes idle rich in Key West; depicts realistically the desperate plight of the unemployed). New York: Scribner, 1937.

1358

Herbst, Josephine. *The Executioner Waits* (concerns a large middle class family after armistice of 1918). New York: Harcourt, Brace, 1934.

1359

————. *The Rope of Gold* (describes economic conditions; U.S.; 1933-1937). New York: Harcourt, Brace, 1939.

1360

Himes, Chester B. *Lonely Crusade* (describes psychological effects of fear on a Negro union organizer in his relationships with workers in an aircraft plant). New York: Alfred A. Knopf, 1947.

1361

Horwitz, Julius. *The Inhabitants* (details the lives of Negroes, Puerto Ricans, and others on relief in New York City). Cleveland: World Pub. Co., 1960.

1362

Howard, George W. (Jason Striker, pseud.) *Haste to Succeed.* New York: Appleton-Century-Crofts, 1961.

1363

Hughes, Rupert. *Miss 318 and Mr. 37* (about department store employees and the need for fire laws in stores; U.S. city; 1910). New York: Revell, 1912.

1364

––––––. *The Giant Wakes: A Novel about Samuel Gompers* (depicts the life of Samuel Gompers, labor leader, and the AFL; U.S.; late 19th and early 20th centuries). Los Angeles: Borden, 1950.

1365

Hull, Morris. *Cannery Anne* (story of cannery workers in central California). Boston: Houghton Mifflin, 1936.

1366

Idell, Albert. *Stephen Hayne* (about coal miners during the economic conflict of German and Irish immigrants; Pennsylvania; 1870s). New York: Sloane, 1951.

1367

Jessey, Cornelia. *Teach the Angry Spirit* (depicts life in the Mexican quarter of Los Angeles; World War II). New York: Crown, 1949.

1368

Jeter, Goetze. *The Strikers* (about a shoe factory; New England; 1930s). Philadelphia: Stokes, 1937.

1369

Johnson, Josephine W. *Jordanstown* (follows small town workers during the Depression; Midwest river town). New York: Simon & Schuster, 1937.

1370

Kapstein, Israel J. *Something of a Hero* (presents effects of industrialism on different people; Midwest; 1907-1929). New York: Alfred A. Knopf, 1941.

1371

Karig, Walter. *Lower Than Angels* (tells of poverty and drabness in the life of a son of a delicatessen owner on Staten Island). New York: Farrar, 1945.

1372

Krech, Hilda S. *The Other Side of the Day* (shows plight of intellectually trained, bored housewife and her struggle to properly adjust her life to part-time work and family duties). New York: Alfred A. Knopf, 1958.

1373
Lanham, Edwin M. *The Stricklands* (about an Oklahoma tenant farmer family; one son union organizer; other son outlaw). Boston: Little, Brown and Co., 1939.

1374
Lawrence, Josephine. *Sound of Running Feet* (concerns clerks in a small real estate office). Philadelphia: Stokes, 1937.

1375
Lee, Edna L. *The Southerners* (depicts a series of labor and promotion problems faced by owner of Georgia cotton mill). New York: Appleton-Century-Crofts, 1953.

1376
Lee, Harry. *Sir and Brother* (about steel workers' labor leader). New York: Appleton-Century-Crofts, 1948.

1377
Levin, Meyer. *Citizens* (covers the Memorial Day massacre; Chicago; 1937). New York: Viking Press, 1940.

1378
Llewellyn, Richard. *How Green Was My Valley* (provides a rich and full story of a mining family in South Wales valley). New York: Macmillan, 1940.

1379
Lumkin, Grace. *A Sign for Cain* (concerns a Negro Communist's organizing of southern Negro and white workers). New York: Lee Furman, 1935.

1380
McDonald, Grace L. (Margaret Graham, pseud.). *Swing Shift* (concerns railroad and cigar workers in the West and South; 1900-1950). New York: Citadel Press, 1951.

1381
McHale, Tom. *Farragan's Retreat** (bizarre, macabre whodunit involving a Philadelphia lace-curtain Irish family driven semi-insane by super-patriotism, bigotry and religious hypocrisy). New York: Viking Press, 1971.

1382
McIntyre, John T. *Ferment*(story of strikebreakers, racketeers, and labor spies in Philadelphia). New York: Farrar, 1937.

1383
McKenney, Ruth. *Jake Home* (about radical coal miner-organizer in Pennsylvania and New York; 1920s and '30s). New York: Harcourt, Brace, 1943.

1384
————. *Industrial Valley* (recounts CIO struggles in rubber industry; Akron, Ohio; 1932-1936). New York: Harcourt, Brace, 1939; Greenwood Press, 1968.

1385
McSorley, Edward. *Our Own Kind* (portrait of Irish-American iron-worker's family in Providence tenement in early 20th century). New York: Harper, 1946.

1386
Magdaleno, Mauricio. *Sunburst* (shows how the exploitation of the Otomi Indians of Hidalgo continued after the revolution in Mexico). New York: Viking Press, 1944.

1387
Maher, Richard. *Gold Must Be Tried by Fire* (describes paper mill workers; N.Y.; 1915). New York: Macmillan, 1917.

1388
Maltz, Albert. *The Black Pit* (A drama about coal miners; Pennsylvania). New York: Putnam, 1935.

1389
––––––. *The Underground Stream* (dramatizes union struggles in Detroit before CIO and NLRA). Boston: Little, Brown and Co., 1940.

1390
Mann , Henry. *Adam Clarke* (depicts grim working conditions of immigrant steel workers; Pennsylvania; 1900s). New York: Popular Book Co., 1904.

1391
Marchand, Margaret. *Pilgrims on the Earth* (about Irish-Americans in a steel town near Pittsburgh). New York: Thomas Y. Crowell, 1940.

1392
Marquand, John P. *The Black Cargo* (narrates adventures of illicit slave trade in New England clipper ship era). New York: Macmillan, 1936.

1393
Meyersburg, Dorothy. *Seventh Avenue* (develops New York garment manufacturer into union-fighter and "runaway"). New York: E.P. Dutton, 1940.

1394
Mitchell, Ruth C. *Of Human Kindness* (about California farm workers and owners; 1930s). New York: Appleton-Century, 1940.

1395
Momaday, N. Scott. *House Made of Dawn* (about an American Indian's cultural and spiritual fight in two worlds: he can neither live the old way nor accept the new). New York: Harper & Row, 1968.

1396
Morgan, Murray C. *Viewless Winds* (about murder of Oregon labor leader's wife; violence between lumber mill workers and owners). New York: E.P. Dutton, 1949.

1397
Morris, Jane K. *Julie* (presents a labor organizer; New York and Chicago; late 19th century). New York: McGraw-Hill, 1952.

1398
Motley, Willard. *We Fished All Night* (about a Chicago labor leader; before and after World War II). New York: Appleton-Century-Crofts, 1951.

1399
Newell, Arthur A. *A Knight of the Toilers* (concerns Eastern miners; 1900s). Philadelphia: F.L. Marsh, 1905.

1400
Newhouse, Edward. *This is Your Day* (about young Communist organizer; upstate New York farms; 1930s). New York: Lee Furman, 1937.

1401
Nichols, Edward J. *Danger! Keep Out* (dramatizes personnel problems, labor problems, the psychology of industrialists, and especially technological unemployment in a Midwest oil refinery). Boston: Houghton Mifflin, 1943.

1402
————. *Hunky Johnny* (depicts a second-generation Slovak-American, raised in Gary, who goes to Chicago and has to face the problems of the Depression). Boston: Houghton Mifflin, 1945.

1403
Norris, Charles G. *Flint* (recounts labor struggles on San Francisco waterfront; 1930s). New York: Doubleday, Doran, 1944.

1404
Norris, Frank. *The Octopus: A Story of California** (dramatizes the battle of San Joaquin, California, farmers with monopolistic railroad). New York: Doubleday, Page, 1901.

1405
————. *The Pit: A Story of Chicago* (about wheat speculation on Chicago stock market). New York: Grove Press, 1956.

1406
O'Brien, Howard V. *New Men for Old* (involves preserving plant workers; Chicago; 1900s). New York: M. Kennerley, 1914.

1407
O'Malley, Michael. *Miner's Hill* (poignant telling of young Irish-American's growing up in lusty, brawling Pennsylvania steel mill town). New York: Harper, 1962.

1408
Partridge, Bellamy (Thomas Bailey, pseud.). *Big Freeze* (centers on building of Croton Aqueduct, New York City; 1840s). New York: Thomas Y. Crowell, 1948.

1409
Paul, Elliot H. *The Stars and Stripes Forever* (describes organizing and strike of manufacturing workers; Connecticut; 1930s). New York: Random House, 1939.

1410
Plunkett, James. *Strumpet City** (depicts the Irish in Dublin in their tumultuous time of trial and triumph, 1907-1914). London: Hutchinson, 1969.

1411
Poole, Ernest. *The Harbor* (tells development of New York harbor through three stages). New York: Macmillan, 1915.

1412
Preston, John H. *The Liberals* (deals with unions, CIO, strikes, anti-Semitism; Connecticut; 1930s). New York: John Day, 1938.

1413
Prosser, William H. *Nine to Five* (pictures life at various levels in offices of business firm in Boston). Boston: Little, Brown and Co., 1953.

1414
Raymond, Margaret T. *Bend in the Road* (describes uncertain period of 1929 "crash" for factory workers in East). New York: Longmans, Green, 1934.

1415
Roberts, Marta. *Tumbleweeds* (traces the life of a Mexican family in California where the father loses his job and the family has to go on relief). New York: Putnam, 1940.

1416
Robinson, Harry P. *Men Born Equal* (concerns 1890s strike to gain political advantages). New York: Harper, 1895.

1417
Roe, Wellington. *The Tree Falls South* (tells tragic story of dust storms and drought in Kansas, and of grim farmers who stage a riot). New York: Putnam, 1937.

1418
Rollins, William. *The Shadow Before* (recounts textile mill strike and effects on major characters). New York: McBride, 1934.

1419
Rölvaag, O.E. *Giants in the Earth*** (sketches life of Norwegian immigrants in the prairie states). New York: Harper, 1927.

1420
Rood, Henry E. *The Company Doctor* (follows coal miners, Molly Maguires, immigration; Pennsylvania; 1890s). Springfield, Mass.: Merriam, 1895.

1421
Ross, Clinton. *The Silent Workman* (about Eastern steelworkers; 1880s). New York: Putnam, 1886.

1422
Roy, Gabrielle. *The Cashier* (describes life of Montreal bank cashier whose tedious white-collar job is wearing him out). New York: Harcourt, 1955.

1423
Russell, Ruth. *Lake Front* (traces Irish family from arrival in Chicago in 1835 through presidential campaign of 1840, the Civil War, Haymarket riot, and railway strike of 1894). Chicago: Rockwell, 1931.

1424
Ryan, Edwin. *One Clear Call* (chronicles one day in the life of Father Clavan, octogenarian parish priest on Brooklyn's waterfront). New York: Macmillan, 1962.

1425
Rylee, Robert. *The Ring and the Cross* (sheds light on political significance of acts by members of AFL unions, the KKK, conservative churches, and industrialists' associations). New York: Alfred A. Knopf, 1947.

1426
Sandoz, Mari. *Capital City* (describes politics, labor, and strife in the capital of a high-plains state, Kanewa). Boston: Little, Brown and Co., 1939.

1427
Saxton, Alexander P. *Great Midland* (involves railroad workers, IWWs, Communists; Chicago; before World War II). New York: Appleton-Century-Crofts, 1948.

1428
————. *Bright Web in the Darkness* (depicts struggle of Negro shipyard workers to gain union recognition; San Francisco; World War II). New York: St. Martin's Press, 1958.

1429
Scarborough, Dorothy. *Can't Get A Red Bird* (describes country customs, farmer cooperatives). New York: Harper, 1929.

1430
Schulberg, Budd. *Waterfront* (discloses longshoremen's lives, rackets, official investigations; New York Harbor; 1950s). New York: Random House, 1955.

1431
Scott, Leroy. *The Walking Delegate* (covers ironworkers' union problems; New York; early 1900s). New York: Doubleday, Page, 1905.

1432
Simon, Charlie M. *The Share-Cropper* (presents plight of sharecroppers; Arkansas; 1930s). New York: E.P. Dutton, 1937.

1433
Sinclair, Upton B. *King Coal* (deals with exploitation of workers; Colorado coal fields). New York: Macmillan, 1917.

1434
————. *Boston* (fictionalized report on the Sacco-Vanzetti case in Massachusetts). New York: Boni, 1928.

1435
————. *Little Steel* (depicts steel barons' fight against unions). New York: Farrar and Rinehart, 1938.

1436
————. *The Jungle** (concerns a packing house worker turned Socialist by conditions and mistreatment of fellows; Chicago). New York: Harper, 1951.

1437

Skidmore, Hubert. *Hawk's Nest* (recounts West Virginia tunnel-drilling; silicosis). New York: Doubleday, Doran, 1941.

1438

Skinner, Burrhus F. *Walden Two* (based on life in a modern American Utopia). New York: Macmillan, 1948.

1439

Slade, Caroline. *The Triumph of Willie Pond* (makes indignant and convincing presentation of plight of the unemployed with families). New York: Vanguard Press, 1940.

1440

————. *Lilly Crackell* (makes case study of generous and beautiful woman born to life of horrible poverty). New York: Vanguard Press, 1943.

1441

Smith, Betty. *A Tree Grows in Brooklyn** (story of a young Irish girl's coming of age in the squalor and poverty of the Brooklyn slums, 1902-1919). New York: Harper & Row, 1943.

1442

Smith, Cecil Woodham. *The Great Hunger: Ireland 1845-1849** (tells gripping story of the Irish famine of the 1840s, a disaster that killed a million and a half people, drove another million to the New World). New York: Harper & Row, 1962.

1443

Smith, Francis H. *Tom Grogan* (about stevedores; east coast; 1800s). Boston: Houghton Mifflin, 1896.

1444

Smith, William Dale. *A Multitude of Men.* New York: Simon & Schuster, 1959.

1445

Smitter, Wessel. *F.O.B., Detroit* (describes a man's life inside and out of an auto factory). New York: Harper, 1938.

1446

Solzhenitsyn, Aleksander. *One Day in the Life of Ivan Denisovich** (represents a true account of Soviet labor camp life under Stalin). Translated by Ralph Parker. New York: E.P. Dutton, 1963.

1447

Spadoni, Andriana. *Not All Rivers* (about a woman's decision to fight for social justice, after realizing that being an "indignant intellectual" is not enough). New York: Doubleday, 1937.

1448

Spivak, John. *Georgia Nigger* (exposes the convict-lease system and the tortures and cruelties of chain-gang prisons). New York: Harcourt, 1932.

1449

Steele, James. *Conveyor* (gives effect of "speed-up" on auto workers; Midwest; 1930s). New York: International Publishers, 1935.

1450

Stegner, Wallace. *The Preacher and the Slave* (fictionalizes and expands biography of Joe Hill, Wobbly poet and musician, for his final years, 1910-1916). Boston: Houghton Mifflin, 1950.

1451

Steinbeck, John. *In Dubious Battle** (concerns California fruit pickers; 1930s). New York: Covici-Friede, 1936.

1452

————. *Of Mice and Men* (follows two men hired to harvest barley to a tragic ending; Salinas Valley, California; 1930s). New York; Modern Library, 1937.

1453

————. *The Grapes of Wrath** (relates displacement of Oklahoma farm family; 1930s). New York: Viking Press, 1939.

1454

Still, James. *River of Earth* (vividly pictures hard life of the people in the hills and coal camps of Kentucky). New York: Viking Press, 1940.

1455

Stilwell, Hart. *Border City* (story of racial intolerance and corrupt politics in a city on the border between Mexico and the United States). New York: Doubleday, 1945.

1456

Stone, Irving. *Adversary in the House* (fictionalizes the life of Eugene V. Debs). New York: Doubleday, 1947.

1457

Stowe, Harriet Beecher. *Uncle Tom's Cabin* (remains a classic propaganda novel, complete with Uncle Tom, Little Eva and Simon Legree). Boston: J.P. Jewett, 1852.

1458

Stribling, Thomas S. *The Forge* (treats a middle class family at the time of the Civil War). New York: Doubleday, 1931.

1459

————. *The Store* (portrays the atmosphere of a small town in Alabama—the folkways, class distinctions, religions, and business practices). New York: Doubleday, 1932.

1460

Styron, William. *The Confessions of Nat Turner** (fictionalizes life and death of runaway slave; slave rebellion). New York: Random House, 1967.

1461

Swados, Harvey. *On the Line* (depicts lives and inner conflicts of eight men on assembly line in auto factory). Boston: Atlantic, Little Brown, 1957.

1462
Swarthout, Glendon F. *Willow Run* (about Willow Run aircraft workers; 1940s). New York: Thomas Y. Crowell, 1943.

1463
Sykes, Hope W. *Second Hoeing* (pictures unending toil of a German-Russian family in the beet fields of Colorado). New York: Putnam, 1935.

1464
Taber, Gladys. *A Star to Steer By* (centers around mill strike; Wisconsin; 1930s). Philadelphia: Macrae Smith, 1938.

1465
Teller, Charlotte. *The Cage* (deals with lumber workers; Haymarket riot; Chicago; 1880s). New York: D. Appleton, 1907.

1466
Thorseth, Matthea. *Color of Ripening* (depicts Norwegian-American labor leader in IWW; Pacific Northwest; 1915). Seattle: Superior Publishers, 1949.

1467
Tillett, Dorothy (John S. Strange, pseud.). *Angry Dust* (about UMW representative during post-World War II reconversion). New York: Doubleday, 1946.

1468
Tippet, Thomas. *Horse Shoe Bottoms* (presents human problems of English miner as leader in coal mine unionization; Illinois). New York: Harper, 1935.

1469
Tobenkin, Elias. *House of Conrad* (describes three generations of a German immigrant family in New York). Philadelphia: Stokes, 1918.

1470
Tomasi, Mari. *Like Lesser Gods* (story of Italian workers in the granite quarries of Vermont). New York: Bruce, 1949.

1471
Tourgee, Albion W. *Murvale Eastman, Christian Socialist* (deals with horsecar drivers in 1880s; Christian Socialism, theme). New York: Fords, Howard, and Hulbert, 1890.

1472
————. *Bricks without Straw* (pictures Negro problems at time of Freedman's Bureau, Ku Klux Klan). First publ. 1890. Baton Rouge: Louisiana State University Press, 1969.

1473
Traven, Bruno. *The Rebellion of the Hanged* (tells story of the inhuman exploitation of Mexican mahogany loggers in latter days of Díaz regime; and of their revolt). New York: Alfred A. Knopf, 1952.

1474
Travers, Robert. *A Funeral for Sabella* (about politics, union rivalries and violent death in a big city. Main character is Harry Cooke, undertaker in charge of the body of Pete Sabella, a longshoreman found at the bottom of a harbor in a casing of cement). New York: Harcourt, Brace, 1952.

1475
Turner, George K. *The Taskmasters* (concerns industrial feudalism in New England mills; 1890s). New York: McClure, Phillips, 1902.

1476
Van Vorst, Marie. *Amanda of the Mill* (exposes child labor in textile mills; South Carolina; turn of the century). New York: Dodd, Mead, 1905.

1477
Vasquez, Richard. *Chicano** (provides brilliant panorama of a proud people in search of their soul, their past and their future). Garden City: Doubleday, 1970.

1478
Von Rhau, Henry. *Fraternally Yours* (satirizes union racketeering; New York; contemporary). Boston: Houghton Mifflin, 1949.

1479
Walker, Charles R. *Bread and Fire* (gives sociological view of labor conditions in steel town; Pennsylvania and New York; 1920s). Boston: Houghton Mifflin, 1927.

1480
Warren Robert Penn. *All the King's Men* (about a Southern governor/political boss; modeled partly on Huey Long's life). New York: Harcourt, Brace, 1946.

1481
Weatherwax, Clara. *Marching! Marching!* (describes strike for organization among Northwest lumber workers; 1930s). New York: John Day, 1935.

1482
Webster, Henry K. *An American Family: A Novel of Today* (about machinists; Chicago; prior to World War I). Indianapolis: Bobbs-Merrill, 1918.

1483
White, Lionel. *Rafferty* (tells story of a labor leader on the stand before the "Rackets" Committee). New York: E.P. Dutton, 1959.

1484
White, Victor. *Peter Dormanig in America: Steel* (follows young immigrant who goes to Pittsburg to make his way in the steel industry; after World War I). Indianapolis: Bobbs-Merrill, 1954.

1485
Wilder, Robert. *The Wine of Youth* (about an oil town in Texas, especially before and after the crash in 1929). New York: Putnam, 1955.

1486

Williams, Ben Ames. *Owen Glenn* (pictures rise of United Mine Workers in small Ohio mine town; 1890-98). Boston: Houghton Mifflin, 1950.

1487

Wolff, Maritta. *Night Shift* (provides a ruthless, dramatic, fatalistic picture of cruelty and fear in a small factory town in wartime). New York: Random House, 1942.

1488

Wormser, Richard. *All's Fair* (about mine workers' early struggles; 1930s). New York: Modern Age Books, 1937.

1489

Zugsmith, Leane. *A Time to Remember* (describes a strike of white collar workers in a large New York department store). New York: Random House, 1936.

1490

—————. *Summer Soldier* (shows tactics used on liberal "outsiders" in Southern community; 1930s). New York: Random House, 1939.

PART II

ARTICLES

ARTICLES

I. American Labor History

GENERAL HISTORIES

1491
Ashenfelter, Orley, and Pencavel, John H. "American Trade Union Growth: 1900-1960." *Quarterly Journal of Economics* 83(1969):434-48.

1492
Barbash, Jack. "American Unionism: From Protest to Going Concern." *Journal of Social Issues* 2(1968):45-59.

1493
Bernstein, Leonard. "The Working People of Philadelphia from Colonial Times to the General Strike of 1835." *Pennsylvania Magazine of History and Biography* 74(1950):322-39.

1494
Blum, Albert A. "Labor and the Federal Government: 1850-1933." *Current History* 48(1965): p. 328.

1495
————. "Why Unions Grow." *Labor History* 9(1968):39-72.

1496
Bolino, August C. "The Duration of Unemployment: Some Tentative Historical Comparisons." *Quarterly Review of Economics and Business* 6(1966):31-47.

1497
Buck, Paul H. "The Poor Whites of the Ante-Bellum South." *American Historical Review* 31(1925):41-54.

1498
Carter, Paul J., Jr. "Mark Twain and the American Labor Movement." *New England Quarterly* 30(1957):382-88.

1499
Ching, Cyrus S. "Some Instruments of Industrial Peace." In *Labor in the American Economy,* edited by Gordon S. Watkins. *American Academy of Political and Social Science Annals* (1951):179-84.

1500
Cleland, Hugh G. "The Effects of Radical Groups on the Labor Movement." *Pennsylvania History* 26(1959):119-32.

1501

Cox, LaWanda F. "The American Agricultural Wage Earner, 1865-1900: The Emergence of a Modern Labor Problem." *Agricultural History* 22(1948):95-114.

1502

Craypo, Charles. "The National Union Convention as an Internal Appeal Tribunal." *Industrial and Labor Relations Review* 22(1969):487-511.

1503

Denisoff, R. Serge. "The Proletarian Renascence: The Folkness of the Ideological Folk." *Journal of American Folklore* 82(1969):51-65.

1504

Derber, Milton. "The Idea of Industrial Democracy in America: 1915-1935." *Labor History* 8(1967):3-29.

1505

Dorson, Richard M. "The Career of 'John Henry.'" *Western Folklore* 24(1965):155-63.

1506

Estey, Martin S. "Trends in Concentration of Union Membership, 1897-1962." *Quarterly Journal of Economics* 80(1966):343-60.

1507

Fine, Sidney. "The Eight-Hour Day Movement in the United States, 1888-1891." *Mississippi Valley Historical Review* 40(1953):441-62.

1508

Foner, Philip S. "Journal of an Early Labor Organizer." *Labor History* 10(1969):205-27.

1509

Green, Archie. "American Labor Lore: Its Meanings and Uses." *Industrial Relations* 4(1965):51-68.

1510

Griffen, Clyde C. "Rich Laymen and Early Social Christianity." *Church History* 36(1967):45-65.

1511

Gross, James A. "Historian and the Literature of the Negro Worker." *Labor History* 10(1969):536-46.

1512

Handlin, Oscar, and Handlin, Mary F. "Origins of the Southern Labor System." *William and Mary Quarterly, 3rd series* 7(1950):199-222.

1513

Laslett, John H.M. "Socialism and the American Labor Movement: Some New Reflections." *Labor History* 8(1967):136-55.

1514

Leonard, Frank. "'Helping' the Unemployed in the Nineteenth Century: The Case of the American Tramp." *Social Service Review* 40(1966):429-34.

1515
Lieberman, Elias. "Is Labor Mortgaging Its Future? Seven Steps of Labor vis-á-vis Society." *Texas Quarterly* 10(1967):7-33.

1516
Lonsdale, David L. "The Fight for an Eight-Hour Day." *Colorado Magazine* 43(1966):339-53.

1517
McKelvey, Blake. "Penology in the Westward Movement." *Pacific Historical Review* 2(1933):418-38.

1518
Mark, Irving. "The Compassionate American." *American Journal of Economics and Sociology* 24(1965):171-92.

1519
Marshall, Leon S. "The English and American Industrial City of the Nineteenth Century." *Western Pennsylvania Historical Magazine* 20(1937):169-80.

1520
Montgomery, Royal E. "Evolution of American Labor." In *Labor in the American Economy*, edited by Gordon S. Watkins. *American Academy of Political and Social Science Annals* (1951):1-8.

1521
Morris, Richard B. "Labor Controls in Maryland in the Nineteenth Century." *Journal of Southern History* 14(1948):385-400.

1522
Peck, Sidney M. "The Sociology of Unionism: An Appraisal." *American Journal of Economics and Sociology* 25(1966):53-67.

1523
Perline, Martin M. "The Trade Union Press: An Historical Analysis." *Labor History* 10(1969):107-14.

1524
Perlman, Selig. "The Basic Philosophy of the American Labor Movement." In *Labor in the American Economy*, edited by Gordon S. Watkins. *American Academy of Political and Social Science Annals* (1951):57-63.

1525
Peterson, Florence. "Causes of Industrial Unrest." In *Labor in the American Economy*, edited by Gordon S. Watkins. *American Academy of Political and Social Science Annals* (1951):25-31.

1526
Radosh, Ronald. "The Corporate Ideology of American Labor Leaders from Gompers to Hillman." *Studies on the Left* 6(1966):66-88.

1527
Reichert, William O. "Toward a New Understanding of Anarchism." *Western Political Quarterly* 20(1967):856-65.

1528
Reuss, Richard A. "The Roots of American Left-Wing Interest in Folksong." *Labor History* 12(1971):259-79.

1529
Reuther, Walter P. "Practical Aims and Purposes of American Labor." In *Labor in the American Economy*, edited by Gordon S. Watkins. *American Academy of Political and Social Science Annals* (1951):64-74.

1530
Rezneck, Samuel. "The Social History of an American Depression, 1837-1843." *American Historical Review* 40(1935):662-87.

1531
————. "Patterns of Thought and Action in an American Depression, 1882-1886." *American Historical Review* 61(1956):284-307.

1532
Rodnitzky, Jerome L. "The Evolution of the American Protest Song." *Journal of Popular Culture* 3(1969):35-45.

1533
Rowland, Donald. "The United States and the Contract Labor Question in Hawaii, 1862-1900." *Pacific Historical Review* 2(1933):249-69.

1534
Seidman, Joel; London, Jack; and Karsh, Bernard. "Why Workers Join Unions." In *Labor in the American Economy*, edited by Gordon S. Watkins. *American Academy of Political and Social Science Annals* (1951):75-84.

1535
Soffer, Benson. "A Theory of Trade Union Development: The Role of the 'Autonomous' Workman." *Labor History* 1(1960):141-63.

1536
Soltow, Lee. "Economic Inequality in the United States in the Period from 1790 to 1860." *Journal of Economic History* 31(1971):822-39.

1537
Stone, Harry W. "Beginnings of the Labor Movement in the Pacific Northwest." *Oregon Historical Quarterly* 47(1946):155-64.

1538
Taft, Philip. "Labor History and the Labor Movement Today." *Labor History* 7(1966):70-77.

1539
————. "Violence in American Labor Disputes." *American Academy of Political and Social Science Annals* 364(1966):127-40.

1540
Troy, Leo. "Trade Union Membership, 1897-1962." *Review of Economics and Statistics* 47(1965):93-113.

1541
Van Auken, Sheldon. "A Century of the Southern Plantation." *Virginia Magazine of History and Biography* 58(1950):356-87.

1542
Wood, Norman J. "Industrial Relations Policies of American Management, 1900-1933." *Business History Review* 34(1960):403-20.

PERIODS OF DEVELOPMENT

Workers in Early America (Colonial America)

1543
Adams, Donald R., Jr. "Wage Rates in Philadelphia, 1790-1830." *Journal of Economic History* 27(1967):608-10.

1544
————. "Wage Rates in the Early National Period: Philadelphia, 1785-1830." *Journal of Economic History* 28(1968):404-26.

1545
Barber, Ruth Kerns. "Indian Labor in the Spanish Colonies." *New Mexico Historical Review* 7(April 1932):105-42; (July 1932):233-72; (October 1932):311-47.

1546
Bernstein, Leonard. "The Working People of Philadelphia from Colonial Times to the General Strike of 1835." *Pennsylvania Magazine of History and Biography* 74(1950):322-39.

1547
Bining, Arthur Cecil. "The Iron Plantations of Early Pennsylvania." *Pennsylvania Magazine of History and Biography* 57(1933):117-37.

1548
Butler, James Davie. "British Convicts Shipped to American Colonies." *American Historical Review* 2(1896):12-33.

1549
Champagne, Robert J. "Liberty Boys and Mechanics of New York City, 1764-1774." *Labor History* 8(1967):115-35.

1550
Deutsch, Albert. "The Sick Poor in Colonial Times." *American Historical Review* 46(1941):560-79.

1551
Fant, H.B. "The Labor Policy of the Trustees for Establishing the Colony of Georgia in America." *Georgia Historical Quarterly* 16(1932):1-16.

1552
Griffin, Richard W. "Poor White Laborers in Southern Cotton Factories, 1789-1865." *South Carolina Historical Magazine* 61(1960):26-40.

1553
Haywood, C. Robert. "Mercantilism and Colonial Slave Labor, 1700-1763." *Journal of Southern History* 23(1957):454-64.

1554
Jernegan, Marcus W. "Slavery and the Beginnings of Industrialism in the American Colonies." *American Historical Review* 25(1920):220-40.

1555
Jervey, Theodore D. "The White Identured Servants of South Carolina." *South Carolina Historical Magazine* 12(1911):163-71.

1556
Jonas, Manfred. "Wages in Early Colonial Maryland." *Maryland Historical Magazine* 51(1956):27-38.

1557
Kisch, Guido. "German Jews in White Labor Servitude in America." *Publication of the American Jewish Historical Society* 34(1937):11-49.

1558
Lemisch, Jesse. "Jack Tar in the Streets: Merchant Seamen in the Politics of Revolutionary America." *William and Mary Quarterly, 3rd series* 25(1968):371-407.

1559
————. "Listening to the 'Inarticulate': William Widger's Dream and the Loyalties of American Revolutionary Seamen in British Prisons." *Journal of Social History* 3(1969):1-29.

1560
Lynd, Staughton. "The Mechanics in New York Politics, 1774-1788." *Labor History* 5(1964):225-46.

1561
McKee, Samuel, Jr. "Indentured Servitude in Colonial New York." *New York History* 12(1931):149-59.

1562
Mackey, Howard. "The Operation of the English Old Poor Law in Colonial Virginia." *Virginia Magazine of History and Biography* 72(1965):29-40.

1563
Miller, William. "The Effects of the American Revolution on Indentured Servitude." *Pennsylvania History* 7(1940):131-41.

1564
Mohl, Raymond A. "Poverty in Early America, a Reappraisal: The Case of Eighteenth-Century New York City." *New York History* 50(1969):4-27.

1565
————. "Poverty, Politics, and the Mechanics of New York City, 1803." *Labor History* 12(1971):38-51.

1566
Montgomery, David. "The Working Classes of the Pre-Industrial American City, 1780-1830." *Labor History* 9(1968):3-22.

1567
Morris, Richard B. "White Bondage in Ante-Bellum South Carolina." *South Carolina Historical Magazine* 49(1948):191-207.

1568
————, and Grossman, Jonathan. "The Regulation of Wages in Early Massachusetts." *New England Quarterly* 11(1938):470-500.

1569
Padgett, James A. "The Status of Slaves in Colonial North Carolina." *Journal of Negro History* 14(1929):300-327.

1570
Palmer, Paul C. "Servant into Slave: The Evolution of the Legal Status of the Negro Laborer in Colonial Virginia." *South Atlantic Quarterly* 65(1966):355-70.

1571
Randall, Edwin T. "Imprisonment for Debt in America: Fact and Fiction." *Mississippi Valley Historical Review* 39(1952):89-102.

1572
Siebert, Wilbur H. "Slavery and White Servitude in East Florida, 1726 to 1776." *Florida Historical Quarterly* 10(1931):3-23.

1573
————. "Slavery in East Florida, 1776 to 1785." *Florida Historical Quarterly* 10(1932):139-61.

1574
Smith, Abbot Emerson, "The Transportation of Convicts to the American Colonies in the Seventeenth Century." *American Historical Review* 39(1934):232-49.

1575
————. "Indentured Servants: New Lights on Some of America's 'First' Families." *Journal of Economic History* 2(1942):40-53.

1576
Sollers, Basil. "Transported Convict Laborers in Maryland during the Colonial Period." *Maryland Historical Magazine* 2(1907):17-47.

1577
Stavisky, Leonard. "The Origins of Negro Craftsmanship in Colonial America." *Journal of Negro History* 32(1947):417-29.

1578
————. "Negro Craftsmanship in Early America." *American Historical Review* 54(1949):315-25.

1579
Stubbs, Jane. "Servant Children in Colonial Virginia." *Virginia Cavalcade* 9(1959):18-23.

1580
Turner, Edward Raymond. "Slavery in Colonial Pennsylvania." *Pennsylvania Magazine of History and Biography* 35(1911):141-51.

1581
Walsh, Richard. "The Charleston Mechanics: A Brief Study, 1760-1776." *South Carolina Historical Magazine* 60(1959):123-44.

1582
Wax, Darold D. "The Demand for Slave Labor in Colonial Pennsylvania." *Pennsylvania History* 34(1967):331-45.

1583
Williams, Edwin L., Jr. "Negro Slavery in Florida." *Florida Historical Quarterly* 28(October 1949):93-110; (January 1950):182-204.

1584
Young, Alfred. "The Mechanics and the Jeffersonians: New York, 1789-1801." *Labor History* 5(1964):247-76.

Workingmen in the Era of Jackson

(1820s-1830s)

1585
Adams, Donald R., Jr. "Wage Rates in the Early National Period: Philadelphia, 1785-1830." *Journal of Economic History* 28(1968):404-26.

1586
Arky, Louis H. "The Mechanics' Union of Trade Associations and the Formation of the Philadelphia Workingmen's Movement." *Pennsylvania Magazine of History and Biography* 76(1952):142-76.

1587
Aurand, Harold W. "The Workingmen's Benevolent Association." *Labor History* 7(1966):19-34.

1588
Bernstein, Leonard. "The Working People of Philadelphia from Colonial Times to the General Strike of 1835." *Pennsylvania Magazine of History and Biography* 74(1950):322-39.

1589
Darling, Arthur B. "The Workingmen's Party in Massachusetts, 1833-1834." *American Historical Review* 29(1923):81-86.

1590
Fink, Gary M. "The Paradoxical Experiences of St. Louis Labor during the Depression of 1837." *Missouri Historical Society* 26(1969):53-63.

1591
Gettleman, Marvin E., and Conlon, Noel P., eds. "Responses to the Rhode Island Workingmen's Reform Agitation of 1833." *Rhode Island History* 28(1969):75-94.

1592
Harrison, John F.C. " 'The Steam Engine of the New Moral World': Owenism and Education, 1817-1829." *Journal of British Studies* 6(1967):76-98.

1593
Jackson, Sidney L. "Labor, Education, and Politics in the 1830s." *Pennsylvania Magazine of History and Biography* 66(1942):279-93.

1594
Morais, Herbert M. "The Medical Profession and Workers' Health in Early Industrial America (1835-1860)." *Journal of Occupational Medicine* 7(1965):203-10.

1595
Morris, Richard B. "Andrew Jackson, Strikebreaker." *American Historical Review* 55(1949):54-68.

1596
Nadworny, Milton J. "New Jersey Workingmen and the Jacksonians." *New Jersey Historical Society Proceedings* 67(1949):185-98.

1597
Neufeld, Maurice F. "Realms of Thought and Organized Labor in the Age of Jackson." *Labor History* 10(1969):5-43

1598
Paulson, Peter. "The Tammany Society and the Jeffersonian Movement in New York City, 1795-1800." *New York History* 34(1953):72-84.

1599
Pessen, Edward. "Thomas Skidmore, Agrarian Reformer in the Early American Labor Movement." *New York History* 35(1954):280-96.

1600
——————. "The Workingmen's Movement of the Jacksonian Era." *Mississippi Valley Historical Review* 43(1956):428-43.

1601
——————. "The Workingmen's Party Revisited." *Labor History* 4(1963):203-26.

1602
Randall, Edwin T. "Imprisonment for Debt in America: Fact and Fiction." *Mississippi Valley Historical Review* 39(1952):89-102.

1603
Reese, James V. "The Early History of Labor Organizations in Texas, 1838-1876." *Southwestern Historical Quarterly* 72(1968):1-20.

1604
Rezneck, Samuel. "The Social History of an American Depression, 1837-1843." *American Historical Review* 40(1935):662-87.

1605
Rosenberg, Nathan. "Anglo-American Wage Differences in the 1820s." *Journal of Economic History* 27(1967):221-29.

1606
Schlegel, Marvin W. "The Workingmen's Benevolent Association: First Union of Anthracite Miners." *Pennsylvania History* 10(1943):243-67.

1607
Sullivan, William A. "Philadelphia Labor during the Jackson Era." *Pennsylvania History* 15(1948):305-20.

1608

––––––. "The Pittsburgh Workingmen's Party." *Western Pennsylvania Historical Magazine* 34(1951):151-61.

Establishing Utopian Communities

(1840s-1850s)

1609

Angle, Paul M. "An Illinois Paradise: The Icarians at Nauvoo." *Chicago History* 7(1965):199-209.

1610

Arrington, Leonard J. "Cooperative Community in the North: Brigham City, Utah." *Utah Historical Quarterly* 33(1965):198-217.

1611

Feuer, Lewis S. "The Influence of the American Communist Colonies on Engels and Marx." *Western Political Quarterly* 19(1966):456-74.

1612

Foner, Philip S. "Journal of an Early Labor Organizer." *Labor History* 10(1969):205-27.

1613

Gitelman, Howard M. "The Waltham System and the Coming of the Irish." *Labor History* 8(1967):227-53.

1614

Harrison, John F.C. "The Owenite Socialist Movement in Britain and the United States: A Comparative Study." *Labor History* 9(1968):323-37.

1615

Kellogg, Miner K. "Miner K. Kellogg: Recollections of New Harmony," edited by Lorna L. Sylvester. *Indiana Magazine of History* 64(1968):39-64.

1616

LeWarne, Charles P. "Equality Colony: The Plan to Socialize Washington." *Pacific Northwest Quarterly* 59(1968):137-46.

1617

Lockwood, Maren. "The Experimental Utopia in America." *Daedalus* 94(1965):401-18.

1618

Schafer, Joseph. "The Wisconsin Phalanx." *Wisconsin Magazine of History* 19(1936):454-74.

1619

Temin, Peter. "Labor Scarcity and the Problem of American Industrial Efficiency in the 1850s: A Reply." *Journal of Economic History* 28(1968):124-25.

1620

Wilson, Harold F. "The North American Phalanx: An Experiment in Communal Living." *New Jersey Historical Society Proceedings* 70(1952):188-209.

1621

Wilson, J.B. "The Antecedents of Brook Farm." *New England Quarterly* 15(1942):320-31.

1622

Wolski, Kalikst. "A Visit to the North American Phalanx." Translated by Marion Moore Coleman. *New Jersey Historical Society Proceedings* 83(1965):149-60.

Slavery (Up to 1865)

1623

Alexander, Herbert B. "Brazilian and United States Slavery Compared." *Journal of Negro History* 7(1922):349-64.

1624

Bradford, S. Sydney. "The Negro Ironworker in Ante-Bellum Virginia." *Journal of Southern History* 25(1959):194-206.

1625

Bruce, Kathleen. "Slave Labor in the Virginia Iron Industry." *William and Mary Quarterly* 6(1926):289-302; 7(1927):21-31.

1626

Carsel, Wilfred. "The Slaveholders' Indictment of Northern Wage Slavery." *Journal of Southern History* 6(1940):504-20.

1627

Cathey, Clyde W. "Slavery in Arkansas." *Arkansas Historical Quarterly* 3(Spring 1944):66-90;(Summer 1944):150-63.

1628

Davis, T.R. "Negro Servitude in the United States." *Journal of Negro History* 8(1923):247-83.

1629

Eckenrode, H.J. "Negroes in Richmond in 1864." *Virginia Magazine of History and Biography* 46(1938):193-200.

1630

Flanders, Ralph B. "Planters' Problems in Ante-Bellum Georgia." *Georgia Historical Quarterly* 14(1930):17-40.

1631

Genovese, Eugene D. "The Medical and Insurance Costs of Slaveholding in the Cotton Belt." *Journal of Negro History* 45(1960):141-55.

1632

Green, Fletcher M. "Gold Mining in Ante-Bellum Virginia." *Virginia Magazine of History and Biography* 45(July 1937):227-35; (October 1937):357-66.

1633
Handlin, Oscar, and Handlin, Mary F. "Origins of the Southern Labor System." *William and Mary Quarterly, 3rd series* 7(1950):199-222.

1634
Haywood, C. Robert. "Mercantilism and Colonial Slave Labor, 1700-1763." *Journal of Southern History* 23(1957):454-64.

1635
Henry, H.M. "The Slave Laws of Tennessee." *Tennessee Historical Quarterly, 1st series* 2(1916):175-203.

1636
Hofstadter, Richard. "U.B. Phillips and the Plantation Legend." *Journal of Negro History* 29(1944):109-24.

1637
House, Albert V. "Labor Management Problems on Georgia Rice Plantations, 1840-1860." *Agricultural History* 28(1954):149-55.

1638
Jordan, Weymouth T. "The Management Rules of an Alabama Black Belt Plantation, 1848-1862." *Agricultural History* 18(1944):53-64.

1639
Jernegan, Marcus W. "Slavery and the Beginnings of Industrialism in the American Colonies." *American Historical Review* 25(1920):220-40.

1640
McDougle, Ivan E. "Slavery in Kentucky." *Journal of Negro History* 3(1918):211-328.

1641
McKelvey, Blake. "Penal Slavery and Southern Reconstruction." *Journal of Negro History* 20(1935):153-79.

1642
Moody, V. Alton. "Slavery on Louisiana Sugar Plantations." *Louisiana Historical Quarterly* 7(1924):191-301.

1643
Nelson, Earl J. "Missouri Slavery, 1861-1865." *Missouri Historical Review* 28(1934):260-74.

1644
Padgett, James A. "The Status of Slaves in Colonial North Carolina." *Journal of Negro History* 14(1929):300-327.

1645
Palmer, Paul C. "Servant into Slave: The Evolution of the Legal Status of the Negro Laborer in Colonial Virginia." *South Atlantic Quarterly* 65(1966):355-70.

1646
Phillips, Ulrich B. "Slave Crime in Virginia." *American Historical Review* 20(1915):336-40.

1647
————. "Plantations with Slave Labor and Free." *Agricultural History* 12(1938):77-95.

1648
Rayback, Joseph G. "The American Workingman and the Antislavery Crusade." *Journal of Economic History* 3(1943):152-63.

1649
Reid, Robert D. "The Negro in Alabama during the Civil War." *Journal of Negro History* 35(1950):265-88.

1650
Russel, Robert R. "The Economic History of Negro Slavery in the United States." *Agricultural History* 11(1937):308-21.

1651
————. "The General Effects of Slavery upon Southern Economic Progress." *Journal of Southern History* 4(1938):34-54.

1652
————. "The Effects of Slavery upon Nonslaveholders in the Ante-Bellum South." *Agricultural History* 15(1941):112-26.

1653
Russell, John H. "Colored Freemen as Slave Owners in Virginia." *Journal of Negro History* 1(1916):233-42.

1654
Siebert, Wilbur H. "Slavery and White Servitude in East Florida, 1726 to 1776." *Florida Historical Quarterly* 10(1931):3-23.

1655
————. "Slavery in East Florida, 1776 to 1785." *Florida Historical Quarterly* 10(1932):139-61.

1656
Smith, Robert Worthington. "Was Slavery Unprofitable in the Ante-Bellum South?" *Agricultural History* 20(1946):62-64.

1657
Snow, William J. "Utah Indians and Spanish Slave Trade." *Utah Historical Quarterly* 2(1929):67-90.

1658
Starobin, Robert. "Disciplining Industrial Slaves in the Old South." *Journal of Negro History* 53(1968):111-28.

1659
Stavisky, Leonard. "The Origins of Negro Craftsmanship in Colonial America." *Journal of Negro History* 32(1947):417-29.

1660
Stealey, John Edmund III. "The Responsibilities and Liabilities of the Bailee of Slave Labor in Virginia." *American Journal of Legal History* 12(1968):336-53.

1661
Taylor, Paul S. "Plantation Laborer before the Civil War." *Agricultural History* 28(1954):1-21.

1662
Trexler, Harrison A. "Slavery in Missouri Territory." *Missouri Historical Review* 3(1909):179-98.

1663
Turner, Edward Raymond. "Slavery in Colonial Pennsylvania." *Pennsylvania Magazine of History and Biography* 35(1911):141-51.

1664
Van Auken, Sheldon. "A Century of the Southern Plantation." *Virginia Magazine of History and Biography* 58(1950):356-87.

1665
Walz, Robert B. "Arkansas Slaveholdings and Slaveholders in 1850." *Arkansas Historical Quarterly* 12(1953):38-74.

1666
Wax, Darold D. "The Demand for Slave Labor in Colonial Pennsylvania." *Pennsylvania History* 34(1967):331-45.

1667
Williams, Edwin L., Jr. "Negro Slavery in Florida." *Florida Historical Quarterly* 28(October 1949):93-110;(January 1950):182-204.

1668
Woolfolk, George Ruble. "Taxes and Slavery in the Ante-Bellum South." *Journal of Southern History* 26(1960):180-200.

Labor During the Civil War

(1861-1865)

1669
Carmichael, Maude. "Federal Experiments with Negro Labor on Abandoned Plantations in Arkansas: 1862-1865." *Arkansas Historical Quarterly* 1(1942):101-16.

1670
Eckenrode, H.J. "Negroes in Richmond in 1864." *Virginia Magazine of History and Biography* 46(1938):193-200.

1671
Gitelman, Howard M. "The Labor Force at Waltham Watch during the Civil War Era." *Journal of Economic History* 25(1965):214-43.

1672
Harding, Leonard. "The Cincinnati Riots of 1862." *Cincinnati Historical Society* 25(1967):229-39.

1673
Lofton, Williston H. "Northern Labor and the Negro during the Civil War." *Journal of Negro History* 34(1949):251-73.

1674
Man, Albon P., Jr. "Labor Competition and the New York Draft Riots of 1863." *Journal of Negrờ History* 36(1951):375-405.

1675
Nelson, Earl J. "Missouri Slavery, 1861-1865." *Missouri Historical Review* 28(1934):260-74.

1676
Nolen, Russell M. "The Labor Movement in St. Louis from 1860 to 1890." *Missouri Historical Review* 34(1940):157-81.

1677
Reid, Robert D. "The Negro in Alabama during the Civil War." *Journal of Negro History* 35(1950):265-88.

Formation of National Unions

(1850s-1860s)

1678
Grob, Gerald N. "Reform Unionism: The National Labor Union." *Journal of Economic History* 14(1954):126-42.

1679
Hall, John Philip. "The Knights of St. Crispin in Massachusetts, 1869-1878." *Journal of Economic History* 18(1958):161-75.

An Era of Socio-Economic Transformation and Violent Protest

(1865-1899)

1680
Akin, William E. "Arbitration and Labor Conflict: The Middle Class Panacea, 1886-1900." *The Historian* 29(1967):565-83.

1681
Aurand, Harold W. "The Anthracite Strike of 1887-1888." *Pennsylvania History* 35(1968):169-85.

1682
Bechtol, Paul T., Jr. "The 1880 Labor Dispute in Leadville." *Colorado Magazine* 47(1970):312-25.

1683
Belissary, Constantine G. "Behavior Patterns and Aspirations of the Urban Working Classes of Tennessee in the Immediate Post-Civil War Era." *Tennessee Historical Quarterly* 14(1955):24-42.

1684
Bethel, Elizabeth. "The Freedmen's Bureau in Alabama." *Journal of Southern History* 14(1948):49-92.

1685
Bliss, Willard F. "The Rise of Tenancy in Virginia." *Virginia Magazine of History and Biography* 58(1950):427-41.

1686
Brinks, Herbert J. "Marquette Iron Range Strike, 1895." *Michigan History* 50(1966):293-305.

1687
Brommel, Bernard J. "Eugene V. Debs: The Agitator as Speaker." *Central States Speech Journal* 20(1969):202-14.

1688
————. "Deb's Cooperative Commonwealth Plan for Workers." *Labor History* 12(1971):560-69.

1689
Busch, Francis X. "The Haymarket Riot and the Trial of the Anarchists." *Illinois State Historical Society Journal* 48(1955):247-70.

1690
Carter, Everett. "The Haymarket Affair in Literature." *American Quarterly* 2(1950):270-78.

1691
Doeringer, Peter B. "Piece Rate Wage Structures in the Pittsburgh Iron and Steel Industry—1880-1900." *Labor History* 9(1968):262-74.

1692
Eckert, Edward K. "Contract Labor in Florida during Reconstruction." *Florida Historical Quarterly* 47(1968):34-50.

1693
Gaboury, William Joseph. "From Statehouse to Bull Pen: Idaho Populism and the Coeur d'Alene Troubles of the 1890s." *Pacific Northwest Quarterly* 58(1967):14-22.

1694
Griffin, Richard W. "Problems of the Southern Cotton Planters after the Civil War." *Georgia Historical Quarterly* 39(1955):103-17.

1695
Greene, Victor R. "A Study of Slavs, Strikes and Unions: The Anthracite Strike of 1897." *Pennsylvania History* 31(1964):199-215.

1696
Grogan, Dennis S. "Unionization in Boulder and Weld Counties to 1890." *Colorado Magazine* 44(1967):324-41.

1697
Gutman, Herbert G. "Trouble on the Railroads in 1873-1874: Prelude to the 1877 Crisis?" *Labor History* 2(1961):215-35.

1698
————. "Reconstruction in Ohio: Negroes in the Hocking Valley Coal Mines in 1873 and 1874." *Labor History* 3(1962):243-64.

1699

––––––. "The Tompkins Square 'Riot' in New York City on January 13, 1874: A Reexamination of Its Causes and Its Aftermath." *Labor History* 6(1965):44-70.

1700

––––––. "Documents on Negro Seamen during the Reconstruction Period." *Labor History* 7(1966):307-11.

1701

––––––. "Protestantism and the American Labor Movement: The Christian Spirit in the Gilded Age." *American Historial Review* 72(1966):74-101.

1702

––––––, ed. "English Labor Views the American Reconstruction: An Editorial in *The Bee-Hive* (London), Sept. 26, 1874." *Labor History* 9(1968):110-12.

1703

––––––. "Five Letters of Immigrant Workers from Scotland to the United States, 1867-1869: William Latta, Daniel M'Lachlan, and Allan Pinkerton." *Labor History* 9(1968):384-408.

1704

Hacker, Barton C. "The United States Army as a National Police Force: The Federal Policing of Labor Disputes, 1877-1898." *Military Affairs* 33(1969):255-64.

1705

Hogg, J. Bernard. "Public Reaction to Pinkertonism and the Labor Question." *Pennsylvania History* 11(1944):171-99.

1706

Hopkins, Richard J. "Occupational and Geographic Mobility in Atlanta, 1870-1896." *Journal of Southern History* 34(1968):200-213.

1707

House, Albert V., Jr. "A Reconstruction Share-Cropper Contract on a Georgia Rice Plantation." *Georgia Historical Quarterly* 26(1942):156-65.

1708

Johnson, Michael R. "Albert R. Parsons: An American Architect of Syndicalism." *Midwest Quarterly* 9(1968):195-206.

1709

Kirk, Clara, and Kirk, Rudolf. "William Dean Howells, George William Curtis, and the 'Haymarket Affair.' " *American Literature* 40(1968):487-98.

1710

Kreuter, Kent, and Kreuter, Gretchen. "The Lure of Law and Order: Cushman K. Davis and the Pullman Strike." *Mid-America* 51(1969):194-204.

1711

Lane, Ann J. "Recent Literature on the Molly Maguires." *Science and Society* 30(1966):309-19.

1712

Lindsey, Almont. "Paternalism and the Pullman Strike." *American Historical Review* 44(1939):272-89.

1713

Lonsdale, David L. "The Fight for an Eight-Hour Day." *Colorado Magazine* 43(1968):339-53.

1714

Low, W.A. "The Freedmen's Bureau and Civil Rights in Maryland." *Journal of Negro History* 37(1952):221-47.

1715

McKelvey, Blake. "Penal Slavery and Southern Reconstruction." *Journal of Negro History* 20(1935):153-79.

1716

McMurry, Donald L. "Labor Policies of the General Managers' Association of Chicago, 1886-1894." *Journal of Economic History* 13(1953):160-78.

1717

Matison, Sumner Eliot. "The Labor Movement and the Negro during Reconstruction." *Journal of Negro History* 33(1948):426-68.

1718

May, J. Thomas. "The Freedmen's Bureau at the Local Level: A Study of a Louisiana Agent." *Louisiana History* 9(1968):5-19.

1719

Morgan, H. Wayne. "The Utopia of Eugene V. Debs." *American Quarterly* 11(1959):120-35.

1720

Nolen, Russell M. "The Labor Movement in St. Louis from 1860 to 1890." *Missouri Historical Review* 34(1940):157-81.

1721

Ozanne, Robert. "Union-Management Relations: McCormick Harvesting Machine Company, 1862-1886." *Labor History* 4(1963):132-60.

1722

Rezneck, Samuel. "Patterns of Thought and Action in an American Depression, 1882-1886." *American Historical Review* 61(1956):284-307.

1723

Rhodes, James Ford. "The Molly Maguires in the Anthracite Region of Pennsylvania." *American Historical Review* 15(1910):547-61.

1724

Richardson, Joe M. "The Freedmen's Bureau and Negro Labor in Florida." *Florida Historical Quarterly* 39(1960):167-74.

1725

Saloutos, Theodore. "Southern Agriculture and the Problems of Readjustment: 1865-1877." *Agricultural History* 30(1956):58-76.

1726

Shelton, Brenda K. "The Grain Shovellers' Strike of 1899." *Labor History* 9(1968):210-38.

1727
Shugg, Roger Wallace. "The New Orleans General Strike of 1892." *Louisiana Historical Quarterly* 21(1938):547-60.

1728
Sisk, Glenn Nolen. "Social Classes in the Alabama Black Belt, 1870-1910." *Alabama Historical Quarterly* 20(1958):653-55.

1729
Suggs, George G., Jr. "Catalyst for Industrial Change: The WFM, 1893-1903." *Colorado Magazine* 45(1968):322-39.

1730
Taylor, A.A. "The Negro in South Carolina during the Reconstruction." *Journal of Negro History* 9(July 1924):241-364; (October 1924):381-569.

1731
————. "The Negro in the Reconstruction of Virginia." *Journal of Negro History* 11(April 1926):243-415; (July 1926):425-537.

1732
Tebeau, C.W. "Some Aspects of Planter-Freedman Relations, 1865-1880." *Journal of Negro History* 21(1936):130-50.

1733
Thomason, Frank. "The Bellevue Stranglers." *Idaho Yesterdays* 13(1969):26-32.

1734
Turner, Ralph V., and Rodgers, William Warren. "Arkansas Labor in Revolt: Little Rock and the Great Southwestern Strike." *Arkansas Historical Quarterly* 24(1965):29-46.

1735
Wagstaff, Thomas. "Call Your Old Master—'Master': Southern Political Leaders and Negro Labor during Presidential Reconstruction." *Labor History* 10(1969):323-45.

1736
Wish, Harvey. "Governor Altgeld Pardons the Anarchists." *Illinois State Historical Society Journal* 31(1938):424-48.

1737
————. "The Pullman Strike: A Study in Industrial Warfare." *Illinois State Historical Society Journal* 32(1939):288-312.

1738
Yearley, Clifton K., Jr. "The Baltimore and Ohio Railroad Strike of 1877." *Maryland Historical Magazine* 51(1956):188-211.

1739
Zeichner, Oscar. "The Transition from Slave to Free Agricultural Labor in the Southern States." *Agricultural History* 13(1939):22-32.

Rise and Decline of the Knights of Labor

(1869-1890)

1740

Bloch, Herman D. "Labor and the Negro, 1866-1910." *Journal of Negro History* 50(1965):163-84.

1741

Browne, Henry J. "Terence V. Powderly and Church-Labor Difficulties of the Early 1880s." *Catholic Historical Review* 32(1946):1-27.

1742

Engberg, George B. "The Knights of Labor in Minnesota." *Minnesota History* 22(1941):367-90.

1743

Faherty, William B. "The Clergyman and Labor Progress: Cornelius O'Leary and the Knights of Labor." In *The Church and the American Labor Movement: Four Episodes: 1880s-1920s. Labor History* 11(1970):175-89.

1744

Foner, Philip S., ed. "The Knights of Labor." *Journal of Negro History* 53(1968):70-77.

1745

Grob, Gerald N. "Terence V. Powderly and the Knights of Labor." *Mid-America* 34(1957):39-55.

1746

————. "The Knights of Labor and the Trade Unions, 1878-1886." *Journal of Economic History* 18(1958):176-92.

1747

————. "The Knights of Labor, Politics, and Populism." *Mid-America* 40(1958):3-21.

1748

Harvey, Katherine A. "The Knights of Labor in the Maryland Coal Fields, 1878-1882." *Labor History* 10(1969):555-83.

1749

Kessler, Sidney H. "The Organization of Negroes in the Knights of Labor." *Journal of Negro History* 37(1952):248-76.

1750

Marcus, Irvin M. "The Southern Negro and the Knights of Labor." *Labor History Bulletin* 30(1967):5-7.

1751

Marshall, F. Ray, and Van Adams, Arvil. "Negro Employment in Memphis." In *Equal Employment Opportunity: Comparative Community Experience. Industrial Relations* 9(1970):308-23.

1752

Matison, Sumner Eliot. "The Labor Movement and the Negro during Reconstruction." *Journal of Negro History* 33(1948):426-68.

1753
Rodgers, William Warren. "Negro Knights of Labor in Arkansas: A Case Study of the 'Miscellaneous' Strike." *Labor History* 10(1969):498-505.

The American Federation of Labor

(1885-1955)

1754
Akin, William E. "Arbitration and Labor Conflict: The Middle Class Panacea, 1886-1900." *The Historian* 29(1967):565-83.

1755
Bloch, Herman D. "Craft Unions and the Negro in Historical Perspective." *Journal of Negro History* 43(1958):10-33.

1756
————. "Labor and the Negro, 1866-1910." *Journal of Negro History* 50(1965):163-84.

1757
Dick, W.M. "Samuel Gompers and American Concensus." *Canadian Historical Association Papers* (1969):129-40.

1758
Gitelman, H.M. "Adolph Strasser and the Origins of Pure and Simple Unionism." *Labor History* 6(1965):71-83.

1759
Greenbaum, Fred. "The Social Ideas of Samuel Gompers." *Labor History* 7(1966):35-61.

1760
Griffen, Clyde. "Christian Socialism Instructed by Gompers." *Labor History* 12(1971):195-213.

1761
Hill, Herbert. "In the Age of Gompers and After—Racial Practices of Organized Labor." *New Politics* 4(1965):26-46.

1762
Lawrence, James R. "The American Federation of Labor and the Philippine Independence Question, 1920-1935." *Labor History* 7(1966):62-69.

1763
Levenstein, Harvey A. "The AFL and Mexican Immigration in the 1920s: An Experiment in Labor Diplomacy." *Hispanic American Historical Review* 48(1968):206-19.

1764
————. "Samuel Gompers and the Mexican Labor Movement." *Wisconsin Magazine of History* 51(1968):155-63.

1765
Lewis, Doris K. "Union-Sponsored Middle-Income Housing: 1927-65." *Monthly Labor Review* 88(1965):629-36.

1766

McKee, Delber L. "Samuel Gompers, the A.F. of L., and Imperialism, 1895-1900." *The Historian* 21(1959):187-99.

1767

Mandel, Bernard. "Gompers and Business Unionism, 1873-90." *Business History Review* 28(1954):264-75.

1768

————. "Samuel Gompers and the Negro Workers, 1886-1914." *Journal of Negro History* 40(1955):34-60.

1769

Matison, Sumner Eliot. "The Labor Movement and the Negro during Reconstruction." *Journal of Negro History* 33(1948):426-68.

1770

Pawa, Jay M. "The 'Jefferson Borden' Pirates and Samuel Gompers: Aftermath of a Mutiny." *American Neptune* 27(1967):46-60.

1771

Radosh, Ronald. "The Corporate Ideology of American Labor Leaders from Gompers to Hillman." *Studies on the Left* 6(1966):66-88.

1772

Scheinberg, Stephen J. "Theodore Roosevelt and the A.F. of L.'s Entry into Politics, 1906-1908." *Labor History* 3(1962):131-48.

1773

Skeels, Joyce G. "The Early American Federation of Labor and Monetary Reform." *Labor History* 12(1971):530-50.

1774

Taft, Philip. "Differences in the Executive Council of the American Federation of Labor." *Labor History* 5(1964):40-56.

1775

Walker, Roger. "The AFL and Child-Labor Legislation." *Labor History* 11(1970):323-40.

1776

Whittaker, William George. "Samuel Gompers, Anti-Imperialist." *Pacific Historical Review* 38(1969):429-45.

1777

Williamson, John. "Some Strands from the Past: The YWL Meets Gompers." *Political Affairs* 44(1965):36-45.

The Progressive and Not So Progressive Era

(1900-1914)

1778

Asher, Robert. "Business and Workers' Welfare in the Progressive Era: Workmen's Compensation Reform in Massachusetts, 1880-1911." *Business History* 43(1969):452-75.

1779
Auerbach, Jerold S. "Progressives at Sea: The La Follette Act of 1915."
    Labor History 2(1961):344-60.

1780
Beck, William. "Law and Order during the 1913 Copper Strike." *Michigan
    History* 54(1970):275-92.

1781
Betten, Neil. "Strike on the Mesabi—1907." *Minnesota History*
    40(1967):340-47.

1782
Bryant, Keith L., Jr. "Kate Barnard, Organized Labor, and Social Justice in
    Oklahoma during the Progressive Era." *Journal of Southern History*
    35(1969):145-64.

1783
Brooks, Tom. "The Terrible Triangle Fire." *American Heritage*
    8(1957): p. 54.

1784
Dubofsky, Melvyn. "Organized Labor and the Immigrant in New York City,
    1900-1918." *Labor History* 2(1961):182-201.

1785
————. "Success and Failure of Socialism in New York City,
    1900-1918: A Case Study." *Labor History* 9(1968):361-75.

1786
Elazar, Daniel J., ed. "Working Conditions in Chicago in the Early 20th
    Century: Testimony before the Illinois Senatorial Vice Committee,
    1913." *American Jewish Archives* 21(1969):149-71.

1787
Elliott, Russell R. "Labor Troubles in the Mining Camp at Goldfield, Nevada,
    1906-1908." *Pacific Historical Review* 19(1950):369-84.

1788
Garraty, John A. "The United States Steel Corporation versus Labor: The
    Early Years." *Labor History* 1(1960):3-38.

1789
Harris, Sheldon H. "Letters from West Virginia: Management's Version of
    the 1902 Coal Strike." *Labor History* 10(1969):229-40.

1790
Heath, Frederick M. "Labor and the Progressive Movement in Connecticut."
    Labor History 12(1971):52-67.

1791
Ingham, John N. "A Strike in the Progressive Era: McKees Rocks, 1909."
    Pennsylvania Magazine of History and Biography 90(1966):353-77.

1792
Larner, John Williams, Jr. "The Glass House Boys: Child Labor Conditions in
    Pittsburgh's Glass Factories, 1890-1917." *Western Pennsylvania Historical
    Magazine* 48(1965):355-64.

1793

Mann, Arthur. "British Social Thought and American Reformers of the Progressive Era." *Mississippi Valley Historical Review* 42(1956):672-92.

1794

Moore, R. Laurence. "Flawed Fraternity—American Socialist Response to the Negro, 1901-1912." *The Historian* 32(1969):1-18.

1795

Morgan, George T., Jr. "No Compromise—No Recognition: John Henry Kirby, the Southern Lumber Operators' Association, and Unionism in the Piney Woods, 1906-1916." *Labor History* 10(1969):193-204.

1796

Olin, Spencer C., Jr. "European Immigrant and Oriental Alien: Acceptance and Rejection by the California Legislature of 1913." *Pacific Historical Review* 35(1966):303-15.

1797

Porter, Eugene O. "The Colorado Coal Strike of 1913: An Interpretation." *The Historian* 12(1949):3-27.

1798

Saxton, Alexander. "San Francisco Labor and the Populist and Progressive Insurgencies." *Pacific Historical Review* 34(1965):421-38.

1799

Scheinberg, Stephen J. "Theodore Roosevelt and the A.F. of L.'s Entry into Politics, 1906-1908." *Labor History* 3(1962):131-48.

1800

————. "Progressivism in Industry: The Welfare Movement in the American Factory." *Canadian Historical Association Papers* (1967):184-97.

1801

Shover, John L. "The Progressives and the Working Class Vote in California." *Labor History* 10(1969):584-601.

1802

Sizer, Samuel A. " 'This is Union Man's Country': Sebastian County, 1914." *Arkansas Historical Quarterly* 27(1968):306-29.

1803

Smith, Russell E. "The March of the Mill Children." *Social Science Review* 41(1967):298-303.

1804

Stambler, Moses. "The Effect of Compulsory Education and Child Labor Laws on High School Attendance in New York City, 1898-1917." *History of Education Quarterly* 8(1968):189-214.

1805

Suggs, George G., Jr. "Prelude to Industrial Warfare: The Colorado City Strike." *Colorado Magazine* 44(1967):241-62.

1806
Sullivan, William A. "The 1913 Revolt of the Michigan Copper Miners."
  Michigan History 43(1959):294-314.

1807
Tuttle, William M., Jr. "Some Strikebreakers' Observations of Industrial
  Warfare." *Labor History* 7(1966):193-96.

1808
——————. "Labor Conflict and Racial Violence: The Black Worker in
  Chicago, 1894-1919." *Labor History* 10(1969):408-32.

1809
Walker, Kenneth R. "The Era of Industrialization: Capital and Labor in the
  Midwest in 1901." *Northwest Ohio Quarterly* 37(1965):49-60.

1810
Wesser, Robert F. "Conflict and Compromise: The Workmen's Compensation Movement in New York, 1890s-1913." *Labor History*
  12(1971):345-72.

1811
Wiebe, Robert H. "The Anthracite Strike of 1902: A Record of Confusion."
  Mississippi Valley Historical Review 48(1961):229-51.

1812
Worthman, Paul B. "A Black Worker and the Bricklayers' and Masons' Union,
  1903." *Journal of Negro History* 54(1969):398-404.

1813
Zimmerman, Jane. "The Penal Reform Movement in the South during the
  Progressive Era, 1890-1917." *Journal of Southern History*
  17(1951):462-92.

Industrial Workers of the World

(1905-1920)

1814
Anderson, Bryce W. "The Bomb at the Governor's Gate." *American West*
  2(1965):p. 12.

1815
Anderson, Rondo W. "Joe Hill—the Legend after Fifty Years." *Western
  Folklore* 25(1966):129-30.

1816
Betten, Neil. "Riot, Revolution, Repression in the Iron Range Strike of
  1916." *Minnesota History* 41(1968):82-94.

1817
Brazier, Richard. "The Mass IWW Trial of 1918: A Retrospect." *Labor
  History* 7(1966):178-92.

1818

——————. "The Story of the IWWs 'Little Red Songbook.' " *Labor History* 9(1968):91-105.

1819

Clark, Norman H. "Everett, 1916, and After." *Pacific Northwest Quarterly* 57(1966):57-64.

1820

Conlin, Joseph R. "The IWW and the Socialist Party." *Science and Society* 31(1967):22-36.

1821

——————. "The IWW and the Question of Violence." *Wisconsin Magazine of History* 51(1968):316-26.

1822

——————. "The Haywood Case: An Enduring Riddle." *Pacific Northwest Quarterly* 59(1968):23-32.

1823

Dubofsky, Melvyn. "The Origins of Western Working Class Radicalism, 1890-1905." *Labor History* 7(1966):131-54.

1824

——————. "James H. Hawley and the Origins of the Haywood Case." *Pacific Northwest Quarterly* 58(1967):23-32.

1825

Ebner, Michael H. "The Passaic Strike of 1912 and the Two IWWs." *Labor History* 11(1970):452-66.

1826

Gunns, Albert F. "Ray Becker, the Last Centralia Prisoner." *Pacific Northwest Quarterly* 59(1968):88-99.

1827

Gutfeld, Arnon. "The Murder of Frank Little: Radical Labor Agitation in Butte, Montana, 1917." *Labor History* 10(1969):177-92.

1828

Haynes, John E. "Revolt of the Timber Beasts: IWW Strike in Minnesota." *Minnesota History* 42(1971):162-74.

1829

Lindquist, John H., "The Jerome Deportation of 1917." *Arizona and the West* 11(1969):233-46.

1830

——————. and Fraser, James. "A Sociological Interpretation of the Bisbee Deportation." *Pacific Historical Review* 38(1968):401-22.

1831

McClelland, John M., Jr. "Terror on Tower Avenue." *Pacific Northwest Quarterly* 57(1966):65-72.

1832

McClurg, Donald J. "The Colorado Coal Strike of 1927—Tactical Leadership of the IWW." *Labor History* 4(1963):68-69.

1833
Newman, Philip. "The First IWW Invasion of New Jersey." *New Jersey Historical Society Proceedings* 58(1940):268-83.

1834
Rader, Benjamin G. "The Montana Lumber Strike of 1917." *Pacific Historical Review* 36(1967):189-208.

1835
Renshaw, Patrick. "The IWW and the Red Scare, 1917-24." *Journal of Contemporary History* 3(1968):63-72.

1836
Reed, Merl E. "The IWW and Individual Freedom in Western Louisiana, 1913." *Louisiana History* 10(1969):61-69.

1837
————. "Lumberjacks and Longshoremen: The IWW in Louisiana." *Labor History* 13(1972):41-59.

1838
Reuss, Richard A. "The Ballad of 'Joe Hill' Revisited." *Western Folklore* 26(1967):187-88.

1839
Rodnitzky, Jerome L. "The Evolution of the American Protest Song." *Journal of Popular Culture* 3(1969):35-45.

1840
Taft, Philip. "The IWW in the Grain Belt." *Labor History* 1(1960):53-67.

1841
————. "Federal Trials of the IWW." *Labor History* 3(1962):57-91.

1842
————. "Mayor Short and the IWW Agricultural Workers." *Labor History* 7(1966):173-77.

1843
————. "The Bisbee Deportation." *Labor History* 13(1972):3-40.

1844
Tyler, Robert L. "The Everett Free Speech Fight." *Pacific Historical Review* 23(1954):19-30.

1845
————. "Violence at Centralia, 1919." *Pacific Northwest Quarterly* 45(1954):116-24.

1846
————. "The Rise and Fall of an American Radicalism: The IWW." *The Historian* 19(1956):48-65.

1847
————. "The IWW and the West." *American Quarterly* 12(1960):175-87.

1848

Zeiger, Robert H. "Robin Hood in the Silk City: The IWW and the Patterson Strike of 1913." *New Jersey Historical Society Proceedings* 84(1966):182-95.

Labor in the First World War

(1914-1920)

1849

Abell, Aaron. "The Catholic Church and Social Problems in the World War I Era." *Mid-America* 30(1948):139-51.

1850

Betten, Neil. "Riot, Revolution, Repression, in the Iron Range Strike of 1916." *Minnesota History* 41(1968):82-93.

1851

Derber, Milton. "The Idea of Industrial Democracy in America: 1915-1935." *Labor History* 8(1967):3-29.

1852

Elkins, W.F. " 'Unrest among the Negroes,' a British Document of 1919." *Science and Society* 32(1968):66-79.

1853

Flynt, Wayne. "Florida Labor and Political 'Radicalism,' 1919-1920." *Labor History* 9(1968):73-90.

1854

Friedheim, Robert L. "Prologue to a General Strike: The Seattle Shipyard Strike of 1919." *Labor History* 6(1965):121-42.

1855

Grubbs, Frank L., Jr. "Council and Alliance Labor Propaganda: 1917-1919." *Labor History* 7(1966):156-72.

1856

Gutfeld, Arnon. "The Speculator Disaster in 1917: Labor Resurgence at Butte, Montana." *Arizona and the West* 11(1969):27-38.

1857

Hendrickson, Kenneth E., Jr. "The Socialists of Reading, Pennsylvania and World War I: A Question of Loyalty." *Pennsylvania History* 36(1969):430-50.

1858

————. "The Pro-War Socialists and the Drive for Industrial Democracy, 1917-1920." *Labor History* 11(1970):304-22.

1859

Herron, Robert. "The Police Strike of 1918." *Bulletin of the Historical and Philosophical Society of Ohio* 17(1959):181-94.

1860
Long, Durward. "The Open-Closed Shop Battle in Tampa's Cigar Industry, 1919-1921." *Florida Historical Quarterly* 47(1968):101-21.

1861
Lyons, Richard L. "The Boston Police Strike of 1919." *New England Quarterly* 20(1947):147-68.

1862
Murray, Robert K. "Communism and the Great Steel Strike of 1919." *Mississippi Valley Historical Review* 38(1951):445-66.

1863
Rader, Benjamin G. "The Montana Lumber Strike of 1917." *Pacific Historical Review* 36(1967):189-207.

1864
Reuss, Carl F. "The Farm Labor Problem in Washington, 1917-18." *Pacific Northwest Quarterly* 34(1943):339-52.

1865
Scheiber, Jane Lang, and Scheiber, Harry N. "The Wilson Administration and the Wartime Mobilization of Black Americans, 1917-18." *Labor History* 10(1969):433-58.

1866
Shapiro, Stanley. "The Great War and Reform: Liberals and Labor, 1917-19." *Labor History* 12(1971):323-44.

1867
Smith, John S. "Organized Labor and Government in the Wilson Era, 1913-1921: Some Conclusions." *Labor History* 3(1962):265-86.

1868
Tuttle, William M., Jr. "Labor Conflict and Racial Violence: The Black Worker in Chicago, 1894-1919." *Labor History* 10(1969):408-32.

1869
Tyler, Robert L. "The Everett Free Speech Fight." *Pacific Historical Review* 23(1954):19-30.

1870
————. "Violence at Centralia, 1919." *Pacific Northwest Quarterly* 45(1954):116-24.

1871
Vadney, Thomas E. "The Politics of Repression, a Case Study of the Red Scare in New York." *New York History* 49(1968):56-75.

Welfare Capitalism and the Open Shop Campaign

(1921-1929)

1872
Bayard, Charles J. "The 1927-1928 Colorado Coal Strike." *Pacific Historical Review* 32(1963):235-50.

1873
Brown, Giles T. "The West Coast Phase of the Maritime Strike of 1921." *Pacific Historical Review* 19(1950):385-96.

1874
Hawley, Ellis W. "Secretary Hoover and the Bituminous Coal Problem, 1921-1928." *Business History Review* 42(1968):247-70.

1875
Russell, Francis. "How I Changed My Mind about the Sacco-Vanzetti Case." *Antioch Review* 27(1965):592-607.

1876
Shideler, James H. "The La Follette Progressive Party Campaign of 1924." *Wisconsin Magazine of History* 33(1950):444-57.

1877
Wakstein, Allen M. "The Origins of the Open-Shop Movement, 1919-1920." *Journal of American History* 51(1964):460-75.

1878
————. "The National Association of Manufacturers and Labor Relations in the 1920s." *Labor History* 10(1969):163-76.

1879
Wollenberg, Charles. "Huelga, 1928 Style: The Imperial Valley Cantaloupe Workers' Strike." *Pacific Historical Review* 38(1969):45-58.

1880
Zeiger, Robert H. "Pinchot and Coolidge: The Politics of the 1923 Anthracite Crisis." *Journal of American History* 52(1965):566-81.

1881
————. "From Hostility to Moderation: Railroad Labor Policy in the 1920s." *Labor History* 9(1968):23-38.

1882
————. "Senator George Wharton Pepper and Labor Issues in the 1920s." *Labor History* 9(1968):163-83.

1883
————. "Pennsylvania Coal and Politics: The Anthracite Strike of 1925-1926." *Pennsylvania Magazine of History and Biography* 92(1969):244-62.

The Great Depression

(1929-1940)

1884
Betten, Neil Bernard. "Urban Catholicism and Industrial Reform, 1937-1940." *Thought* 44(1969):434-50.

1885
————————. "The Great Depression and the Activities of the Catholic Worker Movement." *Labor History* 12(1971):243-58.

1886
Bubka, Tony. "The Harlan County Coal Strike of 1931." *Labor History* 11(1970):41-57.

1887
Chafe, William H. "Flint and the Great Depression." *Michigan History* 53(1969):225-39.

1888
Fox, Bonnie R. "Unemployment Relief in Philadelphia, 1930-1932: A Study of the Depression's Impact on Voluntarism." *Pennsylvania Magazine of History and Biography* 93(1969):86-108.

1889
Katzman, David M. "Ann Arbor: Depression City." *Michigan History* 50(1966):306-17.

1890
Leab, Daniel J. " 'United We Eat': The Creation and Organization of the Unemployed Councils in 1930." *Labor History* 8(1967):300-315.

1891
Lindmark, Sture. "The Swedish-Americans and the Depression Years, 1929-1932." *Swedish Pioneer Historical Quarterly* 19(1968):3-31.

1892
McCoy, Garnett. "Poverty, Politics and Artists, 1930-1945." *Art in America* 53(1965):88-107.

1893
O'Brien, David. "American Catholics and Organized Labor in the 1930s." *Catholic Historical Review* 52(1966):323-49.

1894
Shover, John L. "The Farmers' Holiday Association Strike, August 1932." *Agricultural History* 39(1965):196-203.

1895
————————. "The Penny-Auction Rebellion: Western Farmers Fight against Foreclosure, 1932-1933." *American West* 2(1965):64-72.

1896
Whisenhunt, Donald W. "The Great Depression in Kentucky: The Early Years." *Kentucky Historical Society Register* 67(1969):55-62.

1897
Williams, John. "Struggles of the Thirties in the South." *Political Affairs* 44(1965):15-25.

1898
Wyatt, Bryant N. "Experimentation as Technique: The Protest Novels of John Steinbeck." *Discourse* 12(1969):143-53.

The New Deal and the Rise of Industrial Unionism

(1933-1940)

1899
Abella, I.M. "The CIO, the Communist Party, and the Formation of the Canadian Congress of Labor, 1936-1941." *Canadian Historical Association Papers* (1969):112-28.

1900
Auerbach, Jerold S. "The La Follette Committee, Labor, and Civil Liberties in the New Deal." *Journal of American History* 51(1964):435-59.

1901
————. "The Influence of the New Deal." *Current History* 47(1965): p. 334.

1902
————. "Southern Tenant Farmers: Socialist Critics of the New Deal." *Labor History* 7(1966):3-18.

1903
Cantor, Louis. "A Prologue to the Protest Movement: The Missouri Sharecropper Roadside Demonstration of 1939." *Journal of American History* 55(1969):804-22.

1904
Carlisle, Rodney. "William Randolph Hearst's Reaction to the American Newspaper Guild: A Challenge to New Deal Labor Legislation." *Labor History* 10(1969):74-99.

1905
Chafe, William H. "Flint and the Great Depression." *Michigan History* 53(1969):225-39.

1906
Dubay, Robert W. "The Civilian Conservation Corps: A Study of Opposition, 1933-1935." *Southern Quarterly* 6(1968):341-58.

1907
Erickson, Herman. "WPA Strike and Trials of 1939." *Minnesota History* 42(1971):202-14.

1908
Fine, Sidney. "The Toledo Chevrolet Strike of 1935." *Ohio Historical Quarterly* 67(1958):326-56.

1909
————. "The Origins of the United Automobile Workers, 1933-1935." *Journal of Economic History* 18(1958):249-82.

1910
————. "The Ford Motor Company and the NRA." *Business History Review* 32(1958):353-85.

1911
————. "The General Motors Sit-Down Strike: A Reexamination." *American Historical Review* 70(1965):691-713.

1912
Gower, Calvin W. " 'Camp William James': A New Deal Blunder?" *New England Quarterly* 38(1965):475-93.

1913
Grubbs, Donald H. "Gardner Jackson, that 'Socialist' Tenant Farmers' Union, and the New Deal." *Agricultural History* 42(1968):125-37.

1914
Henwood, James N.J. "Experiment in Relief: The Civil Works Administration in Pennsylvania." *Pennsylvania History* 39(1972):50-71.

1915
Holley, Donald. "The Negro in the New Deal Resettlement Program." *Agricultural History* 45(1971):179-94.

1916
Howard, J. Woodford, Jr. "Frank Murphy and the Sit-Down Strikes of 1937." *Labor History* 1(1960):103-40.

1917
Johnson, James P. "Reorganizing the United Mine Workers of America in Pennsylvania during the New Deal." *Pennsylvania History* 37(1970):117-32.

1918
Karman, Thomas. "The Flint Sit-Down Strike." *Michigan History* 46(June 1962:97-125; 46(September 1962):223-50.

1919
Komisar, Jerome B. "Social Legislation Policies and Labor Force Behavior." *Journal of Economic Issues* 2(1968):187-99.

1920
Larrowe, Charles P. "The Great Maritime Strike of '34: Part I." *Labor History* 11(1970):403-51.

1921
––––––––. "The Great Maritime Strike of '34: Part II." *Labor History* 12(1971):3-37.

1922
Leab, Daniel J. "The Memorial Day Massacre." *Midcontinent American Studies Journal* 8(1967):3-17.

1923
––––––––. "Toward Unionization: The Newark Ledger Strike of 1934-35." *Labor History* 11(1970):3-22.

1924
Nash, Gerald D. "Franklin D. Roosevelt and Labor: The World War I Origins of Early New Deal Policy." *Labor History* 1(1960):39-52.

1925
Nipp, Robert E. "The Negro in the New Deal Resettlement Program: A Comment." *Agricultural History* 45(1971):195-200.

1926

Olson, James S. "Organized Black Leadership and Industrial Unionism: The Racial Response, 1936-1945." *Labor History* 10(1969):475-86.

1927

Salmond, John A. "The Civilian Conservation Corps and the Negro." *Journal of American History* 52(1965):75-88.

1928

Sofchalk, Donald G. "The Chicago Memorial Day Incident: An Episode of Mass Action." *Labor History* 6(1965):3-43.

1929

Speer, Michael. "The 'Little Steel' Strike: Conflict for Control." *Ohio History* 78(1969):273-87.

1930

Venkataramani, M.S. "Norman Thomas, Arkansas Sharecroppers, and the Roosevelt Agricultural Policies, 1933-1937." *Arkansas Historical Quarterly* 24(1965):3-28.

1931

Wagner, Aubrey J. "TVA Looks at Three Decades of Collective Bargaining." *Industrial and Labor Relations Review* 22(1968):20-30.

1932

Whatley, Larry. "The Works Progress Administration in Mississippi." *Journal of Mississippi History* 30(1968):35-50.

Labor in the Second World War and Early Postwar Period

(1941-1949)

1933

Ayer, Hugh M. "Hoosier Labor in the Second World War." *Indiana Magazine of History* 59(1963):95-120.

1934

Bernstein, Barton J. "The Truman Administration and Its Reconversion Wage Policy." *Labor History* 6(1965):214-31.

1935

—————. "Walter Reuther and the General Motors Strike of 1945-1946." *Michigan History* 49(1965):260-77.

1936

—————. "The Truman Administration and the Steel Strike of 1946." *Journal of American History* 52(1966):791-803.

1937

Blackman, John L., Jr. "Navy Policy toward the Labor Relations of Its War Contractors." *Military Affairs* 18(1954):176-87; 19(1955):21-31.

1938

Blum, Albert A. "Sailor or Worker: A Manpower Dilemma during the Second World War." *Labor History* 6(1965):232-43.

1939
Bond, Elsie M. "Day Care of Children of Working Mothers in New York State during the War Emergency." *New York History* 26(1945):51-77.

1940
Derber, Milton. "Labor-Management in World War II." *Current History* 48(1965):340-45.

1941
Di Bacco, Thomas V. " 'Draft the Strikers (1946) and Seize the Mills (1952)': The Business Reaction." *Duquesne Review* 13(1968):63-75.

1942
Green, William. "The Taft-Hartley Act: A Critical View." In *Labor in the American Economy,* edited by Gordon S. Watkins. *American Academy of Political and Social Science Annals* (1951):200-205.

1943
Kesselman, Louis C. "The Fair Employment Practice Commission Movement in Perspective." *Journal of Negro History* 31(1946):30-46.

1944
Lee, R. Alton. "The Army 'Mutiny' of 1946." *Journal of American History* 53(1966):555-71.

1945
Macdonald, Robert M. "Collective Bargaining in the Postwar Period." *Industrial and Labor Relations Review* 20(1967):553-77.

1946
Murray, Philip. "American Labor and the Threat of Communism." In *Labor in the American Economy,* edited by Gordon S. Watkins. *American Academy of Political and Social Science Annals* (1951):125-30.

1947
Olson, James S. "Organized Black Leadership and Industrial Unionism: The Racial Response, 1936-1945." *Labor History* 10(1969):475-86.

1948
Prickett, James R. "Communism and Factionalism in the United Automobile Workers, 1939-1947." *Science and Society* 32(1968):257-77.

1949
———. "Some Aspects of the Communist Controversy in the CIO." *Science and Society* 33(1969):299-321.

1950
Schramm, LeRoy H. "Union Rivalry in Detroit in World War II." *Michigan History* 54(1970):201-15.

1951
Scruggs, Otey M. "The United States, Mexico, and the Wetbacks. 1942-1947." *Pacific Historical Review* 30(1961):149-64.

1952
———. "The Bracero Program under the Farm Security Administration, 1942-1943." *Labor History* 3(1962):149-68.

1953

————. "Texas and the Bracero Program, 1942-1947." *Pacific Historical Review* 32(1963):251-64.

1954

Stein, Bruno. "Labor's Role in Government Agencies during World War II." *Journal of Economic History* 17(1957):389-408.

1955

Taft, Robert A. "The Taft-Hartley Act: A Favorable View." In *Labor in the American Economy,* edited by Gordon S. Watkins. *American Academy of Political and Social Science Annals* (1951):195-99.

1956

Watkins, Gordon S., ed. "Labor in the American Economy." *American Academy of Political and Social Science Annals* (1951).

Recent and Current Problems and Practices of Labor

(1950s-1970s)

General

1957

Lewis, Doris K. "Union-Sponsored Middle-Income Housing: 1927-65." *Monthly Labor Review* 88(1965):629-36.

1958

Lieberman, Elias. "Is Labor Mortgaging Its Future? Seven Steps of Labor vis-à-vis Society." *Texas Quarterly* 10(1967):7-33.

1959

Means, Joan E. "Fair Employment Practices, Legislation, and Enforcement in the United States." *International Labor Review* 93(1966):211-47.

1960

O'Brien, F.S. "The 'Communist-Dominated' Unions in the United States since 1950." *Labor History* 9(1968):184-209.

1961

Stein, Bruno. "Wage Stabilization in the Korean War Period: The Role of the Subsidiary Wage Boards." *Labor History* 4(1963):161-77.

1962

Taft, Philip. "Labor History and the Labor Movement Today." *Labor History* 7(1966):70-77.

1963

Wolfe, Arthur C. "Trends in Labor Union Voting Behavior, 1948-1969." *Industrial Relations* 9(1969):1-10.

1964

Zagoria, Sam. "The U.S. Worker in the Seventies." *Labor Law Journal* 20(1969):759-62.

Unemployment

1965
Bolino, August C. "The Duration of Unemployment: Some Tentative Historical Comparisons." *Quarterly Review of Economics and Business* 6(1966):31-47.

Union Membership

1966
Bernstein, Irving. "The Growth of American Unions, 1945-1960." *Labor History* 2(1961):131-57.

1967
Blum, Albert A. "Why Unions Grow." *Labor History* 9(1968):39-72.

1968
Estey, Marten S. "Trends in Concentration of Union Membership, 1897-1962." *Quarterly Journal of Economics* 80(1966):343-60.

1969
Gitlow, Abraham L. "The Trade Union Prospect in the Coming Decade." *Labor Law Journal* 21(1970):131-58.

1970
Krislov, Joseph. "Union Organizing of New Units, 1955-1966." *Industrial and Labor Relations Review* 21(1967):31-39.

1971
————————, and Christian, Virgil L., Jr. "Union Organizing and the Business Cycle, 1949-1966." *Southern Economic Journal* 36(1969):185-88.

1972
Shair, David I. "Labor Organizations as Employers: 'Unions-within-Unions.'" *Journal of Business* 43(1970):296-316.

1973
Shister, Joseph. "The Direction of Unionism, 1947-1967: Thrust or Drift?" *Industrial and Labor Relations Review* 20(1967):578-601.

1974
Treckel, Karl F. "The Unionization of Union Organizers and International Representatives." *Labor Law Journal* 22(1971):266-77.

1975
Troy, Leo. "Trade Union Membership, 1897-1962." *Review of Economics and Statistics* 47(1965):93-113.

Collective Bargaining

1976
Briggs, Vernon M. "The Strike Insurance Plan of the Railroad Industry." *Industrial Relations* 6(1967):205-12.

1977
Cook, Alice H., and Gray, Lois S. "Labor Relations in New York City." *Industrial Relations* 5(1966):86-104.

1978
Estafen, Bernard D., and Hinton, Bernard L. "Applied Economics: A Strike Tax." *Business Horizons* 13(1970):35-41.

1979
Fogel, Walter. "Union Impact on Retail Food Wages in California." *Industrial Relations* 6(1966):79-94.

1980
Foster, Harold. "Employers Strike Insurance." *Labor History* 12(1971):483-529.

1981
Goldberg, Joseph P. "Labor-Management since World War II." *Current History* 48(1965): p. 346.

1982
———. "Containerization as a Force for Change on the Waterfront." *Monthly Labor Review* 91(1968):8-13.

1983
James, Ralph, and James, Estelle. "Hoffa's Impact on Teamster Wages." *Industrial Relations* 4(1964):60-76.

1984
Kaufman, Jacob J. "The Railroad Labor Dispute: A Marathon of Maneuver and Improvisation." *Industrial and Labor Relations Review* 18(1965):196-212.

1985
Kelly, Matthew A. "The Contract Rejection Problem: A Positive Labor-Management Approach." *Labor Law Journal* 20(1969):404-15.

1986
Kennedy, Thomas. "Freedom to Strike Is in the Public Interest." *Harvard Business Review* 48(1970):45-57.

1987
Kienast, Philip. "Extended Leisure for Blue-Collar Workers: A Look at the Steelworker's Extended Vacation Program." *Labor Law Journal* 20(1969):641-48.

1988
Helburn, I.B. "Trade Union Response to Profit-Sharing Plans: 1886-1966." *Labor History* 12(1971):68-80.

1989
Lesieur, Fred G., and Puckett, Elbridge S. "The Scanlon Plan Has Proved Itself." *Harvard Business Review* 47(1969):109-18.

1990
Lester, Richard A. "Negotiated Wage Increases, 1951-1967." *Review of Economics and Statistics* 50(1968):173-81.

1991
Levine, Marvin J. "The Railroad Crew Size Controversy Revisited." *Labor Law Journal* 20(1969):373-85.

1992
Macdonald, Robert M. "Collective Bargaining in the Postwar Period." *Industrial and Labor Relations Review* 20(1967):553-77.

1993
Michman, Ronald D. "Union Impact on Retail Management." *Business Horizons* 10(1967):79-84.

1994
Miller, Richard Ulric. "Arbitration of New Contract Wage Disputes: Some Recent Trends." *Industrial and Labor Relations Review* 20(1967):250-64.

1995
Moore, Michael A. "A Community's Crisis: Hillsdale and the Essex Wire Strike." *Indiana Magazine of History* 66(1970):238-62.

1996
Northrup, Herbert R., "The Railway Labor Act: A Critical Reappraisal." *Industrial and Labor Relations Review* 25(1971):3-31.

1997
————. and Young, Harvey A. "The Causes of Industrial Peace Revisited." *Industrial and Labor Relations Review* 22(1968):31-47.

1998
Novitt, Mitchell S. "A Right-to-Work Law: Before and After." *Business Horizons* 12(1969):61-68.

1999
Redenius, Charles. "Structural Instability in Airline Industrial Relations." *Labor Law Journal* 22(1971):558-65.

2000
Ross, Philip. "The Teamsters' Response to Technological Change: The Case of Piggybacking." *Labor Law Journal* 21(May 1970):283-97.

2001
————. "Waterfront Labor Response to Technological Change: A Tale of Two Unions." *Labor Law Journal* 21(July 1970):397-419.

2002
Serrin, William. "The Ultimate Shutdown: The Detroit Strike of 1967-1968." *Columbia Journalism Review* 8(1969):36-44.

2003
Simkin, William E. "Positive Approaches to Labor Peace." *Industrial Relations* 4(1964):37-44.

2004
Simons, John H. "The Union Approach to Health and Welfare." *Industrial Relations* 4(1965):61-76.

2005
Slavin, Richard H. "The 'Flint Glass Workers' Union' vs. the Glassware Industry: Union-Management Policies in a Declining Industry." *Labor History* 5(1964):29-39.

2006
Sloane, Arthur A. "Collective Bargaining in Trucking: Prelude to a National Contract." *Industrial and Labor Relations Review* 19(1965):21-40.

2007
————. "National Emergency Strikes: The Danger of Extralegal Success." *Business Horizons* 10(1967):91-96.

2008
Stokes, S.L. "Nonstoppage Strikes: Rationale and Review." *Labor Law Journal* 20(1969):79-84.

2009
Timmins, William M. "The Copper Strike and Collective Bargaining." *Labor Law Journal* 21(1970):28-38.

Professional, Technical and Office Workers

2010
Brown, Martha A. "Collective Bargaining on the Campus: Professors, Associations, and Unions." *Labor Law Journal* 21(1970):167-81.

2011
Dvorak, Eldon J. "Will Engineers Unionize?" *Industrial Relations* 2(1963):45-65.

2012
Estey, Marten. "The Grocery Clerks: Center of Retail Unionism." *Industrial Relations* 7(1968):249-61.

2013
Ferguson, Tracy H. "Collective Bargaining in Universities and Colleges." *Labor Law Journal* 19(1968):778-804.

2014
Garbarino, Joseph W. "Precarious Professors: New Patterns of Representation." *Industrial Relations* 10(1971):1-20.

2015
Glass, Ronald W. "Work Stoppages and Teachers: History and Prospect." *Monthly Labor Review* 90(1967):43-46.

2016
Goldstein, Bernard. "Unionism among Salaried Professionals in Industry." *American Sociological Review* 20(1955):199-205.

2017
Gooding, Judson. "The Fraying White Collar." *Fortune* 82-(1970): p. 78.

2018
Ingerman, Sidney. "Employed Graduate Students Organize at Berkeley." In *Professional and White-Collar Unionism: An International Comparison. Industrial Relations* 5(1965):141-50.

2019
Kasper, Hirschel. "On the Effect of Collective Bargaining on Resource Allocation in Public Schools." *Economic and Business Bulletin* 23(1971):1-9.

2020
Kleingartner, Archie. "Professional and Engineering Unionism." *Industrial Relations* 8(1969):224-35.

2021
Moberly, Robert B. "Causes of Impasse in School Board-Teacher Negotiations." *Labor Law Journal* 21(1970):668-77.

2022
Muir, J. Douglas. "The Strike as a Professional Sanction: The Changing Attitude of the National Education Association." *Labor Law Journal* 19(1968):615-27.

2023
Rehmus, Charles M. "Collective Bargaining and the Market for Academic Personnel." *Quarterly Review of Economics and Business* 8(1968):7-13.

2024
Seidman, Joel, and Cain, Glen G. "Unionized Engineers and Chemists: A Case Study of a Professional Union." *Journal of Business* 37(1964):238-57.

2025
Strauss, George. "Professional or Employee-Oriented: Dilemma for Engineering Unions." *Industrial and Labor Relations Review* 17(1962):519-33.

2026
————. "The AAUP as a Professional Occupational Association." In *Professional and White-Collar Unionism: An International Comparison. Industrial Relations* 5(1965):128-40.

2027
Thornton, Robert J. "The Effects of Collective Negotiations on Teachers' Salaries." *Quarterly Review of Economics and Business* 11(1971):37-46.

2028
Vogel, Alfred. "Your Clerical Workers Are Ripe for Unionism." *Harvard Business Review* 49(1971):48-54.

Public and Non-Profit Employees

2029
Baird, William M. "Barriers to Collective Bargaining in Registered Nursing." *Labor Law Journal* 20(1969):42-46.

2030
Belote, Martha. "Nurses Are Making It Happen." *American Journal of Nursing* 67(1967):285-88.

2031
Cohen, Frederick C. "Labor Features of the Postal Reorganization Act." *Labor Law Journal* 22(1971):44-50.

2032
Committee on Labor Law of the Federal Bar Council. "Federal Public Employee Relations: The Lessons to be Learned from the New York and New Jersey Experiences." *Labor Law Journal* 22(1971):173-85.

2033
Cook, Alice H. "Public Employee Bargaining in New York City." *Industrial Relations* 9(1970):249-67.

2034
Craft, James A. "Fire Fighter Militancy and Wage Disparity." *Labor Law Journal* 21(1970):794-806.

2035
Craver, Charles B. "Bargaining in the Federal Sector." *Labor Law Journal* 19(1968):569-89.

2036
Donoian, Harry A. "Recognition and Collective Bargaining Agreements of Federal Employee Unions—1963-1969." *Labor Law Journal* 21(1970):597-606.

2037
Gitlow, Abraham L. "Public Employee Unionism in the United States: Growth and Outlook." *Labor Law Journal* 21(1970):766-78.

2038
Hardbeck, George W., and Anderson, John S. "The Impact of Executive Order 10988 on Labor Management Relations." *Labor Law Journal* 20(1969):723-29.

2039
Juris, Hervey A., and Hutchison, Kay B. "The Legal Status of Municipal Police Employee Organizations." *Industrial and Labor Relations Review* 23(1970):352-66.

2040
Loewenberg, J. Joseph. "Development of the Federal Labor-Management Relations Program: Executive Order 10988 and Executive Order 11491." *Labor Law Journal* 21(1970):73-78.

2041
McLaughlin, Richard P. "Collective Bargaining Suggestions for the Public Sector." *Labor Law Journal* 20(1969):131-37.

2042
Mustafa, Husain. "Cost Implications of Public Labor-Management Cooperation." *Labor Law Journal* 21(1970):654-62.

2043
Oberer, Walter E. "The Future of Collective Bargaining in Public Employment." *Labor Law Journal* 20(1969):777-86.

2044
Schmidman, John. "Nurses and Pennsylvania's New Public Employee Bargaining Law." *Labor Law Journal* 22(1971):725-33.

2045
Schneider, B.V.H. "Collective Bargaining and the Federal Civil Service." *Industrial Relations* 3(1964):97-120.

2046
Seidman, Joel. "Collective Bargaining in the Postal Service." *Industrial Relations* 9(1969):11-26.

2047
————. "Nurses and Collective Bargaining." *Industrial and Labor Relations Review* 23(1970):335-51.

2048
Sullivan, Daniel P. "Soldiers in Unions–Protected First Amendment Right?" *Labor Law Journal* 20(1969):581-90.

2049
Wagner, Aubrey J. "TVA Looks at Three Decades of Collective Bargaining." *Industrial and Labor Relations Review* 22(1968):20-30.

2050
Weber, Arnold R. "Paradise Lost; or Whatever Happened to the Chicago Social Workers?" *Industrial and Labor Relations Review* 22(1969):323-38.

2051
Woolf, Donald A. "Labor Problems in the Post Office." *Industrial Relations* 9(1969):27-35.

2052
Young, James E., and Brewer, Betty L. "Strikes by State and Local Government Employees." *Industrial Relations* 9(1970):356-61.

Black Workers

2053
Bloch, Herman D. "Discrimination against the Negro in Employment in New York, 1920-1963." *American Journal of Economics and Sociology* 24(1965):361-82.

2054
Campbell, Joel T., and Belcher, Leon. "Changes in Non-White Employment, 1960-1966." *Phylon* 28(1967):325-37.

2055
Cassell, Frank H. "Chicago 1960-1970: One Small Step Forward." In *Equal Employment Opportunity: Comparative Community Experience. Industrial Relations* 9(1970):277-93.

2056
Doeringer, Peter B., and Piore, Michael J. "Equal Employment Opportunity in Boston." In *Equal Employment Opportunity: Comparative Community Experience. Industrial Relations* 9(1970):324-39.

2057
Hiestand, Dale L. "Equal Employment in New York City." In *Equal Employment Opportunity: Comparative Community Experience. Industrial Relations* 9(1970):294-307.

2058
Marshall, F. Ray, and Van Adams, Arvil. "Negro Employment in Memphis." In *Equal Employment Opportunity: Comparative Community Experience. Industrial Relations* 9(1970):308-23.

2059
Rowan, Richard L. "Negro Employment in the Basic Steel Industry." *Industrial and Labor Relations Review* 23(1969):29-39.

2060
Schmidt, Fred H. "Los Angeles: Show, Little Substance." In *Equal Employment Opportunity: Comparative Community Experience. Industrial Relations* 9(1970):340-55.

2061
Wolters, Raymond. "The Negro in American Industries." *Industrial and Labor Relations Review* 25(1971):116-23.

Mexican-Americans

2062
Bullock, Paul. "Employment Problems of the Mexican-American." *Industrial Relations* 3(1964):37-50.

2063
Fuller, Varden. "A New Era for Farm Labor?" *Industrial Relations* 6(1967):285-302.

2064
Gilmore, N. Ray, and Gilmore, Gladys W. "The Bracero in California." *Pacific Historical Review* 32(1963):265-82.

2065
Glass, Judith Chanin. "Organization in Salinas." *Monthly Labor Review* 91(1968):24-27.

2066
Hansen, Niles M. "Improving Economic Opportunity for the Mexican-Americans." *Economic and Business Bulletin* 22(1969):1-14.

2067
Hawley, Ellis W. "The Politics of the Mexican Labor Issue, 1950-1965." *Agricultural History* 40(1966):157-76.

2068
Jones, Lamar B. "Labor and Management in California Agriculture, 1864-1964." *Labor History* 11(1970):23-40.

2069
Schmidt, Fred H. "Job Caste in the Southwest." *Industrial Relations* 9(1969):100-110.

2070
Taylor, Paul S. "Hand Laborers in the Western Sugar Beet Industry." *Agricultural History* 41(1967):19-26.

2071
————. "California Farm Labor: A Review." *Agricultural History* 42(1968):49-53.

2072
Walker, Kenneth P. "The Pecan Shellers of San Antonio and Mechanization." *Southwestern Historical Quarterly* 69(1965):44-58.

2073
Weaver, Charles N., and Glenn, Norval D. "Job Performance Comparisons: Mexican-American and Anglo Employees." *California Management Review* 13(1970):27-30.

White Blue-Collar Workers

2074
Agassi, Judith Buber. "Women Who Work in Factories." *Dissent* 19(1972):233-39.

2075
Barbash, Jack. "The Tensions of Work." *Dissent* 19(1972):240-48.

2076
Bell, Daniel. "Labor in the Post-Industrial Society." *Dissent* 19(1972):163-89.

2077
Benson, H.W. "Apathy and Other Axioms: Expelling the Union Dissenter from History." *Dissent* 19(1972):211-24.

2078
Brooks, Thomas R. "Breakdown in Newark." *Dissent* 19(1972):128-37.

2079
————. "A Steelworkers' Local in New England." *Dissent* 19(1972):47-52.

2080
Carliner, Lewis. "The White Collar on the Ex-Blue Collar is a Cool Collar." *Dissent* 19(1972):257-63.

2081
Epstein, Joseph. "Blue Collars in Cicero." *Dissent* 19(1972):118-27.

2082
Filiatreau, John. "The White Worker in the South." *Dissent* 19(1972):78-82.

2083
Gooding, Judson. "Blue-Collar Blues on the Assembly Line." *Fortune* 82(July 1970): p. 69.

2084
————. "It Pays to Wake up the Blue-Collar Worker." *Fortune* 82(September 1970): p. 133.

2085
Goodman, Walter. "The Sad Legacy of John L. Lewis." *Dissent* 19(1972):99-106.

2086
Gordon, David M. "From Steam Whistles to Coffee Breaks." *Dissent* 19(1972):197-210.

2087
Greeley, Andrew. "The New Ethnicity & Blue Collars." *Dissent* 19(1972):270-77.

2088
Hamilton, Richard F. "Liberal Intelligentsia and White Backlash." *Dissent* 19(1972):225-32.

2089
Harrington, Michael. "Old Working Class, New Working Class." *Dissent* 19(1972):146-62.

2090
Howe, Irving. "Sweet and Sour Notes: On Workers and Intellectuals." *Dissent* 19(1972):264-69.

2091
Kremen, Bennett. "No Pride in This Dust." *Dissent* 19(1972):21-28.

2092
Krickus, Richard J. "Organizing Neighborhoods: Gary and Newark." *Dissent* 19(1972):107-17.

2093
Kriegel, Leonard. "Silent in the Supermarket." *Dissent* 19(1972):91-98.

2094
Levine, Irving M., and Herman, Judith. "The Life of White Ethnics." *Dissent* 19(1972):286-94.

2095
Margolis, Richard J. "Last Chance for Desegregation." *Dissent* 19(1972):249-56.

2096
Rabinowitz, Dorothy. "The Case of the ILGWU." *Dissent* 19(1972):83-90.

2097
Rosenberg, Bernard. "Torn Apart and Driven Together: Portrait of a UAW Local in Chicago." *Dissent* 19(1972):61-69.

2098
Rosow, Jerome M. "Toward a Brighter Blue Collar." *Manpower* 3(1971):28-32.

2099
Sexton, Brendan. "The Tradition of Reutherism." *Dissent* 19(1972):53-60.

2100
Terkel, Studs. "A Steelworker Speaks." *Dissent* 19(1972):9-20.

2101
Tyler, Gus. "White Workers/Blue Mood." *Dissent* 19(1972):190-96.

2102
Watters, Pat. "Workers, White and Black, in Mississippi." *Dissent* 19(1972):70-77.

2103
Widick, B.J. "Detroit: Black City, Black Unions?" *Dissent* 19(1972):138-45.

2104
Wolfgang, Myra. "Young Women Who Work." *Dissent* 19(1972):29-36.

2105
Wrong, Dennis. "How Important Is Social Class?" *Dissent* 19(1972):278-85.

Women

2106
Allen, A. Dale. "What to Do about Sex Discrimination." *Labor Law Journal* 21(1970):563-76.

2107
Ginzberg, Eli. "Paycheck and Apron—Revolution in Womanpower." In *Women in the Labor Force. Industrial Relations* 7(1968):193-203.

2108
Gordon, Margaret S. "Introduction: Women in the Labor Force." In *Women in the Labor Force. Industrial Relations* 7(1968):187-92.

2109
McNally, Gertrude Bancroft. "Patterns of Female Labor Force Activity." In *Women in the Labor Force. Industrial Relations* 7(1968):204-18.

2110
Munts, Raymond, and Rice, David C. "Women Workers: Protection or Equality." *Industrial and Labor Relations Review* 24(1970):3-13.

2111
Oppenheimer, Valerie Kincade. "The Sex-Labeling of Jobs." In *Women in the Labor Force. Industrial Relations* 7(1968):219-34.

2112
Schonberger, Richard J. "Ten Million U.S. Housewives Want to Work." *Labor Law Journal* 21(1970):374-79.

2113
Wilensky, Harold L. "Women's Work: Economic Growth, Ideology, Structure." In *Women in the Labor Force. Industrial Relations* 7(1968):235-48.

Internal Union Affairs

2114
Applebaum, Leon. "A Comparison of Officer Turnover and Salary Structures in Local Unions." *Labor Law Journal* 20(1969):795-802.

2115
————. "Local Union Financial Structure, 1962-1966." *Labor Law Journal* 22(1971):713-24.

2116
Blaine, Harry R., and Zeller, Frederick A. "Who Uses the UAW Public Review Board?" *Industrial Relations* 4(1965):95-104.

2117
Craypo, Charles. "The National Union Convention as an Internal Appeal Tribunal." *Industrial and Labor Relations Review* 22(1969):487-511.

2118
Hutchinson, John. "The Anatomy of Corruption in Trade Unions." *Industrial Relations* 7(1969):135-50.

2119
James, Ralph, and James, Estelle. "Hoffa's Manipulation of Pension Benefits." *Industrial Relations* 4(1965):46-60.

2120
Kleinsorge, Paul L., and Kerby, William C. "The Pulp and Paper Rebellion: A New Pacific Coast Union." *Industrial Relations* 6(1966):1-20.

2121
Kovarsky, Irving. "Union Discipline." *Labor Law Journal* 19(1968):667-80.

2122
Orr, John A. "The Steelworker Election of 1965—the Reasons for the Upset." *Labor Law Journal* 20(1969):100-112.

2123
Ross, Philip. "Distribution of Power within the ILWU and the ILA." *Monthly Labor Review* 91(1968):1-7.

2124
Turner, Emery C. "What Has Landrum-Griffin Accomplished?" *Labor Law Journal* 20(1969):391-403.

AFL and CIO

2125
Brophy, Jacqueline. "The Merger of the AFL and the CIO in Michigan." *Michigan History* 50(1966):139-57.

2126
Foster, James C. "1954: A CIO Victory?" *Labor History* 12(1971):392-408.

2127
Hutchinson, John. "George Meany and the Wayward." *California Management Review* 14(1971):51-60.

2128
Neufeld, Maurice F. "Structure and Government of the AFL-CIO." *Industrial and Labor Relations Review* 9(1956):371-90.

2129
Pomper, Gerald. "Labor and Congress: The Repeal of Taft-Hartley." *Labor History* 2(1961):323-43.

2130
Seidman, Joel. "Efforts toward Merger, 1935-1955." *Industrial and Labor Relations Review* 9(1956):353-70.

Foreign Policy

2131
Bodenheimer, Suzanne. "The AFL-CIO in Latin America: The Dominican Republic—a Case Study." *Viet-Report* 3(1967): p. 17.

2132
Friedland, William H., and Nelkin, Dorothy. "American Labor: Differences and Policies toward Africa." *Africa Today* 14(1966):13-16.

2133
Hero, Alfred O. "American Negroes and U.S. Foreign Policy, 1937-1967." *Journal of Conflict Resolution* 13(1969):220-51.

2134
————. "Liberalism-Conservatism Revisited: Foreign vs. Domestic Federal Policies, 1937-1967." *Public Opinion Quarterly* 33(1969):339-408.

2135
Lipsitz, Lewis. "Work Life and Political Attitudes: A Study of Manual Workers." *American Political Science Review* 58(1964):951-62.

2136
Windmuller, John P. "Foreign Affairs and the AFL-CIO." *Industrial and Labor Relations Review* 9(1956):419-32.

2137
————. "The Foreign Policy Conflict in American Labor." *Political Science Quarterly* 82(1967):205-34.

SPECIALIZED TOPICS

Biographical and Autobiographical Material

2138
Aiken, John R., and McDonnell, James R. "Walter Rauschenbusch and Labor Reform: A Social Gospeller's Approach." In *The Church and the American Labor Movement: Four Episodes, 1880s-1920s. Labor History* 11(1970):131-50.

2139
Anderson, Rondo W. "Joe Hill—the Legend after Fifty Years." *Western Folklore* 25(1966):129-30.

2140
Bailey, Hugh C. "Edgar Gardner Murphy and the Child Labor Movement." *Alabama Review* 18(1965):47-59.

2141
Barbash, Jack. "John R. Commons and the Americanization of the Labor Problem." *Journal of Economic Issues* 1(1967):161-67.

2142
————. "The ILGWU as an Organization in the Age of Dubinsky." *Labor History,* Spec. Suppl. 9(1968):98-115.

2143
Bean, Walton E. "Boss Ruef, the Union Labor Party, and the Graft Prosecution in San Francisco, 1901-1911." *Pacific Historical Review* 17(1948):443-55.

2144
Bernstein, Barton J. "Walter Reuther and the General Motors Strike of 1945-1946." *Michigan History* 49(1965):260-77.

2145
Blantz, Thomas E., C.S.C. "Father Haas and the Minneapolis Truckers Strike of 1934." *Minnesota History* 42(1970):5-15.

2146
Braeman, John. "Albert J. Beveridge and the First National Child Labor Bill." *Indiana Magazine of History* 60(1964):1-36.

2147
Brommel, Bernard J. "Eugene V. Debs: The Agitator as Speaker." *Central States Speech Journal* 20(1969):202-14.

2148
————. "Deb's Cooperative Commonwealth Plan for Workers." *Labor History* 12(1971):560-69.

2149
Bryant, Keith L., Jr. "Kate Barnard, Organized Labor, and Social Justice in Oklahoma during the Progressive Era." *Journal of Southern History* 35(1969):145-64.

2150
Carman, Harry J. "Terence Vincent Powderly—an Appraisal." Journal of Economic History 1(1941):83-87.

2151
Carrigan, D. Owen. "Martha Moore Avery: Crusader for Social Justice." *Catholic Historical Review* 54(1968):17-38.

2152
Chambers, John W. "The Big Switch: Justice Roberts and the Minimum-Wage Cases." *Labor History* 10(1969):44-73.

2153
Conlin, Joseph R. "The Haywood Case: An Enduring Riddle." *Pacific Northwest Quarterly* 59(1968):23-32.

2154
Cook, Philip L. "Tom M. Girdler and the Labor Policies of Republic Steel Corporation." *Social Science* 42(1967):21-30.

2155
Currie, Harold. "Alan Benson, Salesman of Socialism, 1902-1916." *Labor History* 11(1970):285-303.

2156
Daney, Walter F. "Louis D. Brandeis, Champion of Labor." *The Historian* 6(1944):153-66.

2157
Dick, W.M. "Samuel Gompers and American Consensus." *Canadian Historical Association Papers* (1969):129-40.

2158
Dorson, Richard M. "The Career of 'John Henry.' " *Western Folklore* 24(1965):155-63.

2159
Dubofsky, Melvyn. "James H. Hawley and the Origins of the Haywood Case." *Pacific Northwest Quarterly* 58(1967):23-32.

2160
Engdahl, Walfrid. "Magnus Johnson—Colorful Farmer-Labor Senator from Minnesota." *Swedish Pioneer Historical Quarterly* 16(1965):122-36.

2161
Faherty, William B. "The Clergyman and Labor Progress: Cornelius O'Leary and the Knights of Labor." In *The Church and the American Labor Movement: Four Episodes, 1880s-1920s. Labor History* 11(1970):175-89.

2162
Gitelman, H.M. "Adolph Strasser and the Origins of Pure and Simple Unionism." *Labor History* 6(1965):71-83.

2163
Gorb, Peter. "Robert Owen as a Businessman." *Business History Review* 25(1951):127-48.

2164
Green, Archie. "The Death of Mother Jones." *Labor History* 1(1960):68-80.

2165
Greenbaum, Fred. "The Social Ideas of Samuel Gompers." *Labor History* 7(1966):35-61.

2166
Greenway, John. "Woody Guthrie: The Man, the Land, the Understanding." *American West* 3(1966): p. 24.

2167
Greer, Richard A. "Edward Bellamy, an American Utopian." *The Historian* 4(1941):103-15.

2168
Grenier, Judson A. "Upton Sinclair: A Remembrance." *California Historical Society Quarterly* 48(1969):165-69.

2169
Griffen, Clyde. "Christian Socialism Instructed by Gompers." *Labor History* 12(1971):195-213.

2170
Grubbs, Donald H. "Gardner Jackson, that 'Socialist' Tenant Farmers' Union, and the New Deal." *Agricultural History* 42(1968):125-37.

2171
Gunns, Albert F. "Ray Becker, the Last Centralia Prisoner." *Pacific Northwest Quarterly* 59(1968):88-99.

2172
Gutfeld, Arnon. "The Murder of Frank Little: Radical Labor Agitation in Butte, Montana, 1917." *Labor History* 10(1969):177-92.

2173
Hardman, Jacob B.S. "John L. Lewis, Labor Leader and Man: An Interpretation." *Labor History* 2(1961):3-29.

2174
————. "David Dubinsky, Labor Leader and Man." *Labor History,* Spec. Suppl. 9(1968):43-54.

2175
Harter, Lafayette G., Jr. "John R. Commons: Social Reformer and Institutional Economist." *American Journal of Economics and Sociology* 24(1965):85-96.

2176
Hill, Herbert. "In the Age of Gompers and After—Racial Practices of Organized Labor." *New Politics* 4(1965):26-46.

2177
Hofstadter, Richard. "U.B. Phillips and the Plantation Legend." *Journal of Negro History* 29(1944):109-24.

2178
Hoogenboom, Ari. "Thomas A. Jenckes and Civil Service Reform." *Mississippi Valley Historical Review* 47(1961):636-58.

2179
Johnson, Michael R. "Albert R. Parsons: An American Architect of Syndicalism." *Midwest Quarterly* 9(1968):195-206.

2180
Kellogg, Miner K. "Miner K. Kellogg: Recollections of New Harmony," edited by Lorna Lutes Sylvester. *Indiana Magazine of History* 64(1968):39-64.

2181
Kirk, Clara, and Kirk, Rudolf. "William Dean Howells, George William Curtis and the 'Haymarket Affair.' " *American Literature* 40(1968):487-98.

2182
Kugler, Israel. "The Trade Union Career of Susan B. Anthony." *Labor History* 2(1961):90-100.

2183
Landon, Fred. "Ulrich Bonnell Phillips: Historian of the South." *Journal of Southern History* 5(1939):364-71.

2184
Levenstein, Harvey. "Samuel Gompers and the Mexican Labor Movement." *Wisconsin Magazine of History* 51(1968):155-63.

2185
McFarland, C.K. "Crusade for Child Laborers: 'Mother' Jones and the March of the Mill Children." *Pennsylvania History* 38(1971):283-96.

2186
McKee, Delber L. "Samuel Gompers, the A.F. of L., and Imperialism, 1895-1900." *The Historian* 21(1959):187-99.

2187
McKee, Don K. "Daniel De Leon: A Reappraisal." *Labor History* 1(1960):264-97.

2188
Madison, Charles A. "Edward Bellamy, Social Dreamer." *New England Quarterly* 15(1942):444-66.

2189
Mandel, Bernard. "Gompers and Business Unionism, 1873-90." *Business History Review* 28(1954):264-75.

2190
Mark, Irving. "The Compassionate American." *American Journal of Economics and Sociology* 24(1965):171-92.

2191
Morgan, George T., Jr. "No Compromise—No Recognition: John Henry Kirby, the Southern Lumber Operators' Association, and Unionism in the Piney Woods, 1906-1916." *Labor History* 10(1969):193-204.

2192
Morgan, H. Wayne. "The Utopia of Eugene V. Debs." *American Quarterly* 11(1959):120-35.

2193
Nash, George H. III. "Charles Stelzle: Apostle to Labor." In *The Church and the American Labor Movement: Four Episodes, 1880s-1920s. Labor History* 11(1970):151-74.

2194
Newman, Philip Charles. "Ulrich Bonnell Phillips—the South's Foremost Historian." *Georgia Historical Quarterly* 25(1941):244-61.

2195
Perlman, Selig. "John Rogers Commons, 1862-1945." *Wisconsin Magazine of History* 29(1945):25-31.

2196
Pessen, Edward. "Thomas Skidmore, Agrarian Reformer in the Early American Labor Movement." *New York History* 35(1954):280-96.

2197
Radosh, Ronald. "The Corporate Ideology of American Labor Leaders from Gompers to Hillman." *Studies on the Left* 6(1966):66-88.

2198
Raskin, A.H. "Dubinsky: Herald of Change." *Labor History,* Spec. Suppl. 9(1968):14-25.

2199

Reuss, Richard A. "The Ballad of 'Joe Hill' Revisited." *Western Folklore* 26(1967):187-88.

2200

Rich, J.C. "David Dubinsky: The Young Years." *Labor History*, Spec. Suppl. 9(1968):5-13.

2201

Suggs, George G., Jr. "Religion and Labor in the Rocky Mountain West: Bishop Nicholas C. Matz and the Western Federation of Miners." In *The Church and the American Labor Movement: Four Episodes, 1880s-1920s. Labor History* 11(1970):190-206.

2202

Taft, Philip. "David Dubinsky and the Labor Movement." *Labor History*, Spec. Suppl. 9(1968):26-42.

2203

Toth, Charles W. "Samuel Gompers, Communism, and the Pan American Federation of Labor." *Americas* 23(1967):273-78.

2204

Turaj, Frank. "The Social Gospel in Howells' Novels." *South Atlantic Quarterly* 66(1967):449-64.

2205

Whittaker, William George. "Samuel Gompers, Anti-Imperialist." *Pacific Historical Review* 38(1969):429-45.

2206

Wish, Harvey. "Governor Altgeld Pardons the Anarchists." *Journal of the Illinois State Historical Society* 31(1938):424-48.

2207

Wyatt, Bryant N. "Experimentation as Technique: The Protest Novels of John Steinbeck." *Discourse* 12(1969):143-53.

2208

Zieger, Robert H. "Senator George Wharton Pepper and Labor Issues in the 1920s." *Labor History* 9(1968):163-83.

Immigrant and Minority Groups in the Labor Force

2209

Abell, Aaron I. "American Catholic Reaction to Industrial Conflict: The Arbitral Process, 1885-1900." *Catholic Historical Review* 41(1956): 385-407.

2210

Amundson, Richard J. "Henry S. Sanford and Labor Problems in the Florida Orange Industry." *Florida Historical Quarterly* 43(1965):229-43.

2211

Bailer, Lloyd H. "Organized Labor and Racial Minorities." In *Labor in the American Economy*, edited by Gordon S. Watkins. *American Academy of Political and Social Science Annals* (1951):101-07.

2212
Barber, Ruth Kerns. "Indian Labor in the Spanish Colonies." *New Mexico Historical Review* 7(April 1932):105-42; (July 1932):233-72; (October 1932):311-47.

2213
Belissary, C.G. "Tennessee and Immigration, 1865-1880." *Tennessee Historical Quarterly* 7(1948):229-48.

2214
Bell, Daniel. "Jewish Labor History." *Publication of the American Jewish Historical Society* 46(1957):257-60.

2215
Berthoff, Rowland T. "Southern Attitudes toward Immigration, 1865-1914." *Journal of Southern History* 17(1951):328-60.

2216
Bethel, Elizabeth. "The Freedmen's Bureau in Alabama." *Journal of Southern History* 14(1948):49-92.

2217
Beynon, Erdmann Doane. "The Hungarians of Michigan." *Michigan History* 21(1937):89-102.

2218
Bloch, Herman D. "Craft Unions and the Negro in Historical Perspective." *Journal of Negro History* 43(1958):10-33.

2219
———————. "Discrimination against the Negro in Employment in New York, 1920-1963." *American Journal of Economics and Sociology* 24(1965):361-82.

2220
———————. "Labor and the Negro, 1866-1910." *Journal of Negro History* 50(1965):163-84.

2221
Bohme, Frederick G. "The Italians in New Mexico." *New Mexico Historical Review* 34(1959):98-116.

2222
Braeman, John. "Albert J. Beveridge and the First National Child Labor Bill." *Indiana Magazine of History* 60(1964):1-36.

2223
Brandfon, Robert L. "The End of Immigration to the Cotton Fields." *Mississippi Valley Historical Review* 50(1964):591-611.

2224
Bremner, Robert H. "The Big Flat: History of a New York Tenement House." *American Historical Review* 64(1958):54-62.

2225
Brookman, Donald W. "Prison Labor in Iowa." *Iowa Journal of History* 32(1934):124-65.

2226
Campbell, Joel T., and Belcher, Leon. "Changes in Non-White Employment, 1960-1966." *Phylon* 28(1967):325-37.

2227
Carmichael, Maude. "Federal Experiments with Negro Labor on Abandoned Plantations in Arkansas: 1862-1865." *Arkansas Historical Quarterly* 1(1942):101-16.

2228
Cassell, Frank H. "Chicago 1960-1970: One Small Step Forward." In *Equal Employment Opportunity: Comparative Community Experience. Industrial Relations* 9(1970):277-93.

2229
Caughey, John Walton. "Current Discussion of California's Migrant Labor Problem." *Pacific Historical Review* 8(1939):347-54.

2230
Chmielewski, Edward A. "Polish Settlement in East Minneapolis, Minn." *Polish American Studies* 17(1960):14-27.

2231
Crane, Paul, and Larson, Alfred. "The Chinese Massacre." *Annals of Wyoming* 12(January 1940):47-55; (April 1940):153-61.

2232
David, Henry. "The Jewish Unions and Their Influence upon the American Labor Movement." *Publication of the American Jewish Historical Society* 41(1952):339-45.

2233
———————. "Jewish Labor History: A Problem Paper." *Publication of the American Jewish Historical Society* 46(1957):215-20.

2234
Dickinson, Joan Younger. "Aspects of Italian Immigration to Philadelphia." *Pennsylvania Magazine of History and Biography* 90(1966):445-65.

2235
Doeringer, Peter B., and Piore, Michael J. "Equal Employment Opportunity in Boston." In *Equal Employment Opportunity: Comparative Community Experience. Industrial Relations* 9(1970):324-39.

2236
Dubofsky, Melvyn. "Organized Labor and the Immigrant in New York City, 1900-1918." *Labor History* 2(1961):182-201.

2237
DuFault, David V. "The Chinese in the Mining Camps of California: 1848-1870." *Historical Society of Southern California* 41(1959):155-70.

2238
Dyson, Lowell K. "Radical Farm Organizations and Periodicals in America, 1920-1960." *Agricultural History* 45(1971):111-20.

2239
Eckert, Edward K. "Contract Labor in Florida during Reconstruction." *Florida Historical Quarterly* 47(1968):34-50.

2240
Elkins, W.F. " 'Unrest among the Negroes,' a British Document of 1919."
Science and Society 32(1968):66-79.

2241
Engelsman, John Cornelius. "The Freedmen's Bureau in Louisiana."
Louisiana Historical Quarterly 32(1949):145-224.

2242
England, J. Merton. "The Free Negro in Ante-Bellum Tennessee." *Journal of
Southern History* 9(1943):37-58.

2243
Erenburg, Mark. "Obreros Unidos in Wisconsin." *Monthly Labor Review*
91(1968):17-23.

2244
Fenton, Edwin. "Italians in the Labor Movement." *Pennsylvania History*
26(1959):133-48.

2245
————. "Italian Immigrants in the Stoneworkers' Union." *Labor History*
3(1962):188-207.

2246
Fogel, Walter. "Blacks in Meatpacking: Another View of the Jungle."
Industrial Relations 10(1971):338-53.

2247
Fordyce, Wellington G. "Immigrant Colonies in Cleveland." *Ohio Historical
Quarterly* 45(1936):320-40.

2248
Gilmore, N. Ray, and Gilmore, Gladys W. "The Bracero in California." *Pacific
Historical Review* 32(1963):265-82.

2249
Gitelman, Howard M. "The Waltham System and the Coming of the Irish."
Labor History 8(1967):227-53.

2250
Glass, Judith Chanin. "Organization in Salinas." *Monthly Labor Review*
91(1968):24-27.

2251
Greene, Lorenzo J., ed. "Negro Sharcroppers." *Negro History Bulletin*
31(1968):17-19.

2252
Greene, Victor R. "A Study of Slavs, Strikes and Unions: The Anthracite
Strike of 1897." *Pennsylvania History* 31(1964):199-215.

2253
————. "The Poles and Anthracite Unions in Pennsylvania." *Polish
American Studies* 22(1965):10-16.

2254
Griffin, J. David. "Medical Assistance for the Sick Poor in Ante-Bellum
Savannah." *Georgia Historical Quarterly* 53(1969):463-69.

2255
Griffin, Richard W. "Poor White Laborers in Southern Cotton Factories, 1789-1865." *South Carolina Historical Magazine* 61(1960):26-40.

2256
Grob, Gerald N. "Organized Labor and the Negro Worker, 1865-1900." *Labor History* 1(1960):164-76.

2257
Gross, James A. "Historians and the Literature of the Negro Worker." *Labor History* 10(1969):536-46.

2258
Grossman, Jonathan. "The Molders' Struggle against Contract Prison Labor." *New York History* 23(1942):449-57.

2259
Gutman, Herbert G. "Reconstruction in Ohio: Negroes in the Hocking Valley Coal Mines in 1873 and 1874." *Labor History* 3(1962):243-64.

2260
————. "Documents on Negro Seamen during the Reconstruction Period." *Labor History* 7(1966):307-11.

2261
————. "Five Letters of Immigrant Workers from Scotland to the United States, 1867-1869: William Latta, Daniel M'Lachlan, and Allan Pinkerton." *Labor History* 9(1968):384-408.

2262
————. "Black Coal Miners and the Greenback-Labor Party in Redeemer, Alabama: 1878-1879. The Letters of Warren D. Kelley, Willis Johnson Thomas, 'Dawson,' and Others." *Labor History* 10(1969):506-35.

2263
Halich, Wasyl. "Ukrainians in Western Pennsylvania." *Western Pennsylvania Historical Magazine* 18(1935):139-46.

2264
Harrington, Michael. "Catholics in the Labor Movement: A Case History." *Labor History* 1(1960):231-63.

2265
Hawley, Ellis W. "The Politics of the Mexican Labor Issue, 1950–1965." *Agricultural History* 40(1966):157-76.

2266
Heald, Morrell. "Business Attitudes toward European Immigration, 1880-1900." *Journal of Economic History* 13(1953):291-304.

2267
Helfgott, Roy B. "Trade Unionism among the Jewish Garment Workers of Britain and the United States." *Labor History* 2(1961):202-14.

2268
Hiestand, Dale L. "Equal Employment in New York City." In *Equal Employment Opportunity: Comparative Community Experience. Industrial Relations* 9(1970):294-307.

2269
Hill, Herbert. "In the Age of Gompers and After—Racial Practices of Organized Labor." *New Politics* 4(1965):26-46.

2270
Hinckley, Ted C. "Prospectors, Profits & Prejudice." *American West* 2(1965):58-65.

2271
Holley, Donald. "The Negro in the New Deal Resettlement Program." *Agricultural History* 45(1971):179-94.

2272
Horton, Aimee. "The Highlander Folk School: Pioneer of Integration in the South." *Teachers College Record* 68(1966):242-50.

2273
House, Albert V., Jr. "A Reconstruction Share-Cropper Contract on a Georgia Rice Plantation." *Georgia Historical Quarterly* 26(1942):156-65.

2274
Johnston, Esther. "A Square Mile of New York." *New York Public Library Bulletin* 70(1966):425-36.

2275
Jones, Alton DuMar. "The Child Labor Reform Movement in Georgia." *Georgia Historical Quarterly* 49(1965):396-417.

2276
Jones, Lamar B. "Labor and Management in California Agriculture, 1864-1964." *Labor History* 11(1970):23-40.

2277
Karlin, Jules Alexander. "The Anti-Chinese Outbreak in Tacoma, 1885." *Pacific Historical Review* 23(1954):271-83.

2278
Kesselman, Louis C. "The Fair Employment Practice Commission Movement in Perspective." *Journal of Negro History* 31(1946):30-46.

2279
Kessler, Sidney H. "The Organization of Negroes in the Knights of Labor." *Journal of Negro History* 37(1952):248-76.

2280
Kisch, Guido. "German Jews in White Labor Servitude in America." *Publication of the American Jewish Historical Society* 34(1937):11-49.

2281
Kolehmainen, John Ilmari. "The Finnish Pioneers of Minnesota." *Minnesota History* 25(1944):317-28.

2282
Kolodny, Ralph L. "Ethnic Cleavages in the United States: An Historical Reminder to Social Workers." *Social Work* 14(1969):13-23.

2283
Korman, Gerd. "Americanization at the Factory Gate." *Industrial and Labor Relations Review* 18(1965):396-419.

2284
Kraus, George. "Chinese Laborers and the Construction of the Central Pacific." *Utah Historical Quarterly* 37(1969):41-57.

2285
Langley, Harold D. "The Negro in the Navy and Merchant Service— 1789-1860." *Journal of Negro History* 52(1967):273-86.

2286
Larson, Laurence M. "The Norwegian Element in the Northwest." *American Historical Review* 40(1934):69-81.

2287
Levenstein, Harvey A. "Samuel Gompers and the Mexican Labor Movement." *Wisconsin Magazine of History* 51(1968):155-63.

2288
——————. "The AFL and Mexican Immigration in the 1920s: An Experiment in Labor Diplomacy." *Hispanic American Historical Review* 48(1968):206-19.

2289
Liggett, Malcolm H. "The Efficacy of State Fair Employment Practices Commissions." *Industrial and Labor Relations Review* 22(1969):559-67.

2290
Lindmark, Sture. "The Swedish-Americans and the Depression Years, 1929-1932." *Swedish Pioneer Historical Quarterly* 19(1968):3-31.

2291
Lofton, Williston H. "Northern Labor and the Negro during the Civil War." *Journal of Negro History* 34(1949):251-73.

2292
Long, Durward. " 'La Resistencia': Tampa's Immigrant Labor Union." *Labor History* 6(1965):193-213.

2293
——————. "An Immigrant Co-operative Medical Program in the South, 1887-1963." *Journal of Southern History* 31(1965):416-34.

2294
Low, W.A. "The Freedmen's Bureau and Civil Rights in Maryland." *Journal of Negro History* 37(1952):221-47.

2295
Lucille, Sister. "Polish Farmers and Workers in the United States to 1914." *Polish American Studies* 15(1958):1-9.

2296
McFarland, C.K. "Crusade for Child Laborers: 'Mother' Jones and the March of the Mill Children." *Pennsylvania History* 38(1971):283-96.

2297
McKelvey, Blake. "The Irish in Rochester: An Historical Retrospect." *Rochester History* 19(1957):1-16.

2298
——————. "The Germans of Rochester: Their Traditions and Contributions." *Rochester History* 20(1958):1-28.

2299
Malcolm, Roy. "Anti-Japanese Legislation in California, and the Naturalization of the Japanese." *Historical Society of Southern California* 9(1912-1914):97-103.

2300
Man, Albon P., Jr. "Labor Competition and the New York Draft Riots of 1863." *Journal of Negro History* 36(1951):375-405.

2301
Mandel, Bernard. "Samuel Gompers and the Negro Workers, 1886-1914." *Journal of Negro History* 40(1955):34-60.

2302
Manfredini, Dolores M. "The Italians Come to Herrin." *Illinois State Historical Society Journal* 37(1944):317-28.

2303
Marchbin, Andrew A. "Hungarian Activities in Western Pennsylvania." *Western Pennsylvania Historical Magazine* 23(1940):163-74.

2304
Marcus, Irvin M. "The Southern Negro and the Knights of Labor." *Negro History Bulletin* 30(1967):5-7.

2305
Marsden, K. Gerald. "Patriotic Societies and American Labor: The American Protective Association in Wisconsin." *Wisconsin Magazine of History* 41(1958):287-94.

2306
Marshall, F. Ray, and Van Adams, Arvil. "Negro Employment in Memphis." In *Equal Employment Opportunity: Comparative Community Experience. Industrial Relations* 9(1970):308-23.

2307
Matison, Sumner Eliot. "The Labor Movement and the Negro during Reconstruction." *Journal of Negro History* 33(1948):426-68.

2308
Meier, August, and Rudwick, Elliott. "The Rise of Segregation in the Federal Bureaucracy, 1900-1930." *Phylon* 28(1967):178-84.

2309
Meredith, H.L. "Agrarian Socialism and the Negro in Oklahoma, 1900-1918." *Labor History* 11(1970):277-84.

2310
Merriam, H.G. "Ethnic Settlement of Montana." *Pacific Historical Review* 12(1943):157-68.

2311
Modell, John. "Class or Ethnic Solidarity: The Japanese American Company Union." *Pacific Historical Review* 38(1969):193-206.

2312
Moore, R. Laurence. "Flawed Fraternity—American Socialist Response to the Negro, 1901-1912." *The Historian* 32(1969):1-18.

2313
Morefield, Richard Henry. "Mexicans in the California Mines, 1848-1853." *California Historical Society Quarterly* 35(1956):37-46.

2314
Nelli, Humbert S. "The Italian Padrone System in the United States." *Labor History* 5(1964):153-67.

2315
Nipp, Robert E. "The Negro in the New Deal Resettlement Program: A Comment." *Agricultural History* 45(1971):195-200.

2316
O'Brien, David. "American Catholics and Organized Labor in the 1930s." *Catholic Historical Review* 52(1966):323-49.

2317
Olin, Spencer C., Jr. "European Immigrant and Oriental Alien: Acceptance and Rejection by the California Legislature of 1913." *Pacific Historical Review* 35(1966):303-15.

2318
Olson, James S. "Organized Black Leadership and Industrial Unionism: The Racial Response, 1936-1945." *Labor History* 10(1969):475-86.

2319
Ourada, Patricia K. "The Chinese in Colorado." *Colorado Magazine* 29(1952):273-84.

2320
Palickar, Stephen J. "The Slovaks of Chicago." *Mid-America* 4(1921):180-96.

2321
Papanikolas, Helen Zeese. "Life and Labor among the Immigrants of Bingham Canyon." *Utah Historical Quarterly* 33(1965):289-314.

2322
Perlman, Selig. "Jewish-American Unionism, Its Birth Pangs and Contribution to the General American Labor Movement." *Publication of the American Jewish Historical Society* 41(1952):297-337.

2323
————. "America and the Jewish Labor Movement: A Case of Mutual Illumination." *Publication of the American Jewish Historical Society* 46(1957):221-32.

2324
Picher, Robert L. "The Franco-Americans in Vermont." *Vermont History* 28(1960):59-62.

2325
Porter, Kenneth W. "Negro Labor in the Western Cattle Industry, 1866-1900." *Labor History* 10(1969):346-74.

2326
Rankin, Lois. "Detroit Nationality Groups." *Michigan History* 23(1939):129-205.

2327
Reich, Nathan. "Some Observations on Jewish Unionism." *Publication of the American Jewish Historical Society* 41(1952):347-55.

2328
Reinders, Robert C. "The Free Negro in the New Orleans Economy, 1850-1860." *Louisiana History* 6(1965):273-85.

2329
Remigia, Sister M. "The Polish Immigrant in Detroit to 1914." *Polish American Studies* 2(1945):4-11.

2330
Richardson, Joe M. "The Freedmen's Bureau and Negro Labor in Florida." *Florida Historical Quarterly* 39(1960):167-74.

2331
Rischin, Moses. "The Jewish Labor Movement in America." *Labor History* 4(1963):227-47.

2332
Rodgers, William Warren. "Negro Knights of Labor in Arkansas: A Case Study of the 'Miscellaneous' Strike." *Labor History* 10(1969):498-505.

2333
Rudolph, Frederick. "Chinamen in Yankeedom: Anti-Unionism in Massachusetts in 1870." *American Historical Review* 53(1947):1-29.

2334
Salmond, John A. "The Civilian Conservation Corps and the Negro." *Journal of American History* 52(1965):75-88.

2335
Sandmeyer, Elmer C. "California Anti-Chinese Legislation and the Federal Courts: A Study in Federal Relations." *Pacific Historical Review* 5(1936):189-211.

2336
Savage, W. Sherman. "The Negro on the Mining Frontier." *Journal of Negro History* 30(1945):30-46.

2337
Scheiber, Jane Lang, and Scheiber, Harry N. "The Wilson Administration and the Wartime Mobilization of Black Americans, 1917-18." *Labor History* 10(1969):433-58.

2338
Schmidt, Fred H. "Job Caste in the Southwest." *Industrial Relations* 9(1969):100-10.

2339
————. "Los Angeles: Show, Little Substance." In *Equal Employment Opportunity: Comparative Community Experience. Industrial Relations* 9(1970):340-55.

2340
Scruggs, Otey M. "Evolution of the Mexican Farm Labor Agreement of 1942." *Agricultural History* 34(1960):140-49.

2341
————. "The First Mexican Farm Labor Program." *Arizona and the West* 2(1960):319-26.

2342
————. "The United States, Mexico, and the Wetbacks, 1942-1947." *Pacific Historical Review* 30(1961):149-64.

2343
————. "The Bracero Program under the Farm Security Administration, 1942-1943." *Labor History* 3(1962):149-68.

2344
————. "Texas and the Bracero Program, 1942-1947." *Pacific Historical Review* 32(1963):251-64.

2345
Siekaniec, L.J. "The Polish Colony of Sioux City." *Polish American Studies* 9(1952):24-27.

2346
Sitterson, J. Carlyle. "Hired Labor on Sugar Plantations of the Ante-Bellum South." *Journal of Southern History* 14(1948):192-205.

2347
Snow, William J. "Utah Indians and Spanish Slave Trade." *Utah Historical Quarterly* 2(1929):67-90.

2348
Sorrell, Richard S. "Life, Work and Acculturation Patterns of Eastern European Immigrants in Lackawanna, New York: 1900-1922." *Polish Review* 14(1969):65-91.

2349
Stahl, Annie Lee West. "The Free Negro in Ante-Bellum Louisiana." *Louisiana Historical Quarterly* 25(1942):301-96.

2350
Stavisky, Leonard Price. "The Origins of Negro Craftsmanship in Colonial America." *Journal of Negro History* 32(1947):417-29.

2351
————. "Negro Craftsmanship in Early America." *American Historical Review* 54(1949):315-25.

2352
Stearns, Marjorie R. "The Settlement of the Japanese in Oregon." *Oregon Historical Quarterly* 39(1938):262-69.

2353
Swastek, Joseph. "The Poles in South Bend to 1914." *Polish American Studies* 2(1945):79-88.

2354
Sydnor, Charles S. "The Free Negro in Mississippi before the Civil War." *American Historical Review* 32(1927):769-88.

2355
Taylor, A.A. "The Negro in South Carolina during the Reconstruction." *Journal of Negro History* 9(July 1924):241-364; (October 1924):381-569.

2356
————. "The Negro in the Reconstruction of Virginia." *Journal of Negro History* 11(April 1926):243-415; (July 1926):425-537.

2357
Taylor, A. Elizabeth. "The Origin and Development of the Convict Lease System in Georgia." *Georgia Historical Quarterly* 26(1942):113-28.

2358
————. "The Abolition of the Convict Lease System in Georgia." *Georgia Historical Quarterly* 26(1942):273-87.

2359
Taylor, Paul S. "California Farm Labor: A Review." *Agricultural History* 42(1968):49-54.

2360
Thomas, David G. "Memories of the Chinese Riot." *Annals of Wyoming* 19(1947):105-11.

2361
Tuttle, William M., Jr. "Labor Conflict and Racial Violence: The Black Worker in Chicago, 1894-1919." *Labor History* 10(1969):408-32.

2362
Van Valen, Nelson. "The Bolsheviki and the Orange Growers." *Pacific Historical Review* 22(1953):39-50.

2363
Vucinich, Wayne S. "Yugoslavs in California." *Historical Society of Southern California* 42(1960):287-309.

2364
Wagstaff, Thomas. "Call Your Old Master—'Master': Southern Political Leaders and Negro Labor during Presidential Reconstruction." *Labor History* 10(1969):323-45.

2365
Walker, Joseph E. "A Comparison of Negro and White Labor in a Charcoal Iron Community." *Labor History* 10(1969):487-97.

2366
————. "Negro Labor in the Charcoal Industry of Southeastern Pennsylvania." *Pennsylvania Magazine of History and Biography* 93(1969):466-86.

2367
Wargelin, John. "The Finns in Michigan." *Michigan History* 24(1940):179-203.

2368
Wayman, Dorothy G. "Sacco-Vanzetti: The Unfinished Debate." *American Heritage* 11(1959):89-93.

2369
Wellborn, Mildred. "The Events Leading to the Chinese Exclusion Acts." *Historical Society of Southern California* 9(1912-1914):49-58.

2370
White, Charles P. "Early Experiments with Prison Labor in Tennessee." *East Tennessee Historical Society Publications* 12(1940):45-69.

2371
Wilcox, B.P. "Anti-Chinese Riots in Washington." *Pacific Northwest Quarterly* 20(1929):204-12.

2372
Wilson, Charles Jay. "The Negro in Early Ohio." *Ohio Historical Quarterly* 39(1930):717-68.

2373
Wollenberg, Charles. "Huelga, 1928 Style: The Imperial Valley Cantaloupe Workers' Strike." *Pacific Historical Review* 38(1969):45-58.

2374
Wolters, Raymond. "Section 7a and the Black Worker." *Labor History* 10(1969):459-74.

2375
————. "The Negro in American Industries." *Industrial and Labor Relations Review* 25(1971):116-23.

2376
Worthman, Paul B. "A Black Worker and the Bricklayers' and Masons' Union, 1903." *Journal of Negro History* 54(1969):398-404.

2377
————. "Black Workers and Labor Unions in Birmingham, Alabama, 1897-1904." *Labor History* 10(1969):375-407.

2378
Wynne, Robert E. "American Labor Leaders and the Vancouver Anti-Oriental Riots." *Pacific Northwest Quarterly* 57(1966):172-79.

Cities and States

2379
Adams, Donald R., Jr. "Wage Rates in Philadelphia, 1790-1830." *Journal of Economic History* 27(1967):608-10.

2380
————. "Wage Rates in the Early National Period: Philadelphia, 1785-1830." *Journal of Economic History* 28(1968):404-26.

2381
Allen, James B. "The Company Town: A Passing Phase of Utah's Industrial Development." *Utah Historical Quarterly* 34(1966):138-60.

2382
Amundson, Richard J. "Henry S. Sanford and Labor Problems in the Florida Orange Industry." *Florida Historical Quarterly* 43(1965):229-43.

2383
Angle, Paul M. "An Illinois Paradise: The Icarians at Nauvoo." *Chicago History* 7(1965):199-209.

2384
Appel, John C. "American Labor and the Annexation of Hawaii: A Study in Logic and Economic Interest." *Pacific Historical Review* 23(1954):1-18.

2385
————. "The Unionization of Florida Cigarmakers and the Coming of the War with Spain." *Hispanic American Historical Review* 36(1956):38-49.

2386
Arky, Louis H. "The Mechanics' Union of Trade Associations and the Formation of the Philadelphia Workingmen's Movement." *Pennsylvania Magazine of History and Biography* 76(1952):142-76.

2387
Arrington, Leonard J. "Cooperative Community in the North: Brigham City, Utah." *Utah Historical Quarterly* 33(1965):198-217.

2388
Asher, Robert. "Business and Workers' Welfare in the Progressive Era: Workmen's Compensation Reform in Massachusetts, 1880-1911." *Business History* 43(1969):452-75.

2389
Aurand, Harold W. "The Anthracite Strike of 1887-1888." *Pennsylvania History* 35(1968):169-85.

2390
Ayer, Hugh M. "Hoosier Labor in the Second World War." *Indiana Magazine of History* 59(1963):95-120.

2391
Bayard, Charles J. "The 1927-1928 Colorado Coal Strike." *Pacific Historical Review* 32(1963):235-50.

2392
Bean, Walton E. "Boss Ruef, the Union Labor Party, and the Graft Prosecution in San Francisco, 1901-1911." *Pacific Historical Review* 17(1948):443-55.

2393
Bechtol, Paul T., Jr. "The 1880 Labor Dispute in Leadville." *Colorado Magazine* 47(1970):312-25.

2394
Beck, William. "Law and Order during the 1913 Copper Strike." *Michigan History* 54(1970):275-92.

2395
Belissary, Constantine G. "Tennessee and Immigration, 1865-1880." *Tennessee Historical Quarterly* 7(1948):229-48.

2396
————. "Behavior Patterns and Aspirations of the Urban Working Classes of Tennessee in the Immediate Post-Civil War Era." *Tennessee Historical Quarterly* 14(1955):24-42.

2397
Bernstein, Leonard. "The Working People of Philadelphia from Colonial Times to the General Strike of 1835." *Pennsylvania Magazine of History and Biography* 74(1950):322-39.

2398
Berthoff, Rowland. "The Social Order of the Anthracite Region, 1825-1902." *Pennsylvania Magazine of History and Biography* 89(1965):261-91.

2399
Betten, Neil. "Strike on the Mesabi—1907." *Minnesota History* 40(1967):340-47.

2400
————. "Riot, Revolution, Repression, in the Iron Range Strike of 1916." *Minnesota History* 41(1968):82-93.

2401
Beynon, Erdmann Doane. "The Hungarians of Michigan." *Michigan History* 21(1937):89-102.

2402
Bining, Arthur Cecil. "The Iron Plantations of Early Pennsylvania." *Pennsylvania Magazine of History and Biography* 57(1933):117-37.

2403
Blantz, Thomas E., C.S.C. "Father Haas and the Minneapolis Truckers Strike of 1934." *Minnesota History* 42(1970):5-15.

2404
Bliss, Willard F. "The Rise of Tenancy in Virginia." *Virginia Magazine of History and Biography* 58(1950):427-41.

2405
Bloch, Herman D. "Discrimination against the Negro in Employment in New York, 1920-1963." *American Journal of Economics and Sociology* 24(1965):361-82.

2406
Bohme, Frederick G. "The Italians in New Mexico." *New Mexico Historical Review* 34(1959):98-116.

2407
Bond, Elsie M. "Day Care of Children of Working Mothers in New York State during the War Emergency." *New York History* 26(1945):51-77.

2408
Born, Kate. "Organized Labor in Memphis, Tennessee, 1826-1901." *West Tennessee Historical Society Papers* 21(1967):60-79.

2409
Bradford, S. Sydney. "The Negro Ironworker in Ante-Bellum Virginia." *Journal of Southern History* 25(1959):194-206.

2410
Bremner, Robert H. The Big Flat: History of a New York Tenement House." *American Historical Review* 64(1958):54-62.

2411
Brewer, Thomas B. "State Anti-Labor Legislation: Texas—a Case Study." *Labor History* 11(1970):58-76.

2412
Brinks, Herbert J. "Marquette Iron Range Strike, 1895." *Michigan History* 50(1966):293-305.

2413
Brookman, Donald W. "Prison Labor in Iowa." *Iowa Journal of History* 32(1934):124-65.

2414
Brooks, Tom. "The Terrible Triangle Fire." *American Heritage* 8(1957): p. 54.

2415
Brophy, Jacqueline. "The Merger of the AFL and the CIO in Michigan." *Michigan History* 50(1966):139-57.

2416
Bruce, Kathleen. "Slave Labor in the Virginia Iron Industry." *William and Mary Quarterly* 6(1926):289-302; 7(1927):21-31.

2417
Bryant, Keith L., Jr. "Kate Barnard, Organized Labor, and Social Justice in Oklahoma during the Progressive Era." *Journal of Southern History* 35(1969):145-64.

2418
————. "Labor in Politics: The Oklahoma State Federation of Labor during the Age of Reform." *Labor History* 11(1970):259-76.

2419
Busch, Francis X. "The Haymarket Riot and the Trial of the Anarchists." *Journal of the Illinois State Historical Society* 48(1955):247-70.

2420
Cantor, Louis. "A Prologue to the Protest Movement: The Missouri Sharecropper Roadside Demonstration of 1939." *Journal of American History* 55(1969):804-22.

2421
Carmichael, Maude. "Federal Experiments with Negro Labor on Abandoned Plantations in Arkansas: 1862-1865." *Arkansas Historical Quarterly* 1(1942):101-16.

2422
Cassell, Frank H. "Chicago 1960-1970: One Small Step Forward." In *Equal Employment Opportunity: Comparative Community Experience. Industrial Relations* 9(1970):277-93.

2423
Cathey, Clyde W. "Slavery in Arkansas." *Arkansas Historical Quarterly* 3(Spring 1944):66-90; (Summer 1944):150-63.

2424
Caughey, John Walton. "Current Discussion of California's Migrant Labor Problem." *Pacific Historical Review* 8(1939):347-54.

2425
Chafe, William H. "Flint and the Great Depression." *Michigan History* 53(1969):225-39.

2426
Champagne, Robert J. "Liberty Boys and Mechanics of New York City, 1764-1774." *Labor History* 8(1967):115-35.

2427
Chmielewski, Edward A. "Polish Settlement in East Minneapolis, Minn." *Polish American Studies* 17(1960):14-27.

2428
Clinch, Thomas Anthony. "Coxey's Army in Montana." *Montana: The Magazine of Western History* 15(1965):2-11.

2429
Cook, Alice H. "Public Employee Bargaining in New York City." *Industrial Relations* 9(1970):249-67.

2430
————, and Gray, Lois S. "Labor Relations in New York City." *Industrial Relations* 5(1966):86-104.

2431
Cook, Philip L. "Red Scare in Denver." *Colorado Magazine* 43(1966):309-26.

2432
Cravens, John N. "Two Miners and Their Families in the Thurber-Strawn Coal Mines, 1905-1918." *West Texas Historical Association Year Book* 45(1969):115-26.

2433
Daitsman, George. "Labor and the 'Welfare State' in Early New York." *Labor History* 4(1963):248-56.

2434
Daniels, Roger. "Workers' Education and the University of California, 1921-1941." *Labor History* 4(1963):32-50.

2435
Davies, Kenneth J. "Mormonism and the Closed Shop." *Labor History* 3(1962):169-87.

2436
————. "Utah Labor before Statehood." *Utah Historical Quarterly* 34(1966):202-17.

2437
Dickinson, Joan Younger. "Aspects of Italian Immigration to Philadelphia." *Pennsylvania Magazine of History and Biography* 90(1966):445-65.

2438
Doeringer, Peter B., "Piece Rate Wage Structures in the Pittsburgh Iron and Steel Industry—1880-1900." *Labor History* 9(1968):262-74.

2439
————————, and Piore, Michael J. "Equal Employment Opportunity in Boston." In *Equal Employment Opportunity: Comparative Community Experience. Industrial Relations* 9(1970):324-39.

2440
Dubofsky, Melvyn. "Organized Labor and the Immigrant in New York City, 1900-1918." *Labor History* 2(1961):182-201.

2441
DuFault, David V. "The Chinese in the Mining Camps of California: 1848-1870." *Historical Society of Southern California* 41(1959):155-70.

2442
Ebner, Michael H. "The Passaic Strike of 1912 and the Two IWWs." *Labor History* 11(1970):452-66.

2443
Eckenrode, H.J. "Negroes in Richmond in 1864." *Virginia Magazine of History and Biography* 46(1938):193-200.

2444
Eckert, Edward K. "Contract Labor in Florida during Reconstruction." *Florida Historical Quarterly* 47(1968):34-50.

2445
Elazar, Daniel J., ed. "Working Conditions in Chicago in the Early 20th Century: Testimony before the Illinois Senatorial Vice Committee, 1913." *American Jewish Archives* 21(1969):149-71.

2446
Elliott, Russell R. "Labor Troubles in the Mining Camp at Goldfield, Nevada, 1906-1908." *Pacific Historical Review* 19(1950):369-84.

2447
Engberg, George B. "The Rise of Organized Labor in Minnesota." *Minnesota History* 21(1940):372-94.

2448
————————. "The Knights of Labor in Minnesota. *Minnesota History* 22(1941):367-90.

2449
Engelsman, John Cornelius. "The Freedmen's Bureau in Louisiana." *Louisiana Historical Quarterly* 32(1949):145-224.

2450
England, J. Merton. "The Free Negro in Ante-Bellum Tennessee." *Journal of Southern History* 9(1943):37-58.

2451
Erenburg, Mark. "Obreros Unidos in Wisconsin." *Monthly Labor Review* 91(1968):17-23.

2452
Fant, H.B. "The Labor Policy of the Trustees for Establishing the Colony of Georgia in America." *Georgia Historical Quarterly* 16(1932):1-16.

2453

Fine, Sidney. "The Toledo Chevrolet Strike of 1935." *Ohio Historical Quarterly* 67(1958):326-56.

2454

Fink, Gary M. "The Paradoxical Experiences of St. Louis Labor during the Depression of 1837." *Missouri Historical Society Bulletin* 26(1969):53-63.

2455

Flanders, Ralph B. "Planters' Problems in Ante-Bellum Georgia." *Georgia Historical Quarterly* 14(1930):17-40.

2456

Flynt, Wayne. "Pensacola Labor Problems and Political Radicalism, 1908." *Florida Historical Quarterly* 43(1965):315-32.

2457

————. "Florida Labor and Political 'Radicalism,' 1919-1920." *Labor History* 9(1968):73-90.

2458

Fogel, Walter. "Union Impact on Retail Food Wages in California." *Industrial Relations* 6(1966):79-94.

2459

Fordyce, Wellington G. "Immigrant Colonies in Cleveland." *Ohio Historical Quarterly* 45(1936):320-40.

2460

Fox, Bonnie R. "Unemployment Relief in Philadelphia, 1930-1932: A Study of the Depression's Impact on Voluntarism." *Pennsylvania Magazine of History and Biography* 93(1969):86-108.

2461

Friedheim, Robert L. "Prologue to a General Strike: The Seattle Shipyard Strike of 1919." *Labor History* 6(1965):121-42.

2462

Friedman, Lawrence M., and Spector, Michael M. "Tenement House Legislation in Wisconsin: Reform and Reaction." *American Journal of Legal History* 9(1965):41-63.

2463

Gaboury, William Joseph. "From Statehouse to Bull Pen: Idaho Populism and the Coeur d'Alene Troubles of the 1890s." *Pacific Northwest Quarterly* 58(1967):14-22.

2464

Gephart, Ronald M. "Politicians, Soldiers and Strikes: The Reorganizations of the Nebraska Militia and the Omaha Strike of 1882." *Nebraska History* 46(1965):89-120.

2465

Gettleman, Marvin E., and Conlon, Noel P., eds. "Responses to the Rhode Island Workingmen's Reform Agitation of 1833." *Rhode Island History* 28(1969):75-94.

2466
Gibson, George H. "Labor Piracy on the Brandywine." *Labor History* 8(1967):175-82.

2467
Gilmore, N. Ray, and Gilmore, Gladys W. "The Bracero in California." *Pacific Historical Review* 32(1963):265-82.

2468
Gitelman, Howard M. "The Labor Force at Waltham Watch during the Civil War Era." *Journal of Economic History* 25(1965):214-43.

2469
————. "The Waltham System and the Coming of the Irish." *Labor History* 8(1967):227-53.

2470
Glass, Judith Chanin. "Organization in Salinas." *Monthly Labor Review* 91(1968):24-27.

2471
Glazer, Sidney. "The Michigan Labor Movement." *Michigan History* 29(1945):73-82.

2472
Greene, Victor R. "A Study of Slavs, Strikes and Unions: The Anthracite Strike of 1897." *Pennsylvania History* 31(1964):199-215.

2473
————. "The Poles and Anthracite Unions in Pennsylvania." *Polish American Studies* 22(1965):10-16.

2474
Griffin, J. David. "Medical Assistance for the Sick Poor in Ante-Bellum Savannah." *Georgia Historical Quarterly* 53(1969):463-69.

2475
Grogan, Dennis S. "Unionization in Boulder and Weld Counties to 1890." *Colorado Magazine* 44(1967):324-41.

2476
Gutfeld, Arnon. "The Speculator Disaster in 1917: Labor Resurgence at Butte, Montana." *Arizona and the West* 11(1969):27-38.

2477
————. "The Murder of Frank Little: Radical Labor Agitation in Butte, Montana, 1917." *Labor History* 10(1969):177-92.

2478
Gutman, Herbert G. "Reconstruction in Ohio: Negroes in the Hocking Valley Coal Mines in 1873 and 1874." *Labor History* 3(1962):243-64.

2479
————. "The Tompkins Square 'Riot' in New York City on January 13, 1874: A Reexamination of Its Causes and Its Aftermath." *Labor History* 6(1965):44-70.

2480

—————. "Black Coal Miners and the Greenback-Labor Party in Redeemer, Alabama: 1878-1879. The Letters of Warren D. Kelley, Willis Johnson Thomas, 'Dawson,' and Others." *Labor History* 10(1969):506-35.

2481

Hadcock, Editha. "Labor Problems in the Rhode Island Cotton Mills—1790-1940." *Rhode Island History* 14(July 1955): p. 82; (October 1955):110-19.

2482

Halich, Wasyl. "Ukrainians in Western Pennsylvania." *Western Pennsylvania Historical Magazine* 18(1935):139-46.

2483

Hall, John Philip. "The Knights of St. Crispin in Massachusetts, 1869-1878." *Journal of Economic History* 18(1958):161-75.

2484

Harding, Leonard. "The Cincinnati Riots of 1862." *Cincinnati Historical Society Bulletin* 25(1967):229-39.

2485

Harris, Sheldon H. "Letters from West Virginia: Management's Version of the 1902 Coal Strike." *Labor History* 10(1969):229-40.

2486

Harvey, Katherine A. "The Knights of Labor in the Maryland Coal Fields, 1878-1882." *Labor History* 10(1969):555-83.

2487

Haynes, John E. "Revolt of the Timber Beasts: IWW Strike in Minnesota." *Minnesota History* 42(1971):162-74.

2488

Heath, Frederick M. "Labor and the Progressive Movement in Connecticut." *Labor History* 12(1971):52-67.

2489

Henry, H.M. "The Slave Laws of Tennessee." *Tennessee Historical Quarterly, 1st series* 2(1916):175-203.

2490

Henwood, James N.J. "Experiment in Relief: The Civil Works Administration in Pennsylvania." *Pennsylvania History* 39(1972):50-71.

2491

Herron, Robert. "The Police Strike of 1918." *Bulletin of the Historical and Philosophical Society of Ohio* 17(1959):181-94.

2492

Hiestand, Dale L. "Equal Employment in New York City." In *Equal Employment Opportunity: Comparative Community Experience. Industrial Relations* 9(1970)294-307.

2493

Hinckley, Ted C. "Prospectors, Profits & Prejudice." *American West* 2(1965):58-65.

2494
Hogg, J. Bernard. "Public Reaction to Pinkertonism and the Labor Question." *Pennsylvania History* 11(1944):171-99.

2495
Hoogenboom, Ari. "Pennsylvania in the Civil Service Reform Movement." *Pennsylvania History* 28(1961):268-78.

2496
Hooper, Osman C. "The Coxey Movement in Ohio." *Ohio Historical Quarterly* 9(1900):155-76.

2497
Hopkins, Richard J. "Occupational and Geographic Mobility in Atlanta, 1870-1896." *Journal of Southern History* 34(1968):200-213.

2498
House, Albert V., Jr. "A Reconstruction Share-Cropper Contract on a Georgia Rice Plantation." *Georgia Historical Quarterly* 26(1942):156-65.

2499
————. "Labor Management Problems on Georgia Rice Plantations, 1840-1860." *Agricultural History* 28(1954):149-55.

2500
Hutson, A.C., Jr. "The Overthrow of the Convict Lease System in Tennessee." *East Tennessee Historical Society's Publications* 8(1936):82-103.

2501
Ingham, John N. "A Strike in the Progressive Era: McKees Rocks, 1909." *Pennsylvania Magazine of History and Biography* 90(1966):353-77.

2502
Jervey, Theodore. D. "The White Identured Servants of South Carolina." *South Carolina Historical Magazine* 12(1911):163-71.

2503
Johnson, James P. "Reorganizing the United Mine Workers of America in Pennsylvania during the New Deal." *Pennsylvania History* 37(1970):117-32.

2504
Johnston, Esther. "A Square Mile of New York." *New York Public Library Bulletin* 70(1966):425-36.

2505
Jolley, Harley E. "The Labor Movement in North Carolina, 1880-1922." *North Carolina Historical Review* 30(1953):354-75.

2506
Jonas, Manfred. "Wages in Early Colonial Maryland." *Maryland Historical Magazine* 51(1956):27-38.

2507
Jones, Alton DuMar. "The Child Labor Reform Movement in Georgia." *Georgia Historical Quarterly* 49(1965):396-417.

2508
Jones, Lamar B. "Labor and Management in California Agriculture, 1864-1964." *Labor History* 11(1970):23-40.

2509
Jordan, Weymouth T. "The Management Rules of an Alabama Black Belt Plantation, 1848-1862." *Agricultural History* 18(1944):53-64.

2510
Karlin, Jules Alexander. "The Anti-Chinese Outbreak in Tacoma, 1885." *Pacific Historical Review* 23(1954):271-83.

2511
Karman, Thomas. "The Flint Sit-Down Strike." *Michigan History* 46(June 1962):97-125; (September 1962):223-50.

2512
Katzman, David M. "Ann Arbor: Depression City." *Michigan History* 50(1966):306-17.

2513
Kauer, Ralph. "The Workingmen's Party of California." *Pacific Historical Review* 13(1944):278-91.

2514
Keiser, John H. "The Union Miners Cemetery at Mt. Olive, Illinois—a Spirit-Thread of Labor History." *Illinois State Historical Society Journal* 62(1969):229-66.

2515
Kellogg, Miner K. "Miner K. Kellogg: Recollections of New Harmony," edited by Lorna Lutes Sylvester. *Indiana Magazine of History* 64(1968):39-64.

2516
Kerr, Thomas J. IV. "The New York Factory Investigating Commission and the Minimum-Wage Movement." *Labor History* 12(1971):373-91.

2517
Kolehmainen, John Ilmari. "The Finnish Pioneers of Minnesota." *Minnesota History* 25(1944):317-28.

2518
Kuritz, Hyman. "Criminal Conspiracy Cases in Post-Bellum Pennsylvania." *Pennsylvania History* 17(1950):292-301.

2519
Larner, John Williams, Jr. "The Glass House Boys: Child Labor Conditions in Pittsburgh's Glass Factories, 1890-1917." *Western Pennsylvania Historical Magazine* 48(1965):355-64.

2520
Leab, Daniel J. "Toward Unionization: The Newark Ledger Strike of 1934-35." *Labor History* 11(1970):3-22.

2521
LeWarne, Charles P. "Equality Colony: The Plan to Socialize Washington." *Pacific Northwest Quarterly* 59(1968):137-46.

2522
Lindquist, John H. "The Jerome Deportation of 1917." *Arizona and the West* 11(1969):233-46.

2523
———————, and Fraser, James. "A Sociological Interpretation of the Bisbee Deportation." *Pacific Historical Review* 38(1968):401-22.

2524
Long, Durward. " 'La Resistencia': Tampa's Immigrant Labor Union." *Labor History* 6(1965):193-213.

2525
———————. "The Open-Closed Shop Battle in Tampa's Cigar Industry, 1919-1921." *Florida Historical Quarterly* 47(1968):101-21.

2526
———————. "Labor Relations in the Tampa Cigar Industry, 1885-1911." *Labor History* 12(1971):551-59.

2527
Lonsdale, David L. "The Fight for an Eight-Hour Day." *Colorado Magazine* 43(1968):339-53.

2528
Low, W.A. "The Freedmen's Bureau and Civil Rights in Maryland." *Journal of Negro History* 37(1952):221-47.

2529
Lynd, Staughton. "The Mechanics in New York Politics, 1774-1788." *Labor History* 5(1964):225-46.

2530
Lyons, Richard L. "The Boston Police Strike of 1919." *New England Quarterly* 20(1947):147-68.

2531
Lyons, Schley R. "The Labor Press and Its Audience: The Case of the Toledo *Union Journal.*" *Journalism Quarterly* 46(1969):558-64.

2532
McClelland, John M., Jr. "Terror on Tower Avenue." *Pacific Northwest Quarterly* 57(1966):65-72.

2533
McClurg, Donald J. "The Colorado Coal Strike of 1927–Tactical Leadership of the IWW." *Labor History* 4(1963):68-69.

2534
McDougle, Ivan E. "Slavery in Kentucky." *Journal of Negro History* 3(1918):211-328.

2535
McKee, Samuel, Jr. "Indentured Servitude in Colonial New York." *New York History* 12(1931):149-59.

2536
McKelvey, Blake. "The Germans of Rochester: Their Traditions and Contribution." *Rochester History* 20(1958):1-28.

2537

—————. "The Italians of Rochester: An Historical Review." *Rochester History* 22(1960):1-24.

2538

Mackey, Howard. "The Operation of the English Old Poor Law in Colonial Virginia." *Virginia Magazine of History and Biography* 72(1965):29-40.

2539

McLaughlin, Francis M. "The Development of Labor Peace in the Port of Boston." *Industrial and Labor Relations Review* 20(1967):221-33.

2540

McMurry, Donald L. "Labor Policies of the General Managers' Association of Chicago, 1886-1894." *Journal of Economic History* 13(1953):160-78.

2541

Malcolm, Roy. "Anti-Japanese Legislation in California, and the Naturalization of the Japanese." *Historical Society of Southern California* 9(1912-1914):97-103.

2542

Manfredini, Dolores M. "The Italians Come to Herrin." *Journal of the Illinois State Historical Society* 37(1944):317-28.

2543

Marchbin, Andrew A. "Hungarian Activities in Western Pennsylvania." *Western Pennsylvania Historical Magazine* 23(1940):163-74.

2544

Marsden, K. Gerald. "Patriotic Societies and American Labor: The American Protective Association in Wisconsin." *Wisconsin Magazine of History* 41(1958):287-94.

2545

Marshall, F. Ray, and Jones, Lamar B. "Agricultural Unions in Louisiana." *Labor History* 3(1962):287-306.

2546

—————. and Van Adams, Arvil. "Negro Employment in Memphis." In *Equal Employment Opportunity: Comparative Community Experience. Industrial Relations* 9(1970):308-23.

2547

Marshall, Thomas Maitland. "The Miners' Laws of Colorado." *American Historical Review* 25(1920):426-39.

2548

May, J. Thomas. "The Freedmen's Bureau at the Local Level: A Study of a Louisiana Agent." *Louisiana History* 9(1968):5-19.

2549

Meredith, H.L. "Agrarian Socialism and the Negro in Oklahoma, 1900-1918." *Labor History* 11(1970):277-84.

2550

Merriam, H.G. "Ethnic Settlement of Montana." *Pacific Historical Review* 12(1943):157-68.

2551
Miller, Glenn W., and Ware, Stephen B. "Organized Labor in the Political Process: A Case Study of the Right-to-Work Campaign in Ohio." *Labor History* 4(1963):51-67.

2552
Mohl, Raymond A. "Poverty in Early America, a Reappraisal: The Case of Eighteenth-Century New York City." *New York History* 50(1969):4-27.

2553
————. "Poverty, Politics, and the Mechanics of New York City, 1803." *Labor History* 12(1971):38-51.

2554
Montgomery, David. "The Working Classes of the Pre-Industrial American City, 1780-1830." *Labor History* 9(1968):3-22.

2555
Moody, V. Alton. "Slavery on Louisiana Sugar Plantations." *Louisiana Historical Quarterly* 7(1924):191-301.

2556
Moore, Michael A. "A Community's Crisis: Hillsdale and the Essex Wire Strike." *Indiana Magazine of History* 66(1970):238-62.

2557
Morefield, Richard Henry. "Mexicans in the California Mines, 1848-1853." *California Historical Society Quarterly* 35(1956):37-46.

2558
Morris, Richard B. "White Bondage in Ante-Bellum South Carolina." *South Carolina Historical Magazine* 49(1948):191-207.

2559
————. "Labor Controls in Maryland in the Nineteenth Century." *Journal of Southern History* 14(1948):385-400.

2560
————, and Grossman, Jonathan. "The Regulation of Wages in Early Massachusetts." *New England Quarterly* 11(1938):470-500.

2561
Murray, Robert K. "Communism and the Great Steel Strike of 1919." *Mississippi Valley Historical Review* 38(1951):445-66.

2562
Nadworny, Milton J. "New Jersey Workingmen and the Jacksonians." *New Jersey Historical Society Proceedings* 67(1949):185-98.

2563
Nelson, Daniel. "The Origins of Unemployment Insurance in Wisconsin." *Wisconsin Magazine of History* 51(1968):109-21.

2564
Nelson, Earl J. "Missouri Slavery, 1861-1865." *Missouri Historical Review* 28(1934):260-74.

2565

Newman, Philip. "The First IWW Invasion of New Jersey." *New Jersey Historical Society Proceedings* 58(1940):268-83.

2566

Nolen, Russell M. "The Labor Movement in St. Louis prior to the Civil War." *Missouri Historical Review* 34(1939):18-37.

2567

————. "The Labor Movement in St. Louis from 1860 to 1890." *Missouri Historical Review* 34(1940):157-81.

2568

Olin, Spencer C., Jr. "European Immigrant and Oriental Alien: Acceptance and Rejection by the California Legislature of 1913." *Pacific Historical Review* 35(1966):303-15.

2569

Olson, Frederick I. "The Socialist Party and the Union in Milwaukee." *Wisconsin Magazine of History* 44(Winter 1960-1961):110-16.

2570

Osofsky, Gilbert. "A Decade of Urban Tragedy: How Harlem Became a Slum." *New York History* 46(1965):330-55.

2571

Ourada, Patricia K. "The Chinese in Colorado." *Colorado Magazine* 29(1952):273-84.

2572

Padgett, James A. "The Status of Slaves in Colonial North Carolina." *Journal of Negro History* 14(1929):300-27.

2573

Pahl, Thomas L. "G-string Conspiracy, Political Reprisal or Armed Revolt? The Minneapolis Trotskyite Trial." *Labor History* 8(1967):30-51.

2574

Palickar, Stephen J. "The Slovaks of Chicago." *Mid-America* 4(1921):180-96.

2575

Palmer, Paul C. "Servant into Slave: The Evolution of the Legal Status of the Negro Laborer in Colonial Virginia." *South Atlantic Quarterly* 65(1966):355-70.

2576

Papanikolas, Helen Zeese. "Life and Labor among the Immigrants of Bingham Canyon." *Utah Historical Quarterly* 33(1965):289-314.

2577

Paulson, Peter. "The Tammany Society and the Jeffersonian Movement in New York City, 1795-1800." *New York History* 34(1953):72-84.

2578

Pawar, Sheelwant B. "The Structure and Nature of Labor Unions in Utah, an Historical Perspective, 1890-1920." *Utah Historical Quarterly* 35(1967):236-55.

2579
Perrigo, Lynn I. "Law and Order in Early Colorado Mining Camps." *Mississippi Valley Historical Review* 28(1941):41-62.

2580
Phillips, Ulrich B. "Slave Crime in Virginia." *American Historical Review* 20(1915):336-40.

2581
Picher, Robert L. "The Franco-Americans in Vermont." *Vermont History* 28(1960):59-62.

2582
Pivar, David J. "The Hosiery Workers and the Philadelphia Third Party Impulse." *Labor History* 5(1964):18-28.

2583
Porter, Eugene O. "The Colorado Coal Strike of 1913—an Interpretation." *The Historian* 12(1949):3-27.

2584
Rader, Benjamin G. "The Montana Lumber Strike of 1917." *Pacific Historical Review* 36(1967):189-207.

2585
Rankin, Lois. "Detroit Nationality Groups." *Michigan History* 23(1939):129-205.

2586
Reed, Merl E. "The IWW and Individual Freedom in Western Louisiana, 1913." *Louisiana History* 10(1969):61-69.

2587
————. "Lumberjacks and Longshoremen: The IWW in Louisiana." *Labor History* 13(1972):41-59.

2588
Reese, James V. "The Early History of Labor Organizations in Texas, 1838-1876." *Southwestern Historical Quarterly* 72(1968):1-20.

2589
Reid, Robert D. "The Negro in Alabama during the Civil War." *Journal of Negro History* 35(1950):265-88.

2590
Reinders, Robert C. "The Free Negro in the New Orleans Economy, 1850-1860." *Louisiana History* 6(1965):273-85.

2591
Remigia, Sister M. "The Polish Immigrant in Detroit to 1914." *Polish American Studies* 2(1945):4-11.

2592
Reuss, Carl F. "The Farm Labor Problem in Washington, 1917-18." *Pacific Northwest Quarterly* 34(1943):339-52.

2593
Rhodes, James Ford. "The Molly Maguires in the Anthracite Region of Pennsylvania." *American Historical Review* 15(1910):547-61.

2594
Richardson, Joe M. "The Freedman's Bureau and Negro Labor in Florida." *Florida Historical Quarterly* 39(1960):167-74.

2595
Robinson, Robert M. "San Francisco Teamsters at the Turn of the Century," *California Historical Society Quarterly* 35(March 1956):59-69; (June 1956): 145-53.

2596
Rodgers, William Warren. "Negro Knights of Labor in Arkansas: A Case Study of the 'Miscellaneous' Strike." *Labor History* 10(1969):498-505.

2597
Rowland, Donald. "The United States and the Contract Labor Question in Hawaii, 1862-1900." *Pacific Historical Review* 2(1933):249-69.

2598
Rowley, William D. "The Loup City Riot of 1934: Main Street vs. the 'Far-Out' Left." *Nebraska History* 47(1966):295-327.

2599
Rudolph, Frederick. "Chinamen in Yankeedom: Anti-Unionism in Massachusetts in 1870." *American Historical Review* 53(1947):1-29.

2600
Russell, Francis. "How I Changed My Mind about the Sacco-Vanzetti Case." *Antioch Review* 27(1965):592-607.

2601
Russell, John H. "Colored Freemen as Slave Owners in Virginia." *Journal of Negro History* 1(1916):233-42.

2602
Sandmeyer, Elmer C. "California Anti-Chinese Legislation and the Federal Courts: A Study in Federal Relations." *Pacific Historical Review* 5(1936):189-211.

2603
Saxton, Alexander. "San Francisco Labor and the Populist and Progressive Insurgencies." *Pacific Historical Review* 34(1965):421-38.

2604
Schafer, Joseph. "The Wisconsin Phalanx." *Wisconsin Magazine of History* 19(1936):454-74.

2605
Schmidt, Fred H. "Los Angeles: Show, Little Substance." In *Equal Employment Opportunity: Comparative Community Experience. Industrial Relations* 9(1970):340-55.

2606
Schramm, LeRoy H. "Union Rivalry in Detroit in World War II." *Michigan History* 54(1970):201-15.

2607
Scruggs, Otey M. "Texas and the Bracero Program, 1942-1947." *Pacific Historical Review* 32(1963):251-64.

2608
Shaffer, Ralph E. "Formation of the California Communist Labor Party."
Pacific Historical Review 36(1967):59-78.

2609
Shover, John L. "The Progressives and the Working Class Vote in California."
Labor History 10(1969):584-601.

2610
Shugg, Roger Wallace. "The New Orleans General Strike of 1892." *Louisiana
Historical Quarterly* 21(1938):547-60.

2611
Siebert, Wilbur H. "Slavery and White Servitude in East Florida, 1726 to
1776." *Florida Historical Quarterly* 10(1931):3-23.

2612
————. "Slavery in East Florida, 1776 to 1785." *Florida Historical
Quarterly* 10(1932):139-61.

2613
Siekaniec, L.J. "The Polish Colony of Sioux City." *Polish American Studies*
9(1952):24-27.

2614
Sisk, Glenn Nolen. "Social Classes in the Alabama Black Belt, 1870-1910."
Alabama Historical Quarterly 20(1958):653-55.

2615
Sizer, Samuel A. " 'This is Union Man's Country': Sebastian County, 1914."
Arkansas Historical Quarterly 27(1968):306-29.

2616
Snow, William J. "Utah Indians and Spanish Slave Trade." *Utah Historical
Quarterly* 2(1929):67-90.

2617
Sofchalk, Donald G. "The Chicago Memorial Day Incident: An Episode of
Mass Action." *Labor History* 6(1965):3-43.

2618
————. "Organized Labor and the Iron Ore Miners of Northern
Minnesota, 1907-1936." *Labor History* 12(1971):214-42.

2619
Sollers, Basil. "Transported Convict Laborers in Maryland during the Colonial
Period." *Maryland Historical Magazine* 2(1907):17-47.

2620
Sorrell, Richard S. "Life, Work and Acculturation Patterns of Eastern
European Immigrants in Lackawanna, New York: 1900-1922." *Polish
Review* 14(1969):65-91.

2621
Stahl, Annie Lee West. "The Free Negro in Ante-Bellum Louisiana."
Louisiana Historical Quarterly 25(1942):301-96.

2622
Stavisky, Leonard Price. "Industrialism in Ante-Bellum Charleston." *Journal of Negro History* 36(1951):302-22.

2623
Stealey, John Edmund III. "The Responsibilities and Liabilities of the Bailee of Slave Labor in Virginia." *American Journal of Legal History* 12(1968):336-53.

2624
Stearns, Marjorie R. "The Settlement of the Japanese in Oregon." *Oregon Historical Quarterly* 39(1938):262-69.

2625
Stegner, S. Page. "Protest Songs from the Butte Mines." *Western Folklore* 26(1967):157-67.

2626
Stoveken, Ruth. "The Pine Lumberjacks in Wisconsin." *Wisconsin Magazine of History* 30(1947):322-34.

2627
Stubbs, Jane. "Servant Children in Colonial Virginia." *Virginia Cavalcade* 9(1959):18-23.

2628
Suggs, George G., Jr. "Strike-Breaking in Colorado: Governor James H. Peabody and the Telluride Strike, 1903-1904." *Journal of the West* 5(1966):454-76.

2629
————. "Prelude to Industrial Warfare: The Colorado City Strike." *Colorado Magazine* 44(1967):241-62.

2630
Sullivan, William A. "Philadelphia Labor during the Jackson Era." *Pennsylvania History* 15(1948):305-20.

2631
————. "The Pittsburgh Workingmen's Party." *Western Pennsylvania Historical Magazine* 34(1951):151-61.

2632
————. "The Industrial Revolution and the Factory Operative in Pennsylvania." *Pennsylvania Magazine of History and Biography* 78(1954):476-94.

2633
————. "The 1913 Revolt of the Michigan Copper Miners." *Michigan History* 43(1959):294-314.

2634
Swastek, Joseph. "The Poles in South Bend to 1914." *Polish American Studies* 2(1945):79-88.

2635
Sydnor, Charles S. "The Free Negro in Mississippi before the Civil War." *American Historical Review* 32(1927):769-88.

2636
Taft, Philip. "The Bisbee Deportation." *Labor History* 13(1972):3-40.

2637
Taylor, A.A. "The Negro in South Carolina during the Reconstruction." *Journal of Negro History* 9(July 1924):241-364; (October 1924): 381-569.

2638
————. "The Negro in the Reconstruction of Virginia." *Journal of Negro History* 11(April 1926):243-415; (July 1926):425-537.

2639
Taylor, A. Elizabeth. "The Origin and Development of the Convict Lease System in Georgia." *Georgia Historical Quarterly* 26(1942):113-28.

2640
————. "The Abolition of the Convict Lease System in Georgia." *Georgia Historical Quarterly* 26(1942):273-87.

2641
Taylor, Paul S. "California Farm Labor: A Review." *Agricultural History* 42(1968):49-54.

2642
Thomason, Frank. "The Bellevue Stranglers." *Idaho Yesterdays* 13(1969):26-32.

2643
Trexler, Harrison A. "Slavery in Missouri Territory." *Missouri Historical Review* 3(1909):179-98.

2644
Turner, Edward Raymond. "Slavery in Colonial Pennsylvania." *Pennsylvania Magazine of History and Biography* 35(1911):141-51.

2645
Turner, Ralph V., and Rodgers, William Warren. "Arkansas Labor in Revolt: Little Rock and the Great Southwestern Strike." *Arkansas Historical Quarterly* 24(1965):29-46.

2646
Tuttle, William M., Jr. "Some Strikebreakers' Observations of Industrial Warfare." *Labor History* 7(1966):193-96.

2647
————. "Labor Conflict and Racial Violence: The Black Worker in Chicago, 1894-1919." *Labor History* 10(1969):408-32.

2648
Tyler, Robert L. "The Everett Free Speech Fight." *Pacific Historical Review* 23(1954):19-30.

2649
————. "Violence at Centralia, 1919." *Pacific Northwest Quarterly* 45(1954):116-24.

2650

Venkataramani, M.S. "Norman Thomas, Arkansas Sharecroppers, and the Roosevelt Agricultural Policies, 1933-1937." *Arkansas Historical Quarterly* 24(1965):3-28.

2651

Vucinich, Wayne S. "Yugoslavs in California." *Historical Society of Southern California* 42(1960):287-309.

2652

Walker, Joseph E. "Negro Labor in the Charcoal Industry of Southeastern Pennsylvania." *Pennsylvania Magazine of History and Biography* 93(1969):466-86.

2653

Walker, Kenneth P. "The Pecan Shellers of San Antonio and Mechanization." *Southwestern Historical Quarterly* 69(1965):44-58.

2654

Walz, Robert B. "Arkansas Slaveholdings and Slaveholders in 1850." *Arkansas Historical Quarterly* 12(1953):38-74.

2655

Wargelin, John. "The Finns in Michigan." *Michigan History* 24(1940):179-203.

2656

Wax, Darold D. "The Demand for Slave Labor in Colonial Pennsylvania." *Pennsylvania History* 34(1967):331-45.

2657

Webb, Bernice Larson. "Company Town—Louisiana Style." *Louisiana History* 9(1968):325-39.

2658

Weber, Arnold R. "Paradise Lost; or Whatever Happened to the Chicago Social Workers?" *Industrial and Labor Relations Review* 22(1969):323-38.

2659

Whatley, Larry. "The Works Progress Administration in Mississippi." *Journal of Mississippi History* 30(1968):35-50.

2660

Whisenhunt, Donald W. "The Great Depression in Kentucky: The Early Years." *Kentucky Historical Society Register* 67(1969):55-62.

2661

White, Charles P. "Early Experiments with Prison Labor in Tennessee." *East Tennessee Historical Society Publications* 12(1940):45-69.

2662

Wiebe, Robert H. "The Anthracite Strike of 1902: A Record of Confusion." *Mississippi Valley Historical Review* 48(1961):229-51.

2663

Wilcox, B.P. "Anti-Chinese Riots in Washington." *Pacific Northwest Quarterly* 20(1929):204-12.

2664
Williams, Edwin L., Jr. "Negro Slavery in Florida." *Florida Historical Quarterly* 28(October 1949):93-110; (January 1950):182-204.

2665
Wilson, Charles Jay. "The Negro in Early Ohio." *Ohio Historical Quarterly* 39(1930):717-68.

2666
Witte, Edwin E. "Labor in Wisconsin History." *Wisconsin Magazine of History* 35(1951): p. 83.

2667
Wollenberg, Charles. "*Huelga,* 1928 Style: The Imperial Valley Cantaloupe Workers' Strike." *Pacific Historical Review* 38(1969):45-58.

2668
Worthman, Paul B. "Black Workers and Labor Unions in Birmingham, Alabama, 1897-1904." *Labor History* 10(1969):375-407.

2669
Young, Alfred. "The Mechanics and the Jeffersonians: New York, 1789-1801." *Labor History* 5(1964):247-76.

2670
Zeiger, Robert H. "Robin Hood in the Silk City: The IWW and the Patterson Silk Strike of 1913." *New Jersey Historical Society Proceedings* 84(1966):182-95.

2671
————. "Pennsylvania Coal and Politics: The Anthracite Strike of 1925-1926." *Pennsylvania Magazine of History and Biography* 92(1969):244-62.

2672
Zimmerman, Jane. "The Convict Lease System in Arkansas and the Fight for Abolition." *Arkansas Historical Quarterly* 8(1949):171-88.

Individual Unions, Companies and Occupations

2673
Appel, John C. "The Unionization of Florida Cigarmakers and the Coming of the War with Spain." *Hispanic American Historical Review* 36(1956):38-49.

2674
Auerbach, Jerold S. "Progressives at Sea: The La Follette Act of 1915." *Labor History* 2(1961):344-60.

2675
Aurand, Harold W. "The Anthracite Strike of 1887-1888." *Pennsylvania History* 35(1968):169-85.

2676

Baird, William M. "Barriers to Collective Bargaining in Registered Nursing."
Labor Law Journal 20(1969):42-46.

2677

Barbash, Jack. "The ILGWU as an Organization in the Age of Dubinsky."
Labor History, Spec. Suppl. 9(1968):98-115.

2678

Bayard, Charles J. "The 1927-1928 Colorado Coal Strike." *Pacific Historical
Review* 32(1963):235-50.

2679

Bechtol, Paul T., Jr. "The 1880 Labor Dispute in Leadville." *Colorado
Magazine* 47(1970):312-25.

2680

Beck, William. "Law and Order during the 1913 Copper Strike." *Michigan
History* 54(1970):275-92.

2681

Bell Daniel. "Jewish Labor History." *Publication of the American Jewish
Historical Society* 46(1957):257-60.

2682

Belote, Martha. "Nurses Are Making It Happen." *American Journal of
Nursing* 67(1967):285-88.

2683

Bernstein, Barton J. "Walter Reuther and the General Motors Strike of
1945-1946." *Michigan History* 49(1965):260-77.

2684

Berthoff, Rowland. "The Social Order of the Anthracite Region,
1825-1902." *Pennsylvania Magazine of History and Biography*
89(1965):261-91.

2685

Betten, Neil. "Strike on the Mesabi—1907." *Minnesota History*
40(1967):340-47.

2686

————. "Riot, Revolution, Repression, in the Iron Range Strike of
1916." *Minnesota History* 41(1968):82-93.

2687

Bining, Arthur Cecil. "The Iron Plantations of Early Pennsylvania." *Pennsylvania Magazine of History and Biography* 57(1933):117-37.

2688

Blaine, Harry R., and Zeller, Frederick A. "Who Uses the UAW Public Review
Board?" *Industrial Relations* 4(1965):95-104.

2689

Blantz, Thomas E., C.S.C. "Father Haas and the Minneapolis Truckers Strike
of 1934." *Minnesota History* 42(1970):5-15.

2690
Brandfon, Robert L. "The End of Immigration to the Cotton Fields."
   Mississippi Valley Historical Review 50(1964):591-611.

2691
Brinks, Herbert J. "Marquette Iron Range Strike, 1895." *Michigan History*
   50(1966):293-305.

2692
Briggs, Vernon M. "The Strike Insurance Plan of the Railroad Industry."
   Industrial Relations 6(1967):205-12.

2693
Brooks, Harold C. "Story of the Founding of the Brotherhood of Locomotive
   Engineers." *Michigan History* 27(1943):611-19.

2694
Brooks, Tom "The Terrible Triangle Fire." *American Heritage*
   8(1957): p. 54.

2695
Brown, Giles T. "The West Coast Phase of the Maritime Strike of 1921."
   Pacific Historical Review 19(1950):385-96.

2696
Brown, Martha A. "Collective Bargaining on the Campus: Professors,
   Associations and Unions." *Labor Law Journal* 21(1970):167-81.

2697
Bruce, Kathleen. "Slave Labor in the Virginia Iron Industry," *William and
   Mary Quarterly* 6(1926):289-302; 7(1927):21-31.

2698
Bubka, Tony. "The Harlan County Coal Strike of 1931." *Labor History*
   11(1970):41-57.

2699
Cantor, Louis. "A Prologue to the Protest Movement: The Missouri
   Sharecropper Roadside Demonstration of 1939." *Journal of American
   History* 55(1969):804-22.

2700
Carlisle, Rodney. "William Randolph Hearst's Reaction to the American
   Newspaper Guild: A Challenge to New Deal Labor Legislation." *Labor
   History* 10(1969):74-99.

2701
Cook, Philip L. "Tom M. Girdler and the Labor Policies of Republic Steel
   Corporation." *Social Science* 42(1967):21-30.

2702
Cox, LaWanda F. "The American Agricultural Wage Earner, 1865-1900: The
   Emergence of a Modern Labor Problem." *Agricultural History*
   22(1948):95-114.

2703
Craft, James A. "Fire Fighter Militancy and Wage Disparity." *Labor Law
   Journal* 21(1970):794-806.

2704
Cravens, John N. "Two Miners and Their Families in the Thurber-Strawn Coal Mines, 1905-1918." *West Texas Historical Association Year Book* 45(1969):115-26.

2705
David, Henry. "The Jewish Unions and Their Influence upon the American Labor Movement." *Publication of the American Jewish Historical Society* 41(1952):339-45.

2706
————. "Jewish Labor History: A Problem Paper," *Publication of the American Jewish Historical Society* 46(1957):215-20.

2707
Davis, Allen F. "The Women's Trade Union League: Origins and Organization." *Labor History* 5(1964):3-17.

2708
DuFault, David V. "The Chinese in the Mining Camps of California: 1848-1870." *Historical Society of Southern California* 41(1959):155-70.

2709
Dvorak, Eldon J. "Will Engineers Unionize?" *Industrial Relations* 2(1963):45-65.

2710
Dyson, Lowell K. "Radical Farm Organizations and Periodicals in America, 1920-1960." *Agricultural History* 45(1971):111-20.

2711
Eisner, J.M. "Politics, Legislation, and the ILGWU." *American Journal of Economics and Sociology* 28(1969):301-14.

2712
Elliott, Russell R. "Labor Troubles in the Mining Camp at Goldfield, Nevada, 1906-1908." *Pacific Historical Review* 19(1950):369-84.

2713
Erenburg, Mark. "Obreros Unidos in Wisconsin." *Monthly Labor Review* 91(1968):17-23.

2714
Estey, Marten. "The Grocery Clerks: Center of Retail Unionism." *Industrial Relations* 7(1968):249-61.

2715
Fenton, Edwin. "Italian Immigrants in the Stoneworkers' Union." *Labor History* 3(1962):188-207.

2716
Ferguson, Tracy H. "Collective Bargaining in Universities and Colleges." *Labor Law Journal* 19(1968):778-804.

2717
Fine, Sidney. "The Origins of the United Automobile Workers, 1933-1935." *Journal of Economic History* 18(1958):249-82.

2718
————. "The Ford Motor Company and the NRA." *Business History Review* 32(1958):353-85.

2719
————. "The Toledo Chevrolet Strike of 1935." *Ohio Historical Quarterly* 67(1958):326-56.

2720
————. "The General Motors Sit-Down Strike: A Reexamination." *American Historical Review* 70(1965):691-713.

2721
Fogel, Walter. "Blacks in Meatpacking: Another View of the Jungle." *Industrial Relations* 10(1971):338-53.

2722
Gallaway, Lowell E. "The Origin and Early Years of the Federation of Flat Glass Workers of America." *Labor History* 3(1962):92-102.

2723
Garbarino, Joseph W. "Precarious Professors: New Patterns of Representation." *Industrial Relations* 10(1971):1-20.

2724
Garraty, John A. "The United States Steel Corporation versus Labor: The Early Years." *Labor History* 1(1960):3-38.

2725
Gilmore, N. Ray, and Gilmore, Gladys W. "The Bracero in California." *Pacific Historical Review* 32(1963):265-82.

2726
Gitelman, Howard M. "The Labor Force at Waltham Watch during the Civil War Era." *Journal of Economic History* 25(1965):214-43.

2727
Glass, Judith Chanin. "Organization in Salinas." *Monthly Labor Review* 90(1968):24-27.

2728
Glass, Ronald W. "Work Stoppages and Teachers: History and Prospect." *Monthly Labor Review* 90 (1967):43-46.

2729
Goldberg, Joseph P. "Containerization as a Force for Change on the Waterfront." *Monthly Labor Review* 91(1968):8-13.

2730
Gomberg, William. "Union Policy Experimentation in a Volatile Industry." *Labor History,* Spec. Suppl. 9(1968):69-81.

2731
Green, Archie. "A Discography of American Coal Miners' Songs." *Labor History* 2(1961):101-15.

2732

Green, Fletcher M. "Gold Mining in Ante-Bellum Virginia." *Virginia Magazine of History and Biography* 45(July 1937):227-35; (October 1937): 357-66.

2733

Greene, Lorenzo J., ed. "Negro Sharecroppers." *Negro History Bulletin* 31(1968):17-19.

2734

Greene, Victor R. " A Study in Slavs, Strikes and Unions: The Anthracite Strike of 1897." *Pennsylvania History* 31(1964):199-215.

2735

————. "The Poles and Anthracite Unions in Pennsylvania." *Polish American Studies* 22(1965):10-16.

2736

Griffin, Richard W. "Poor White Laborers in Southern Cotton Factories, 1789-1865." *South Carolina Historical Magazine* 61(1960):26-40.

2737

Gross, James A. "The Making and Shaping of Unionism in the Pulp and Paper Industry." *Labor History* 5(1964):183-208.

2738

Grossman, Jonathan. "The Molders' Struggle against Contract Prison Labor." *New York History* 23(1942):449-57.

2739

Grubbs, Donald H. "Gardner Jackson, that 'Socialist' Tenant Farmers' Union, and the New Deal." *Agricultural History* 42(1968):125-37.

2740

Guimary, Donald L. "Strike-Born Newspapers." *Journalism Quarterly* 46(1969):594-97.

2741

Gutman, Herbert G. "Trouble on the Railroads in 1873-1874: Prelude to the 1877 Crisis?" *Labor History* 2(1961):215-35.

2742

————. "Documents on Negro Seamen during the Reconstruction Period." *Labor History* 7(1966):307-11.

2743

Hadcock, Editha. "Labor Problems in the Rhode Island Cotton Mills— 1790-1940." *Rhode Island History* 14(July 1955): p. 82; (October 1955):110-19.

2744

Hardman, Jacob B.S. "John L. Lewis, Labor Leader and Man: An Interpretation." *Labor History* 2(1961):3-29.

2745

————. "David Dubinsky, Labor Leader and Man." *Labor History*, Spec. Suppl. 9(1968):43-54.

2746
Harris, Sheldon H. "Letters from West Virginia: Management's Version of the 1902 Coal Strike." *Labor History* 10(1969):229-40.

2747
Hawley, Ellis W. "The Politics of the Mexican Labor Issue, 1950-1965." *Agricultural History* 40(1966):157-76.

2748
————. "Secretary Hoover and the Bituminous Coal Problem, 1921-1928." *Business History Review* 42(1968):247-70.

2749
Haynes, John E. "Revolt of the Timber Beasts: IWW Strike in Minnesota." *Minnesota History* 42(1971):162-74.

2750
Helfgott, Roy B. "Trade Unionism among the Jewish Garment Workers of Britain and the United States." *Labor History* 2(1961):202-14.

2751
Hinckley, Ted C. "Prospectors, Profits & Prejudice." *American West* 2(1965):58-65.

2752
Hoogenboom, Ari. "Pennsylvania in the Civil Service Reform Movement." *Pennsylvania History* 28(1961):268-78.

2753
————. "Thomas A. Jenckes and Civil Service Reform." *Mississippi Valley Historical Review* 47(1961):636-58.

2754
Ingerman, Sidney. "Employed Graduate Students Organize at Berkeley." In *Professional and White-Collar Unionism: An International Comparison. Industrial Relations* 5(1965):141-50.

2755
James, Ralph C., and James Estelle. "Hoffa's Manipulation of Pension Benefits." *Industrial Relations* 4(1965):46-60.

2756
————. "The Purge of the Trotskyites from the Teamsters." *Western Political Quarterly* 19(1966):5-15.

2757
Johnson, James P. "Reorganizing the United Mine Workers of America in Pennsylvania during the New Deal." *Pennsylvania History* 37(1970):117-32.

2758
Jones, Lamar B. "Labor and Management in California Agriculture, 1864-1964." *Labor History* 11(1970):23-40.

2759
Juris, Hervey A., and Hutchison, Kay B. "The Legal Status of Municipal Police Employee Organizations." *Industrial and Labor Relations Review* 23(1970):352-66.

2760
Karman, Thomas. "The Flint Sit-Down Strike." *Michigan History* 46(June 1962):97-125; (September 1962):223-50.

2761
Kaufman, Jacob J. "The Railroad Labor Dispute [1959-1964]: A Marathon of Maneuver and Improvisation." *Industrial and Labor Relations Review* 18(1965):196-212.

2762
Keppel, Ann M. "Civil Disobedience on the Mining Frontier." *Wisconsin Magazine of History* 41(1958):185-95.

2763
Kienast, Philip. "Extended Leisure for Blue-Collar Workers: A Look at the Steelworker's Extended Vacation Program." *Labor Law Journal* 20(1969):641-48.

2764
Kleingartner, Archie. "Professional and Engineering Unionism." *Industrial Relations* 8(1969):224-35.

2765
Kleinsorge, Paul L., and Kerby, William C. "The Pulp and Paper Rebellion: A New Pacific Coast Union." *Industrial Relations* 6(1966):1-20.

2766
Kraus, George. "Chinese Laborers and the Construction of the Central Pacific." *Utah Historical Quarterly* 37(1969):41-57.

2767
Langley, Harold D. "The Negro in the Navy and Merchant Service— 1789-1860." *Journal of Negro History* 52(1967):273-86.

2768
Larrowe, Charles P. "A Meteor on the Industrial Relations Horizon: The Foreman's Association of America." *Labor History* 2(1961):259-94.

2769
——————. "The Great Maritime Strike of '34: Part I." *Labor History* 11(1970):403-51.

2770
——————. "The Great Maritime Strike of '34: Part II." *Labor History* 12(1971):3-37.

2771
Leab, Daniel J. "The Memorial Day Massacre." *Midcontinent American Studies Journal* 8(1967):3-17.

2772
——————. "Toward Unionization: The Newark Ledger Strike of 1934-35." *Labor History* 11(1970):3-22.

2773
Lemisch, Jesse. "Jack Tar in the Streets: Merchant Seamen in the Politics of Revolutionary America." *William and Mary Quarterly, 3rd Series* 25(1968):371-407.

2774

—————. "Listening to the 'Inarticulate': William Widger's Dream and the Loyalties of American Revolutionary Seamen in British Prisons." *Journal of Social History* 3(1969):1-29.

2775

Levine, Marvin J. "The Railroad Crew Size Controversy Revisited." *Labor Law Journal* 20(1969):373-85.

2776

Lewis, Doris K. "Union-Sponsored Middle-Income Housing: 1927-65." *Monthly Labor Review* 88(1965):629-36.

2777

Long, Durward. "The Open-Closed Shop Battle in Tampa's Cigar Industry, 1919-1921." *Florida Historical Quarterly* 47(1968):101-21.

2778

—————. "Labor Relations in the Tampa Cigar Industry, 1885-1911." *Labor History* 12(1971):551-59.

2779

Lyons, Richard L. "The Boston Police Strike of 1919." *New England Quarterly* 20(1947):147-68.

2780

Maddala, G.S. "Productivity and Technological Change in the Bituminous Coal Industry, 1919-1954." *Journal of Political Economy* 73(1965):352-65.

2781

Mangum, Garth. "The Development of Local Union Jurisdiction in the International Union of Operating Engineers." *Labor History* 4(1963):257-72.

2782

Marshall, F. Ray, and Jones, Lamar B. "Agricultural Unions in Louisiana." *Labor History* 3(1962):287-306.

2783

Mayer, Thomas. "Some Characteristics of Union Members in the 1880s and 1890s." *Labor History* 5(1964):57-66.

2784

Moberly, Robert B. "Causes of Impasse in School Board-Teacher Negotiations." *Labor Law Journal* 21(1970):668-77.

2785

Moody, V. Alton. "Slavery on Louisiana Sugar Plantations." *Louisiana Historical Quarterly* 7(1924):191-301.

2786

Moore, Michael A. "A Community's Crisis: Hillsdale and the Essex Wire Strike." *Indiana Magazine of History* 66(1970):238-62.

2787

Morefield, Richard Henry. "Mexicans in the California Mines, 1848-1853." *California Historical Society Quarterly* 35(1956):37-46.

2788

Muir, J. Douglas. "The Strike as a Professional Sanction: The Changing Attitude of the National Education Association." *Labor Law Journal* 19(1968):615-27.

2789

Nelson, Daniel. " 'While Waiting for the Government': The Needle Trades Unemployment Insurance Plans." *Labor History* 12(1970):482-99.

2790

Munts, Raymond, and Munts, Mary Louise. "Welfare History of the ILGWU." *Labor History*, Spec. Suppl. 9(1968):82-97.

2791

Myers, Robert J. "The Mine Workers' Welfare and Retirement Fund: Fifteen Years' Experience." *Industrial and Labor Relations Review* 20(1967):265-74.

2792

Nelligan, John E. "The Life of a Lumberman." With Charles M. Sheridan. *Wisconsin Magazine of History* 13(September 1929):3-65; (December 1929):131-85; (March 1930):241-304.

2793

Norton, Nancy P. "Labor in the Early New England Carpet Industry." *Business History Review* 26(1952):19-26.

2794

Olson, Frederick I. "The Socialist Party and the Union in Milwaukee." *Wisconsin Magazine of History* 44(Winter 1960-1961):110-16.

2795

Orr, John A. "The Steelworker Election of 1965—the Reasons for the Upset." *Labor Law Journal* 20(1969):100-112.

2796

Ozanne, Robert. "Union-Management Relations: McCormick Harvesting Machine Company, 1862-1886." *Labor History* 4(1963):132-60.

2797

Pahl, Thomas L. "G-string Conspiracy, Political Reprisal or Armed Revolt? The Minneapolis Trotskyite Trial." *Labor History* 8(1967):30-51.

2798

Pawa, Jay M. "The 'Jefferson Borden' Pirates and Samuel Gompers: Aftermath of a Mutiny." *American Neptune* 27(1967):46-60.

2799

Perlman, Selig. "Jewish-American Unionism, Its Birth Pangs and Contribution to the General American Labor Movement." *Publication of the American Jewish Historical Society* 41(1952):297-337.

2800

——————. "America and the Jewish Labor Movement: A Case of Mutual Illumination." *Publication of the American Jewish Historical Society* 46(1957):221-32.

2801
Perrigo, Lynn I. "Law and Order in Early Colorado Mining Camps."
   Mississippi Valley Historical Review 28(1941):41-62.

2802
Pivar, David J. "The Hosiery Workers and the Philadelphia Third Party
   Impulse." *Labor History* 5(1964):18-28.

2803
Pope, Norma, and Brinker, Paul A. "Recent Developments with the
   Guaranteed Annual Wage: The Ford Settlement." *Labor Law Journal*
   19(1968):555-62.

2804
Porter, Eugene O. "The Colorado Coal Strike of 1913—an Interpretation."
   The Historian 12(1949):3-27.

2805
Porter, Kenneth W. "Negro Labor in the Western Cattle Industry,
   1866-1900." *Labor History* 10(1969):346-74.

2806
Prickett, James R. "Communism and Factionalism in the United Automobile
   Workers, 1939-1947." *Science and Society* 32(1968):257-77.

2807
Purrington, Philip F. "Anatomy of a Mutiny." *American Neptune*
   27(1967):98-110.

2808
Raskin, A.H. "Dubinsky: Herald of Change." *Labor History,* Spec. Suppl.
   9(1968):14-25.

2809
Reed, Merl E. "Lumberjacks and Longshoremen: The IWW in Louisiana."
   Labor History 13(1972):41-59.

2810
Reich, Nathan. "Some Observations on Jewish Unionism." *Publication of the
   American Jewish Historical Society* 41(1952):347-55.

2811
Repas, Robert. "History of the Christian Labor Association." *Labor History*
   5(1964):168-82.

2812
Reuss, Carl F. "The Farm Labor Problem in Washington, 1917-18." *Pacific
   Northwest Quarterly* 34(1943):339-52.

2813
Reynolds, Robert L. "The Coal Kings Come to Judgment." *American
   Heritage* 11(1960): p. 55.

2814
Rezler, Julius. "Labor Organization at Du Pont: A Study in Independent
   Local Unionism." *Labor History* 4(1963):178-95.

2815
Rich, J.C. "David Dubinsky: The Young Years." *Labor History,* Spec. Suppl.
   9(1968):5-13.

2816
Robinson, Robert M. "San Francisco Teamsters at the Turn of the Century." *California Historical Society Quarterly* 35(March 1956):59-69; (June 1956):145-53.

2817
Ross, Philip. "Distribution of Power within the ILWU and the ILA." *Monthly Labor Review* 91(1968):1-7.

2818
———. "The Teamsters' Response to Technological Change: The Case of Piggybacking." *Labor Law Journal* 21(1970):283-97.

2819
———. "Waterfront Labor Response to Technological Change: A Tale of Two Unions." *Labor Law Journal* 21(1970):397-419.

2820
Rothstein, William G. "The American Association of Engineers." *Industrial and Labor Relations Review* 22(1968):48-72.

2821
Rowan, Richard L. "Negro Employment in the Basic Steel Industry." *Industrial and Labor Relations Review* 23(1969):29-39.

2822
Savage, W. Sherman. "The Negro on the Mining Frontier." *Journal of Negro History* 30(1945):30-46.

2823
Schlegel, Marvin W. "The Workingmen's Benevolent Association: First Union of Anthracite Miners." *Pennsylvania History* 10(1943):243-67.

2824
Schmidman, John. "Nurses and Pennsylvania's New Public Employee Bargaining Law." *Labor Law Journal* 22(1971):725-33.

2825
Seidman, Joel. "The ILGWU in the Dubinsky Period." *Labor History*, Spec. Suppl. 9(1968):55-68.

2826
———. "Collective Bargaining in the Postal Service." *Industrial Relations* 9(1969):11-26.

2827
———. "Nurses and Collective Bargaining." *Industrial and Labor Relations Review* 23(1970):335-51.

2828
———, and Cain, Glen G. "Unionized Engineers and Chemists: A Case Study of a Professional Union." *Journal of Business* 37(1964):238-57.

2829
Serrin, William. "The Ultimate Shutdown: The Detroit Strike of 1967-1968." *Columbia Journalism Review* 8(1969):36-44.

2830
Shelton, Brenda K. "The Grain Shovellers' Strike of 1899." *Labor History* 9(1968):210-38.

2831
Sitterson, J. Carlyle. "Hired Labor on Sugar Plantations of the Ante-Bellum South." *Journal of Southern History* 14(1948):192-205.

2832
Skeels, Jack. "The Background of UAW Factionalism." *Labor History* 2(1961):158-81.

2833
Slavin, Richard H. "The 'Flint Glass Workers' Union' vs. the Glassware Industry: Union-Management Policies in a Declining Industry." *Labor History* 5(1964):29-39.

2834
Sloane, Arthur A. "Collective Bargaining in Trucking: Prelude to a National Contract." *Industrial and Labor Relations Review* 19(1965):21-40.

2835
Sofchalk, Donald G. "Organized Labor and the Iron Ore Miners of Northern Minnesota, 1907-1936." *Labor History* 12(1971):214-42.

2836
Soffer, Benson. "The Role of Union Foremen in the Evolution of the International Typographical Union." *Labor History* 2(1961):62-81.

2837
Stegner, S. Page. "Protest Songs from the Butte Mines." *Western Folklore* 26(1967):157-67.

2838
Stoveken, Ruth. "The Pine Lumberjacks in Wisconsin." *Wisconsin Magazine of History* 30(1947):322-34.

2839
Strauss, George. "Professional or Employee-Oriented: Dilemma for Engineering Unions." *Industrial and Labor Relations Review* 17(1962):519-33.

2840
––––––. "The AAUP as a Professional Occupational Association." In *Professional and White-Collar Unionism: An International Comparison. Industrial Relations* 5(1965):128-40.

2841
Suggs, George G., Jr. "Strike-Breaking in Colorado: Governor James H. Peabody and the Telluride Strike, 1903-1904." *Journal of the West* 5(1966):454-76.

2842
––––––. "Catalyst for Industrial Change: The WFM,1893-1903." *Colorado Magazine* 45(1968):322-39.

2843

––––––. "Religion and Labor in the Rocky Mountain West: Bishop Nicholas C. Matz and the Western Federation of Miners." In *The Church and the American Labor Movement: Four Episodes, 1880s-1920s. Labor History* 11(1970):190-206.

2844

Sullivan, Daniel P. "Soldiers in Unions—Protected First Amendment Rights?" *Labor Law Jouranl* 20(1969):581-90.

2845

Sullivan, William A. "The Industrial Revolution and the Factory Operative in Pennsylvania." *Pennsylvania Magazine of History and Biography* 78(1954):476-94.

2846

––––––. "The 1913 Revolt of the Michigan Copper Miners." *Michigan History* 43(1959):294-314.

2847

Taft, Philip. "David Dubinsky and the Labor Movement." *Labor History,* Spec. Suppl. 9(1968):26-42.

2848

––––––. "The Bisbee Deportation." *Labor History* 13(1972):3-40.

2849

Taylor, Paul S. "Hand Laborers in the Western Sugar Beet Industry." *Agricultural History* 41(1967):19-26.

2850

––––––. "California Farm Labor: A Review." *Agricultural History* 42(1968):49-54.

2851

Thomason, Frank. "The Bellevue Stranglers." *Idaho Yesterdays* 13(1969):26-32.

2852

Timmins, William M. "The Copper Strike and Collective Bargaining." *Labor Law Journal* 21(1970):28-38.

2853

Troy, Leo. "Labor Representation on American Railways." *Labor History* 2(1961):295-322.

2854

Tyler, Robert L. "The United States Government as Union Organizer: The Loyal Legion of Loggers and Lumbermen." *Mississippi Valley Historical Review* 47(1960):434-51.

2855

Van Valen, Nelson. "The Bolsheviki and the Orange Growers." *Pacific Historical Review* 22(1953):39-50.

2856

Varg, Paul A. "The Political Ideas of the American Railway Union." *The Historian* 10(1948):85-100.

2857
Walker, Joseph E. "A Comparison of Negro and White Labor in a Charcoal Iron Community." *Labor History* 10(1969):487-97.

2858
Weber, Arnold R. "Paradise Lost; or Whatever Happened to the Chicago Social Workers?" *Industrial and Labor Relations Review* 22(1969):323-38.

2859
Woolf, Donald A. "Labor Problems in the Post Office." *Industrial Relations* 9(1969):27-35.

2860
Wollenberg, Charles. "*Huelga,* 1928 Style: The Imperial Valley Cantaloupe Workers' Strike." *Pacific Historical Review* 38(1969):45-58.

2861
Yearley, Clifton K., Jr. "The Baltimore and Ohio Railroad Strike of 1877." *Maryland Historical Magazine* 51(1956):188-211.

2862
Young, Dallas M. "Origin of the Progressive Mine Workers of America." *Journal of the Illinois State Historical Society* 40(1947):313-30.

2863
Young, James E., and Brewer, Betty L. "Strikes by State and Local Government Employees." *Industrial Relations* 9(1970):356-61.

2864
Zieger, Robert H. "Pinchot and Coolidge: The Politics of the 1923 Anthracite Crisis." *Journal of American History* 52(1965):566-81.

2865
———————. "From Hostility to Moderation: Railroad Labor Policy in the 1920s." *Labor History* 9(1968):23-38.

Labor and the Law

2866
Auerbach, Jerold S. "The La Follette Committee, Labor and Civil Liberties in the New Deal." *Journal of American History* 51(1964):435-59.

2867
Asher, Robert. "Business and Workers' Welfare in the Progressive Era: Workmen's Compensation Reform in Massachusetts, 1880-1911." *Business History* 43(1969):452-75.

2868
Blum, Albert A. "Labor and the Federal Government: 1850-1933." *Current History* 48(1965): p. 328.

2869
Braeman, John. "Albert J. Beveridge and the First National Child Labor Bill." *Indiana Magazine of History* 60(1964):1-36.

2870
Bremner, Robert H. "The Background of the Norris-La Guardia Act." *The Historian* 9(1947):171-80.

2871
Brewer, Thomas B. "State Anti-Labor Legislation: Texas: A Case Study." *Labor History* 11(1970):58-76.

2872
Cassell, Frank H. "Chicago 1960-1970: One Small Step Forward." In *Equal Employment Opportunity: Comparative Community Experience. Industrial Relations* 9(1970):277-93.

2873
Chambers, John W. "The Big Switch: Justice Roberts and the Minimum-Wage Cases." *Labor History* 10(1969):44-73.

2874
Daney, Walter F. "Louis D. Brandeis, Champion of Labor." *The Historian* 6(1944):153-66.

2875
Doeringer, Peter B., and Piore, Michael J. "Equal Employment Opportunity in Boston." In *Equal Employment Opportunity: Comparative Community Experience. Industrial Relations* 9(1970):324-39.

2876
Drescher, Naula McGann. "Organized Labor and the Eighteenth Amendment." *Labor History* 8(1967):280-99.

2877
Felt, Jeremy P. "The Child Labor Provisions of the Fair Labor Standards Act." *Labor History* 11(1970):467-81.

2878
Fine, Sidney. "Frank Murphy, the Thornhill Decision, and Picketing as Free Speech." *Labor History* 6(1965):99-120.

2879
Green, William. "The Taft-Hartley Act: A Critical View." In *Labor in the American Economy*, edited by Gordon S. Watkins. *American Academy of Political and Social Science Annals* (1951):200-205.

2880
Hacker, Barton C. "The United States Army as a National Police Force: The Federal Policing of Labor Disputes, 1877-1898." *Military Affairs* 33(1969):255-64.

2881
Hiestand, Dale L. "Equal Employment in New York City." In *Equal Employment Opportunity: Comparative Community Experience. Industrial Relations* 9(1970):294-307.

2882
Hogg, J. Bernard. "Public Reaction to Pinkertonism and the Labor Question." *Pennsylvania History* 11(1944):171-99.

2883
Hutchinson, John. "The Anatomy of Corruption in Trade Unions." *Industrial Relations* 7(1969):135-50.

2884
Kerr, Thomas J. IV. "The New York Factory Investigating Commission and the Minimum-Wage Movement." *Labor History* 12(1971):373-91.

2885
Kesselman, Louis C. "The Fair Employment Practice Commission Movement in Perspective." *Journal of Negro History* 31(1946):30-46.

2886
Kuritz, Hyman. "Criminal Conspiracy Cases in Post-Bellum Pennsylvania." *Pennsylvania History* 17(1950):292-301.

2887
Kutler, Stanley I. "Chief Justice Taft, Judicial Unanimity, and Labor: The Coronado Case." *The Historian* 24(1961):68-83.

2888
————. "Labor, the Clayton Act, and the Supreme Court." *Labor History* 3(1962):19-38.

2889
Liggett, Malcolm H. "The Efficacy of State Fair Employment Practices Commissions." *Industrial and Labor Relations Review* 22(1969):559-67.

2890
Mackey, Howard. "The Operation of the English Old Poor Law in Colonial Virginia." *Virginia Magazine of History and Biography* 72(1965):29-40.

2891
Man, Albon P., Jr. "Labor Competition and the New York Draft Riots of 1863." *Journal of Negro History* 36(1951):375-405.

2892
Marshall, F. Ray, and Van Adams, Arvil. "Negro Employment in Memphis." In *Equal Employment Opportunity: Comparative Community Experience. Industrial Relations* 9(1970):308-23.

2893
Marshall, Thomas Maitland. "The Miners' Laws of Colorado." *American Historical Review* 25(1920):426-39.

2894
Means, Joan E. "Fair Employment Practices, Legislation and Enforcement in the United States." *International Labor Review* 93(1966):211-47.

2395
Murphy, Paul L. "Labor-Management Relations: Constitutional Assumptions." *Current History* 48(1965): p. 353.

2896
Murray, Robert K. "Public Opinion, Labor, and the Clayton Act." *The Historian* 21(1959):255-70.

2897
Nelson, Daniel. "The Origins of Unemployment Insurance in Wisconsin." *Wisconsin Magazine of History* 51(Winter 1967-1968):109-21.

2898
Pomper, Gerald. "Labor and Congress: The Repeal of Taft-Hartley." *Labor History* 2(1961):323-43.

2899
Randall, Edwin T. "Imprisonment for Debt in America: Fact and Fiction." *Mississippi Valley Historical Review* 39(1952):89-102.

2900
Roche, John P. "Entrepreneurial Liberty and the Fourteenth Amendment." *Labor History* 4(1963):3-31.

2901
Rowley, William D. "The Loup City Riot of 1934: Main Street vs. the 'Far-Out' Left." *Nebraska History* 47(1966):295-327.

2902
Sandmeyer, Elmer C. "California Anti-Chinese Legislation and the Federal Courts: A Study in Federal Relations." *Pacific Historical Review* 5(1936):189-211.

2903
Schmidt, Fred H. "Los Angeles: Show, Little Substance." In *Equal Employment Opportunity: Comparative Community Experience. Industrial Relations* 9(1970):340-55.

2904
Spengler, Joseph J. "Right to Work: A Backward Glance." *Journal of Economic History* 28(1968):171-96.

2905
Stambler, Moses. "The Effect of Compulsory Education and Child Labor Laws on High School Attendance in New York City, 1898-1917." *History of Education Quarterly* 8(1968):189-214.

2906
Taft, Philip. "Violence in American Labor Disputes." *American Academy of Political and Social Science Annals* 364(1966):127-40.

2907
Taft, Robert A. "The Taft-Hartley Act: A Favorable View." In *Labor in the American Economy*, edited by Gordon S. Watkins. *American Academy of Political and Social Science Annals* (1951):195-99.

2908
Tarrow, Sidney G. "Lochner versus New York: A Political Analysis." *Labor History* 5(1964):277-312.

2909
Trattner, Walter I. "The First Federal Child Labor Law (1916)." *Social Science Quarterly* 50(1969):507-24.

2910
Walker, Roger. "The AFL and Child-Labor Legislation." *Labor History* 11(1970):323-40.

2911
Weinstein, James. "Big Business and the Origins of Workmen's Compensation." *Labor History* 8(1967):156-74.

2912
Wesser, Robert F. "Conflict and Compromise: The Workmen's Compensation Movement in New York, 1890s-1913." *Labor History* 12(1971):345-72.

2913
Wolters, Raymond. "Section 7a and the Black Worker." *Labor History* 10(1969):459-74.

2914
Yellowitz, Irwin. "The Origins of Unemployment Reform in the United States." *Labor History* 9(1968):338-60.

Labor and Politics

2915
Appel, John C. "American Labor and the Annexation of Hawaii: A Study in Logic and Economic Interest." *Pacific Historical Review* 23(1954):1-18.

2916
Arky, Louis H. "The Mechanics' Union of Trade Associations and the Formation of the Philadelphia Workingmen's Movement." *Pennsylvania Magazine of History and Biography* 76(1952):142-76.

2917
Auerbach, Jerold S. "The La Follette Committee, Labor and Civil Liberties in the New Deal." *Journal of American History* 51(1964):435-59.

2918
——————. "Southern Tenant Farmers: Socialist Critics of the New Deal." *Labor History* 7(1966):3-18.

2919
Aurand, Harold W. "The Workingmen's Benevolent Association." *Labor History* 7(1966):19-34.

2920
Bean, Walton E. "Boss Ruef, the Union Labor Party, and the Graft Prosecution in San Francisco, 1901-1911." *Pacific Historical Review* 17(1948):443-55.

2921
Bedford, Henry F. "The 'Haverhill Social Democrat': Spokesman for Socialism." *Labor History* 2(1961):82-89.

2922
Bernstein, Barton J. "The Truman Administration and Its Reconversion Wage Policy." *Labor History* 6(1965):214-31.

2923

————————. "The Truman Administration and the Steel Strike of 1946." *Journal of American History* 52(1966):791-803.

2924

Blantz, Thomas E., C.S.C. "Father Haas and the Minneapolis Truckers Strike of 1934." *Minnesota History* 42(1970):5-15.

2925

Blum, Albert A. "Labor and the Federal Government: 1850-1933." *Current History* 48(1965): p. 328.

2926

Bodenheimer, Suzanne. "The AFL-CIO in Latin America: The Dominican Republic–a Case Study." *Viet-Report* 3(1967): p. 17.

2927

Braeman, John. "Albert J. Beveridge and the First National Child Labor Bill." *Indiana Magazine of History* 60(1964):1-36.

2928

Bremner, Robert H. "The Background of the Norris-La Guardia Act." *The Historian* 9(1947):171-80.

2929

Bryant, Keith L., Jr. "Labor in Politics: The Oklahoma State Federation of Labor during the Age of Reform." *Labor History* 11(1970):259-76.

2930

Cleland, Hugh G. "The Effects of Radical Groups on the Labor Movement." *Pennsylvania History* 26(1959):119-32.

2931

Conlin, Joseph R. "The IWW and the Socialist Party." *Science and Society* 31(1967):22-36.

2932

Cook, Philip L. "Red Scare in Denver." *Colorado Magazine* 43(1966):309-26.

2933

Darling, Arthur B. "The Workingmen's Party in Massachusetts, 1833-1834." *American Historical Review* 29(1923):81-86.

2934

Daitsman, George. "Labor and the 'Welfare State' in Early New York." *Labor History* 4(1963):248-56.

2935

Davies, Kenneth J. "Mormonism and the Closed Shop." *Labor History* 3(1962):169-87.

2936

Dubofsky, Melvyn. "Success and Failure of Socialism in New York City, 1900-1918: A Case Study." *Labor History* 9(1968):361-75.

2937

Eisner, J.M. "Politics, Legislation, and the ILGWU." *American Journal of Economics and Sociology* 28(1969):301-14.

2938
Engdahl, Walfrid. "Magnus Johnson—Colorful Farmer-Labor Senator from Minnesota." *Swedish Pioneer Historical Quarterly* 16(1965):122-36.

2939
Fine, Sidney. "The Eight-Hour Day Movement in the United States, 1888-1891." *Mississippi Valley Historical Review* 40(1953):441-62.

2940
Flynt, Wayne. "Pensacola Labor Problems and Political Radicalism, 1908." *Florida Historical Quarterly* 43(1965):315-32.

2941
————. "Florida Labor and Political 'Radicalism,' 1919-1920." *Labor History* 9(1968):73-90.

2942
Friedland, William H., and Nelkin, Dorothy. "American Labor: Differences and Policies toward Africa." *Africa Today* 14(1966):13-16.

2943
Gephart, Ronald M. "Politicians, Soldiers and Strikes: The Reorganizations of the Nebraska Militia and the Omaha Strike of 1882." *Nebraska History* 46(1965):89-120.

2944
Grob, Gerald N. "The Knights of Labor, Politics, and Populism." *Mid-America* 40(1958):3-21.

2945
Grossman, Jonathan. "The Molders' Struggle against Contract Prison Labor." *New York History* 23(1942):449-57.

2946
Grubbs, Frank L., Jr. "Council and Alliance Labor Propaganda: 1917-1919." *Labor History* 7(1966):156-72.

2947
Gutman, Herbert G. "Black Coal Miners and the Greenback-Labor Party in Redeemer, Alabama: 1878-1879. The Letters of Warren D. Kelley, Willis Johnson Thomas, 'Dawson,' and Others." *Labor History* 10(1969):506-35.

2948
Handley, William J. "American Labor and World Affairs." In *Labor in the American Economy,* edited by Gordon S. Watkins. *American Academy of Political and Social Science Annals* (1951):131-38.

2949
Hawley, Ellis W. "The Politics of the Mexican Labor Issue, 1950-1965." *Agricultural History* 40(1966):157-76.

2950
Hendrickson, Kenneth E., Jr. "The Socialists of Reading, Pennsylvania and World War I—a Question of Loyalty." *Pennsylvania History* 36(1969):430-50.

2951

————. "The Pro-War Socialists and the Drive for Industrial Democracy, 1917-1920." *Labor History* 11(1970):304-22.

2952

Hero, Alfred O. "American Negroes and U.S. Foreign Policy, 1937-1967." *Journal of Conflict Resolution* 13(1969):220-51.

2953

————. "Liberalism-Conservatism Revisited: Foreign vs. Domestic Federal Policies, 1937-1967." *Public Opinion Quarterly* 33(1969):399-408.

2954

Howard, J. Woodford, Jr. "Frank Murphy and the Sit-Down Strikes of 1937." *Labor History* 1(1960):103-40.

2955

Hutson, A.C., Jr. "The Overthrow of the Convict Lease System in Tennessee." *East Tennessee Historical Society's Publications* 8(1936):82-103.

2956

Jackson, Sidney L. "Labor, Education, and Politics in the 1830s." *Pennsylvania Magazine of History and Biography* 66(1942):279-93.

2957

James, Ralph C., and James, Estelle. "The Purge of the Trotskyites from the Teamsters." *Western Political Quarterly* 19(1966):5-15.

2958

Kauer, Ralph. "The Workingmen's Party of California." *Pacific Historical Review* 13(1944):278-91.

2959

Kaufman, Jacob J. "The Railroad Labor Dispute: A Marathon of Maneuver and Improvisation." *Industrial and Labor Relations Review* 18(1965):196-212.

2960

Komisar, Jerome B. "Social Legislation Policies and Labor Force Behavior." *Journal of Economic Issues* 2(1968):187-99.

2961

Kroll, Jack. "Labor's Political Role." In *Labor in the American Economy*, edited by Gordon S. Watkins. *American Academy of Political and Social Science Annals* (1951):118-22.

2962

Laslett, John H.M. "Reflections on the Failure of Socialism in the American Federation of Labor." *Mississippi Valley Historical Review* 50(1964):634-51.

2963

————. "Socialism and the American Labor Movement: Some New Reflections." *Labor History* 8(1967):136-55.

2964
Leiserson, Avery. "Organized Labor as a Pressure Group." In *Labor in the American Economy*, edited by Gordon S. Watkins. *American Academy of Political and Social Science Annals* (1951):108-17.

2965
Lemisch, Jesse. "Jack Tar in the Streets: Merchant Seamen in the Politics of Revolutionary America." *William and Mary Quarterly, 3rd series.* 25(1968):371-407.

2966
————. "Listening to the 'Inarticulate': William Widger's Dream and the Loyalties of American Revolutionary Seamen in British Prisons." *Journal of Social History* 3(1969):1-29.

2967
Levenstein, Harvey A. "The AFL and Mexican Immigration in the 1920s: An Experiment in Labor Diplomacy." *Hispanic American Historical Review* 48(1968):206-19.

2968
Lipsitz, Lewis. "Work Life and Political Attitudes: A Study of Manual Workers." *American Political Science Review* 58(1964):951-62.

2969
Lynd, Staughton. "The Mechanics in New York Politics, 1774-1788." *Labor History* 5(1964):225-46.

2970
Malcolm, Roy. "Anti-Japanese Legislation in California, and the Naturalization of the Japanese." *Historical Society of Southern California* 9(1912-1914):97-103.

2971
Miller, Glenn W., and Ware, Stephen B. "Organized Labor in the Political Process: A Case Study of the Right-to-Work Campaign in Ohio." *Labor History* 4(1963):51-67.

2972
Miller, William. "The Effects of the American Revolution on Indentured Servitude." *Pennsylvania History* 7(1940):131-41.

2973
Mitchell, Daniel J.B. "Labor and the Tariff Question." *Industrial Relations* 9(1970):268-76.

2974
Mohl, Raymond A. "Poverty, Politics, and the Mechanics of New York City, 1803." *Labor History* 12(1971):38-51.

2975
Murray, Robert K. "Communism and the Great Steel Strike of 1919." *Mississippi Valley Historical Review* 38(1951):445-66.

2976
————. "Public Opinion, Labor, and the Clayton Act." *The Historian* 21(1959):255-70.

2977

Nash, Gerald D. "Franklin D. Roosevelt and Labor: The World War I Origins of Early New Deal Policy." *Labor History* 1(1960):39-52.

2978

Nelson, Daniel. "The Origins of Unemployment Insurance in Wisconsin." *Wisconsin Magazine of History* 51(1968):109-21.

2979

O'Brien, F.S. "The 'Communist-Dominated' Unions in the United States since 1950." *Labor History* 9(1968):184-209.

2980

Olson, Frederick I. "The Socialist Party and the Union in Milwaukee." *Wisconsin Magazine of History* 44(Winter 1960-1961):110-16.

2981

O'Neill, William L. "Labor Radicalism and the 'Masses.' " *Labor History* 7(1966):197-208.

2982

Pahl, Thomas L. "G-string Conspiracy, Political Reprisal or Armed Revolt? The Minneapolis Trotskyite Trial." *Labor History* 8(1967):30-51.

2983

Pessen, Edward. "Thomas Skidmore, Agrarian Reformer in the Early American Labor Movement." *New York History* 35(1954):280-96.

2984

————. "The Workingmen's Movement of the Jacksonian Era." *Mississippi Valley Historical Review* 43(1956):428-43.

2985

————. "The Workingmen's Party Revisited." *Labor History* 4(1963):203-26.

2986

Pivar, David J. "The Hosiery Workers and the Philadelphia Third Party Impulse." *Labor History* 5(1964):18-28.

2987

Pomper, Gerald. "Labor and Congress: The Repeal of Taft-Hartley." *Labor History* 2(1961):323-43.

2988

Prickett, James R. "Communism and Factionalism in the United Automobile Workers, 1939-1947." *Science and Society* 32(1968):257-77.

2989

Reichert, William O. "Toward a New Understanding of Anarchism." *Western Political Quarterly* 20(1967):856-65.

2990

Renshaw, Patrick. "The IWW and the Red Scare, 1917-1924." *Journal of Contemporary History* 3(1968):63-72.

2991

Rollins, Alfred B., Jr. "Franklin Roosevelt's Introduction to Labor." *Labor History* 3(1962):3-18.

2992
Russell, Francis. "How I Changed My Mind about the Sacco-Vanzetti Case." *Antioch Review* 27(1965):592-607.

2993
Saxton, Alexander. "San Francisco Labor and the Populist and Progressive Insurgencies." *Pacific Historical Review* 34(1965):421-38.

2994
Scheinberg, Stephen J. "Theodore Roosevelt and the A.F. of L.'s Entry into Politics, 1906-1908." *Labor History* 3(1962):131-48.

2995
Scruggs, Otey M. "The First Mexican Farm Labor Program." *Arizona and the West* 2(1960):319-26.

2996
————. "Evolution of the Mexican Farm Labor Agreement of 1942." *Agricultural History* 34(1960):140-49.

2997
————. "The United States, Mexico, and the Wetbacks, 1942-1947." *Pacific Historical Review* 30(1961):149-64.

2998
Shaffer, Ralph E. "Formation of the California Communist Labor Party." *Pacific Historical Review* 36(1967):59-78.

2999
Shideler, James H. "The La Follette Progressive Party Campaign of 1924." *Wisconsin Magazine of History* 33(1950):444-57.

3000
Shover, John L. "The Progressives and the Working Class Vote in California." *Labor History* 10(1969):584-601.

3001
Smith, John S. "Organized Labor and Government in the Wilson Era; 1913-1921: Some Conclusions." *Labor History* 3(1962):265-86.

3002
Stein, Bruno. "Wage Stabilization in the Korean War Period: The Role of the Subsidiary Wage Boards." *Labor History* 4(1963):161-77.

3003
Suggs, George G., Jr. "Strike-Breaking in Colorado: Governor James H. Peabody and the Telluride Strike, 1903-1904." *Journal of the West* 5(1966):454-76.

3004
Sullivan, William A. "Philadelphia Labor during the Jackson Era." *Pennsylvania History* 15(1948):305-20.

3005
Tarrow, Sidney G. "Lochner versus New York: A Political Analysis." *Labor History* 5(1964):277-312.

3006

Taylor, A. Elizabeth. "The Abolition of the Convict Lease System in Georgia." *Georgia Historical Quarterly* 26(1942):273-87.

3007

Toth, Charles W. "The Pan American Federation of Labor: Its Political Nature." *Western Political Quarterly* 18(1965):615-20.

3008

————. "Samuel Gompers, Communism, and the Pan American Federation of Labor." *Americas* 23(1967):273-78.

3009

Tyler, Robert L. "The United States Government as Union Organizer: The Loyal Legion of Loggers and Lumbermen." *Mississippi Valley Historical Review* 47(1960):434-51.

3010

Vadney, Thomas E. "The Politics of Repression, a Case Study of the Red Scare in New York." *New York History* 49(1968):56-75.

3011

Varg, Paul A. "The Political Ideas of the American Railway Union." *The Historian* 10(1948):85-100.

3012

Wayman, Dorothy G. "Sacco-Vanzetti: The Unfinished Debate." *American Heritage* 11(1959):89-93.

3013

Wellborn, Mildred. "The Events Leading to the Chinese Exclusion Acts." *Historical Society of Southern California* 9(1912-1914):49-58.

3014

Williamson, John. "Some Strands from the Past: The YWL Meets Gompers." *Political Affairs* 44(1965):36-45.

3015

Windmuller, John P. "Foreign Affairs and the AFL-CIO." *Industrial and Labor Relations Review* 9(1956):419-32.

3016

————. "The Foreign Policy Conflict in American Labor." *Political Science Quarterly* 82(1967):205-34.

3017

————. "Internationalism in Eclipse: The ICFTU after Two Decades." *Industrial and Labor Relations Review* 23(1970):510-27.

3018

Wish, Harvey. "Governor Altgeld Pardons the Anarchists." *Journal of the Illinois State Historical Society* 31(1938):424-48.

3019

Wolfe, Arthur C. "Trends in Labor Union Voting Behavior, 1948-1969." *Industrial Relations* 9(1969):1-10.

3020
Yellowitz, Irwin. "The Origins of Unemployment Reform in the United States." *Labor History* 9(1968):338-60.

3021
Young, Alfred. "The Mechanics and the Jeffersonians: New York, 1789-1801." *Labor History* 5(1964):247-76.

3022
Zieger, Robert H. "Pinchot and Coolidge: The Politics of the 1923 Anthracite Crisis." *Journal of American History* 52(1965):566-81.

3023
————. "Senator George Wharton Pepper and Labor Issues in the 1920s." *Labor History* 9(1968):163-83.

3024
————. "Pennsylvania Coal and Politics: The Anthracite Strike of 1925-1926." *Pennsylvania Magazine of History and Biography* 92(1969):244-62.

3025
Zimmerman, Jane. "The Convict Lease System in Arkansas and the Fight for Abolition." *Arkansas Historical Quarterly* 8(1949):171-88.

II. Comparative Labor Movements

GENERAL SURVEYS

3026
Bates, Robert H. "Approaches to the Study of Unions and Development." *Industrial Relations* 9(1970):365-78.

3027
Butler, Arthur D. "Labor Costs in the Common Market." *Industrial Relations* 6(1967):166-83.

3028
Derber, Milton. "Crosscurrents in Workers Participation." In *Workers Participation in Management: An International Comparison. Industrial Relations* 9(1970):123-36.

3029
Evans, Archibald H. "Work and Leisure, 1919-1969." *International Labour Review* 99(1969):35-60.

3030
Goodman, Stephen H. "Trade Unions and Political Parties: The Case of East Africa." *Economic Development and Cultural Change* 17(1969):338-45.

3031
International Labor Office. "Agricultural Policy in Scandinavian Countries." *International Labour Review* 81(1960):25-46.

3032

————. "Industrial Injury Trends over Three Decades." *International Labour Review* 83(1961):248-72.

3033

Kassalow, Everett M. "The Prospects for White-Collar Union Growth." In *Professional and White-Collar Unionism: An International Comparison. Industrial Relations* 5(1965):34-47.

3034

Mouly, Jean. "Changing Concepts of Wage Policy." *International Labour Review* 100(1969):1-22.

3035

Orizet, Jean. "The Cooperative Movement since the First World War." *International Labour Review* 100(1969):23-50.

3036

Parmeggiani, Luigi. "Past Development and Present Trends in Occupational Medicine." *International Labour Review* 88(1963):107-28.

3037

Perrin, Guy. "Reflections on Fifty Years of Social Security." *International Labour Review* 99(1969): p. 249.

3038

Riach, P.A. "Equal Pay and Equal Opportunity." *The Journal of Industrial Relations* 11(1969):99-110.

3039

Schregle, Johannes. "Workers Participation in Management." In *Workers Participation in Management: An International Comparison. Industrial Relations* 9(1970):117-22.

3040

Spyropoulos, Georges. "An Outline of Developments and Trends in Labour Relations." *International Labour Review* 99(1969):315-86.

3041

Strauss, George, and Rosenstein, Eliezer. "Workers Participation: A Critical View." In *Workers Participation in Management: An International Comparison. Industrial Relations* 9(1970):197-214.

3042

Wallin, Michael. "Labour Administration: Origins and Development." *International Labour Review* 100(1969):51-110.

SPECIFIC COUNTRIES

Argentina

3043

International Labor Office. "The Settlement of Labor Disputes in Argentina." *International Labour Review* 104(1971):77-96.

Australia

3044

Bentley, Philip R. "Strike Incidence in the Australian Stevedoring Industry—the Government's Search for a Solution." *The Journal of Industrial Relations* 11(1969):111-124.

3045

Buckley, K. "Arbitration—its History and Process." *The Journal of Industrial Relations* 13(1971):96-103.

3046

Campbell, D.V.A. "Trades Unions and Automation in Australia." *The Journal of Industrial Relations* 11(1969):223-30.

3047

Chambers, E.A. "Problems of Communication in Industrial Relations: Communication between the Tribunals and the Parties." *The Journal of Industrial Relations* 12(1970):1-8.

3048

Chan, Kenneth. "The Origins of Compulsion in Australia: The Case of Victoria, 1888-1894." *The Journal of Industrial Relations* 13(1971):155-63.

3049

De Vyver, Frank T. "The 1920 Civil Service and Teachers' Strike in Western Australia." *The Journal of Industrial Relations* 7(1965):281-97.

3050

Gordon, B.J. "A Classification of Regional and Sectoral Dispute Patterns in Australian Industry, 1945-1964." *The Journal of Industrial Relations* 10(1968):233-42.

3051

————, and McShane, R.W. "Stability and Instability in Australian Strike Patterns, 1947-1966." *The Journal of Industrial Relations* 13(1971):188-94.

3052

Hince, Kevin W. "Unions on the Shop Floor." *The Journal of Industrial Relations* 9(1967):214-23.

3053

Holden, W. Sprague. "The Anatomy of Two Newspaper Industrial Disputes: U.S. and Australian." *The Journal of Industrial Relations* 9(1967):1-12.

3054

Hotchkiss, W.E. "The Broken Hill Mines Agreement—a Study of Some Objective Factors in Industrial Negotiation." *The Journal of Industrial Relations* 12(1970):9-19.

3055

Hughes, Helen. "Industrial Relations in the Australian Iron and Steel Industry, 1876-1962." *The Journal of Industrial Relations* 4(1962):120-36.

3056
Hunter, Thelma. "The Employment of Women in Australia." *The Journal of Industrial Relations* 3(1961):94-104.

3057
Kelley, Allen G. "Internal Migration and Economic Growth, Australia, 1865-1935." *Journal of Economic History* 25(1965):333-54.

3058
Macarthy, Peter G. "Wage Determination in New South Wales, 1890-1921." *The Journal of Industrial Relations* 10(1968):189-205.

3059
――――――. "Employers, the Tariff and Legal Wage Regulation in Australia–1890-1910." *The Journal of Industrial Relations* 12(1970):182-93.

3060
Martin, Ross M. "Australian Professional and White-Collar Unions." In *Professional and White-Collar Unionism: An International Comparison. Industrial Relations* 5(1965):93-102.

3061
――――――. "Class Identification and Trade Union Behaviour: The Case of Australian White Collar Unions." *The Journal of Industrial Relations* 7(1965):131-48.

3062
Oxnam, Desmond W. "Issues in Industrial Conflict: Australian Experience, 1913-1963." *The Journal of Industrial Relations* 9(1967):13-25.

3063
――――――. "The Changing Pattern of Strike Settlements in Australia: 1913-1963." *The Journal of Industrial Relations* 10(1968):11-24.

3064
Sharpe, Ian G. "The Growth of Australian Trade Unions: 1937-1969." *The Journal of Industrial Relations* 13(1971):138-54.

3065
Wigglesworth, E.C. "The Incidence and Distribution of Occupational Injuries in the States of Australia, 1965-66." *The Journal of Industrial Relations* 12(1970):20-38.

3066
Woodward, A.E. "Industrial Relations in the '70s." *The Journal of Industrial Relations* 12(1970):115-29.

3067
Wootten, J.H. "The Role of the Tribunals." *The Journal of Industrial Relations* 12(1970):130-44.

3068
Young, Irwin. "Changes within the NSW Branch of the Australian Workers' Union 1919-1924." *The Journal of Industrial Relations* 6(1964):51-60.

Belguim

3069
Blanpain, Roger. "Recent Trends in Collective Bargaining in Belgium."
International Labour Review 104(1971):111-30.

3070
Pêtre, René. "Workers' Labour Inspection Delegates in Belgium with
Particular Reference to Mining." *International Labour Review*
97(1968):429-46.

3071
Troclet, L.-E., and Vogel-Polsky, E. "The Influence of International Labor
Conventions on Belgian Labor Legislation." *International Labour Review*
98(1968):389-424.

Brazil

3072
Alexander, Herbert B. "Brazilian and United States Slavery Compared."
Journal of Negro History 7(1922):349-64.

Canada

3073
Abella, I.M. "The CIO, the Communist Party and the Formation of the
Canadian Congress of Labour, 1936-1941." *Canadian Historical Association Papers* (1969):112-28.

3074
Cormick, Gerald W. "The Collective Bargaining Experience of Canadian
Registered Nurses." *Labor Law Journal* 20(1969):667-82.

3075
Vanderkamp, John. "Economic Activity and Strikes in Canada." *Industrial
Relations* 9(1970):215-30.

Chile

3076
Bauer, Arnold J. "Chilean Rural Labor in the Nineteenth Century." *American
Historical Review* 76(1971):1059-83.

China

3077
Hoffmann, Charles. "Work Incentives in Communist China." *Industrial
Relations* 3(1964):81-98.

Czechoslovakia

3078

Stieber, Jack, and Paukert, Liba. "Manpower and Technological Change in Czechoslovakia." *Industrial Relations* 8(1968):91-107.

3079

Windmuller, John P. "Czechoslovakia and the Communist Union Model." *British Journal of Industrial Relations* 9(1971):33-54.

Finland

3080

Rinne, Rof. "Industrial Relations in Postwar Finland." *International Labour Review* 89(1964):461-81.

France

3081

Delamotte, Yves. "Recent Collective Bargaining Trends in France." *International Labour Review* 103(1971):351-78.

3082

Lorwin, Val R. "Reflections on the History of the French and American Labor Movements." *Journal of Economic History* 17(1957):25-44.

3083

Meyers, Frederic. "Job Reinstatement: France and the U.S." *Industrial Relations* 2(1963):97-114.

3084

Stearns, Peter N. "Patterns of Industrial Strike Activity in France during the July Monarchy." *American Historical Review* 70(1965):371-94.

Germany

3085

Fuhrig, Wolf D. "A Quasi-Union: West Germany University Association." In *Professional and White-Collar Unionism: An International Comparison. Industrial Relations* 5(1965):116-27.

3086

Hartmann, Heinz. "Codetermination in West Germany." In *Workers Participation in Management: An International Comparison. Industrial Relations* 9(1970):137-47.

3087

Reichel, Hans. "Recent Trends in Collective Bargaining in the Federal Republic of Germany." *International Labour Review* 104(1971):469-88.

3088

Rimlinger, Gaston V. "The Economics of Postwar German Social Policy." *Industrial Relations* 6(1967):184-204.

3089
Skrzypczak, Henryk. "Some Strategic and Tactical Problems of the German Free Trade Union Movement during the Weimar Republic." *Internationale Wissenschaftliche Korrespondenz zur Geschichte der Deutschen Arbeiterbewegung.* 13(1971):26-45.

Great Britain

3090
Bain, George Sayers. "The Growth of White-Collar Unionism in Great Britain." *British Journal of Industrial Relations* 4(1966):304-35.

3091
Blaug, Mark. "The Myth of the Old Poor Law and the Making of the New." *Journal of Economic History* 23(1963):151-84.

3092
————. "The Poor Law Report Reexamined." *Journal of Economic History* 24(1964):229-45.

3093
Bretten, G.R. "Reform of the British System of Industrial Relations." *Labor Law Journal* 20(1969):113-19.

3094
Burns, Eveline M. "Social Security in Britain—Twenty Years after Beveridge." *Industrial Relations* 2(1963):15-32.

3095
Cameron, G.C. "Postwar Strikes in the North-East Shipbuilding and Ship-Repairing Industry 1946-1961." *British Journal of Industrial Relations* 2(1964):1-22.

3096
Davidson, R.B. "Immigration and Unemployment in the United Kingdom, 1955-1962." *British Journal of Industrial Relations* 1(1963):43-61.

3097
Derber, Milton. "Collective Bargaining in Great Britain and the United States." *Quarterly Review of Economics and Business* 8(1968):55-66.

3098
Edelstein, J. David. "Democracy in a National Union: The British AEU." *Industrial Relations* 4(1965):105-25.

3099
Gallaway, Lowell E., and Vedder, Richard K. "Emigration from the United Kingdom to the United States: 1860-1913." *Journal of Economic History* 31(1971):885-97.

3100
Gilbert, Bentley B. "Winston Churchill versus the Webbs: The Origins of British Unemployment Insurance." *American Historical Review* 71(1966):846-62.

3101
Goodman, J.F.B. "Strikes in the United Kingdom: Recent Statistics and Trends." *International Labour Review* 95(1967):465-81.

3102
——————. "The Report of the Royal Commission on Trade Unions and Employers' Associations in Britain and Its Implications." *The Journal of Industrial Relations* 10(1968):222-32.

3103
Grunfield, Cyril. "Political Independence in British Trade Unions: Some Legal Aspects." *British Journal of Industrial Relations* 1(1963):23-42.

3104
Handy, L.J. "Absenteeism and Attendance in the British Coal-Mining Industry: An Examination of Postwar Trends." *British Journal of Industrial Relations* 6(1968):27-50.

3105
Handsaker, Morrison, and Handsaker, Marjorie L. "Arbitration in Great Britain." *Industrial Relations* 1(1961):117-36.

3106
Harrison, John F.C. "The Owenite Socialist Movement in Britain and the United States: A Comparative Study." *Labor History* 9(1968):323-37.

3107
Jencks, Clinton E. "British Coal: Labor Relations since Nationalization." *Industrial Relations* 6(1966):95-110.

3108
Johnston, G.A. "The Influence of International Labour Standards on Legislation and Practice in the United Kingdom." *International Labour Review* 97(1968):465-88.

3109
McCarthy, W.E.J., and Clifford, B.A. "The Work of Industrial Courts of Inquiry: A Study of Existing Provisions and Past Practices." *British Journal of Industrial Relations* 4(1966):39-58.

3110
Mann, Arthur. "British Social Thought and American Reformers of the Progressive Era." *Mississippi Valley Historical Review* 42(1956):672-92.

3111
Marshall, Leon S. "The English and American Industrial City of the Nineteenth Century." *Western Pennsylvania Historical Magazine* 20(1937):169-80.

3112
Miernyk, William H. "Experience under the British Local Employment Acts of 1960 and 1963." *Industrial and Labor Relations Review* 20(1966):30-49.

3113
Prandy, Ken. "Professional Organization in Great Britain." In *Professional and White-Collar Unionism: An International Comparison. Industrial Relations* 5(1965):67-79.

3114
Rosenberg, Nathan. "Anglo-American Wage Differences in the 1820s." *Journal of Economic History* 27(1967):221-29.

3115
Ross, Arthur M. "Prosperity and British Industrial Relations." *Industrial Relations* 2(1963):63-94.

3116
Thomson, Andrew W.J. "The Injunction in Trades Disputes in Britain before 1910." *Industrial and Labor Relations Review* 19(1966):213-23.

3117
————. "Collective Bargaining under Incomes Legislation: The Case of Britain's Buses." *Industrial and Labor Relations Review* 24(1971):389-406.

3118
Warner, Malcolm. "Organizational Background and 'Union Parliamentarianism'—an Examination of British and American Cases." *The Journal of Industrial Relations* 12(1970):205-17.

3119
Whittingham, T.G., and Gottschalk, A.W. "Proposals for Change in the British System of Industrial Relations." *The Journal of Industrial Relations* 12(1970):52-71.

3120
Young, Irwin. "The NSW—one Big Union, 1918-1919." *The Journal of Industrial Relations* 6(1964):226-38.

India

3121
Dufty, N.F. "The Evolution of the Indian Industrial Relations System." *The Journal of Industrial Relations* 7(1965):40-49.

3122
International Labor Office. "Agricultural Labor in India." *International Labour Review* 85(1962):148-62.

3123
Mathur, J.S. "India's Labour Policy." *The Journal of Industrial Relations* 8(1966):283-97.

3124
Pandey, S.M. "Inter-Union Rivalry in India: An Analysis." *The Journal of Industrial Relations* 9(1967):140-54.

3125
Papola, T.S. "The Place of Collective Bargaining in Industrial Relations Policy in India." *The Journal of Industrial Relations* 10(1968):25-33.

Ireland

3126
Sams, K.I. "The Creation of the Irish Congress of Trade Unions." *The Journal of Industrial Relations* 8(1966):68-78.

Israel

3127
Ben-David, Joseph. "Professionals and Unions in Israel." In *Professional and White-Collar Unionism: An International Comparison. Industrial Relations* 5(1965):48-66.

3128
Metcalf, David. "Wage Policy in Israel." *British Journal of Industrial Relations* 8(1970):213-23.

3129
Rosenstein, Eliezer. "Histadrut's Search for a Participation Program." In *Workers Participation in Management: An International Comparison. Industrial Relations* 9(1970):170-86.

Italy

3130
Archibugi, Franco. "Recent Trends in Women's Work in Italy." *International Labour Review* 81(1960):285-318.

3131
Giugni, Gino. "Recent Trends in Collective Bargaining in Italy." *International Labour Review* 104(1971):307-28.

3132
Riva-Sanseverino, Luisa. "The Influence of International Labour Conventions on Italian Labor Legislation." *International Labour Review* 83(1961):576-601.

Japan

3133
Evans, Robert, Jr. "Evolution of the Japanese System of Employer-Employee Relations, 1868-1945." *Business History Review* 44(1970):110-25.

3134
Handsaker, Morrison, and Handsaker, Marjorie. "The ILO and Japanese Public Employee Unions." *Industrial Relations* 7(1967):80-91.

3135
Kogi, Kazutaka. "Social Aspects of Shift Work in Japan." *International Labour Review* 104(1971):415-33.

3136
Levine, Solomon B. "The White-Collar, Blue-Collar Alliance in Japan." In *Professional and White-Collar Unionism: An International Comparison. Industrial Relations* 5(1965):103-15.

3137
Okita, Saburo. "Manpower Policy in Japan." *International Labour Review* 90(1964):45-58.

3138
Taira, Koji. "The Labour Market in Japanese Development." *British Journal of Industrial Relations* 2(1964):209-27.

3139
————. "Urban Poverty, Ragpickers, and the 'Ants' Villa' in Tokyo." *Economic Development and Cultural Change* 17(1969):155-77.

Mexico

3140
Kessing, Donald B. "Structural Change Early in Development: Mexico's Changing Industrial and Occupational Structure from 1895 to 1950." *Journal of Economic History* 29(1969):716-38.

3141
Miller, Richard V. "Labor Legislation and Mexican Industrial Relations." *Industrial Relations* 7(1968):171-82.

3142
Ramos, Fernando Yllanes. "The Social Rights Enshrined in the Mexican Constitution of 1917." *International Labour Review* 96(1967):590-608.

3143
Sonnichsen, C.L. "Colonel William C. Greene and the Strike at Cananea, Sonora, 1906." *Arizona and the West* 13(1971):343-68.

Netherlands

3144
Albeda, W. "Recent Trends in Collective Bargaining in the Netherlands." *International Labour Review* 103(1971):247-68.

3145
Oettinger, Martin P. "Nationwide Job Evaluation in the Netherlands." *Industrial Relations* 4(1964):45-59.

New Guinea

3146
Martin, R.M. "Tribesmen into Trade Unionists: The African Experience and the Papua-New Guinea Prospect." *The Journal of Industrial Relations* 11(1969):125-72.

3147
Turner, Basil. "Background to Industrial Relations during the Early Stages of Industrial Development: Some New Guinea Experience." *The Journal of Industrial Relations* 11(1969):243-52.

New Zealand

3148
Brissenden, Paul F. "Disputes Settlement in New Zealand." *Industrial Relations* 3(1964):47-62.

3149
Child, John. "Wages Policy and Wage Movements in New Zealand, 1914-23." *The Journal of Industrial Relations* 13(1971):164-76.

3150
Howells, J.M. "Concentration and Growth in New Zealand Unions." *The Journal of Industrial Relations* 12(1970):39-51.

3151
Sorrell, G.H. "Industrial Relations in New Zealand." *The Journal of Industrial Relations* 3(1961):117-30.

3152
Stewart, P.J. "New Zealand and the Pacific Labor Traffic, 1870-1874." *Pacific Historical Review* 30(1961):47-60.

Nigeria

3153
Abiodun, M.O. "Industrial Relations in Nigeria." *The Journal of Industrial Relations* 3(1961):44-53.

3154
Berg, Elliot J. "Urban Real Wages and the Nigerian Trade Union Movement, 1939-1960: A Comment." *Economic Development and Cultural Change* 17(1969):604-17.

3155
Warren, W.M. "Urban Real Wages and the Nigerian Trade Union Movement, 1939-1960: Rejoinder." *Economic Development and Cultural Change* 17(1969):618-33.

Norway

3156
Dahl, Karl Nandrup. "The Influence of ILO Standards on Norwegian Legislation." *International Labour Review* 90(1964):226-51.

3157
Fivelsdal, Egil. "White-Collar Unions and the Norwegian Labor Movement." In *Professional and White-Collar Unionism: An International Comparison. Industrial Relations* 5(1965):80-92.

3158
Thorsrud, Einar, and Emery, Fred E. "Industrial Democracy in Norway." In *Workers Participation in Management: An International Comparison. Industrial Relations* 9(1970):187-96.

3159
Ulsaker, Berger. "Local Labour Inspection in Norway." *International Labour Review* 96(1967):557-80.

Pakistan

3160
Raza, M. Ali. "Industrial Disputes and Their Settlement in Pakistan." *The Journal of Industrial Relations* 9(1967):224-44.

Philippines

3161
Calderón, Cicero D. "From Compulsory Arbitration to Collective Bargaining in the Philippines." *International Labour Review* 81(1960):1-24.

Poland

3162
Rosner, Jan. "The Influence of International Labour Conventions on Polish Legislation." *International Labour Review* 92(1965):353-79.

Puerto Rico

3163
Whittaker, William George. "The Santiago Iglesias Case, 1901-1902: Origins of American Trade Union Involvement in Puerto Rico." *The Americas* 24(1968):378-93.

Rumania

3164
Păcurarŭ I. "Planned Development and Labor Force Structure in Rumania 1950-65." *International Labour Review* 94(1966):535-49.

Russia

3165
Giffin, Frederick C. "In Quest of an Effective Program of Factory Legislation in Russia: The Years of Preparation, 1859-1880." *The Historian* 29(1967):175-85.

3166
Von Lave, Theodore H. "Russian Peasants in the Factory." *Journal of Economic History* 21(1961):61-80.

Singapore

3167

Raza, M. Ali. "Singapore's Industrial Relations and Public Policy: Management of Successive Crises." *The Journal of Industrial Relations* 12(1970):218-37.

South Africa

3168

Chapin, Gene L.; Vedder, Richard K.; and Gallaway, Lowell E. "The Determinants of Migration to South Africa, 1950-1967." *South African Journal of Economics* 38(1970):374-81.

3169

Clack, Garfield. "Industrial Peace in South Africa." *British Journal of Industrial Relations* 1(1963):94-106.

3170

De Vyver, Frank T. "Labour Relations in South African Industry." *The Journal of Industrial Relations* 2(1960):109-18.

3171

Pursell, Donald E. "South African Labor Policy: 'New Deal' for Nonwhites?" *Industrial Relations* 10(1971):36-48.

Spain

3172

Oroza, Guillermo Moreda. "Fishermen's Guilds in Spain." *International Labour Review* 94(1966):465-76.

Sudan

3173

Osman, Omer M. "Recent Changes in Labour Legislation in the Sudan." *International Labour Review* 86(1962):235-46.

Sweden

3174

Clayton, Rennie E. "Collective Bargaining in Sweden." *The Journal of Industrial Relations* 1(1959):98-110.

3175

Kassalow, Everett M. "Professional Unionism in Sweden." *Industrial Relations* 8(1969):119-34.

3176

Rehn, Gösta, and Lundberg, Erik. "Employment and Welfare: Some Swedish Issues." *Industrial Relations* 2(1963):1-14.

Switzerland

3177
Berenstein, Alexandre. "Union Security and the Scope of Collective Agreements in Switzerland." *International Labour Review* 85(1962):101-20.

3178
Janjic, Marion. "Women's Employment and Conditions of Work in Switzerland." *International Labour Review* 96(1967):292-317.

Syria

3179
Atasi, Nadr. "Minimum Wage Fixing and Wage Structure in Syria." *International Labour Review* 98(1968):337-54.

Tunisia

3180
Abdeljaouad, Amor. "The Influence of International Labour Conventions on Tunisian Legislation." *International Labour Review* 91(1965):191-200.

Yugoslavia

3181
Leeman, Wayne A. "Syndicalism in Yugoslavia." *Economic Development and Cultural Change* 18(1970):230-39.

3182
Mesa-Lago, Carmelo. "Unemployment in a Socialist Economy: Yugoslavia." *Industrial Relations* 10(1971):49-69.

3183
Obradovic, Josip. "Participation and Work Attitudes in Yugoslavia." In *Workers Participation in Management: An International Comparison. Industrial Relations* 9(1970):161-69.

3184
Rus, Veljko. "Influence Structure in Yugoslav Enterprise." In *Workers Participation in Management: An International Comparison. Industrial Relations* 9(1970):148-60.

INDEX OF AUTHORS